PRAISE FOR *EVOLVING TOWARD PEACE*

With an authority that grows from years of experience, Jalaja Bonheim helps us understand how we can *be* the change we hope to move toward. Absorbing, inspiring and practical, her book is grounded in psychology, anthropology and neuroscience.

> Jean Shinoda Bolen, MD, author, *Goddesses in Everywoman* and *The Millionth Circle*

Jalaja Bonheim has written a lucid, inspiring vision, based on her direct experience, of how to unlock the potential of the human heart for the benefit of all. *Evolving Toward Peace* shows how we can awaken the deep wisdom already inside us. A deeply insightful and important work.

> James Baraz, co-author of *Awakening Joy: 10 Steps That Will Put You on the Road to Real Happiness*, and co-founding teacher, Spirit Rock Meditation Center.

What a powerful book! Revealing a path to peace within and without, *Evolving Towards Peace* is a much-needed offering to the world.

> Dorothy Firman, Ed.D, co-author, *Chicken Soup for the Mother & Daughter Soul* and *Chicken Soup for the Father and Son Soul*

This penetrating and deeply kind book, based on Jalaja Bonheim's invaluable experience of working with circles of people from around the world, shows how we can create a sane and peaceful world for ourselves and the children of the future.

Sherry Ruth Anderson, author, *The Cultural Creatives* and *Ripening Time*

With beauty, grace and insight, Jalaja Bonheim peels away layers of encrusted cultural conditioning to reveal a shining jewel: the evolutionary potential of the human race when it taps into its own heart. Read this book and it may change your way of thinking.

Liz Walker, Co-founder, Executive Director, EcoVillage at Ithaca, author of *Choosing a Sustainable Future*

EVOLVING TOWARD PEACE

AWAKENING THE GLOBAL HEART

EVOLVING TOWARD PEACE

AWAKENING THE GLOBAL HEART

Jalaja Bonheim, Ph.D.

Two Harbors Press

Minneapolis, MN

Two Harbors Press
322 First Avenue N, 5th floor
Minneapolis, MN 55401
612.455.2293
www.TwoHarborsPress.com

ISBN-13: 978-1-62652-360-9
LCCN: 2013915721

Contributor's names have been changed to protect their identity.

"Whoever you are ..." from *The Book of Images* by Rainer Maria Rilke, author's translation.

"Take an axe to the prison wall ..." excerpt from "Quietness" by Rumi, *These Branching Moments*, ©1988 John Mayne & Coleman Barks. Used by permission of Copper Beach Press.

"The Small Ruby" from *The Kabir Book: Forty-Four of the Ecstatic Poems of Kabir*, Versions by Robert Bly, © 1977 Robert Bly. Reprinted by permission of Beacon Press Books, Boston.

"Gate 4-A" from *Honeybee* by Naomi Shihab Nye, ©2008 by Naomi Shihab Nye. Used by permission of HarperCollins Publishers.

Distributed by Itasca Books

Cover Design: Ryan McGuire, Bells Design
Cover Photograph: Design Pics / Ron Nickel
Author Photograph: Jari Poulin
Typeset by: Benjamin Carrancho

Printed in the United States of America

The knowledge of the heart is in no book and is not to be found in the mouth of any teacher, but grows out of you like the green seed from the dark earth.

—C.G. Jung

Table of Contents

INTRODUCTION

In the hearts of people today there is a deep longing for peace. When the true spirit of peace is thoroughly dominant, it becomes an inner experience with unlimited possibilities. Only when this really happens—when the spirit of peace awakens and takes possession of men's hearts, can humanity be saved from perishing.

—Albert Schweitzer

Ten years old, we're in what's supposed to be math class. But math is the last thing on our minds. Our teacher, a young woman with curly black hair, whom we adore, has just informed us that in the case of a nuclear attack, we are to hide beneath our desks.

An eerie silence descends on our class as we stare at her with wide eyes. Clearly uncomfortable, her own eyes dart anxiously from one child to the next, as if looking for reassurance in our answering gazes.

I study my desk doubtfully, running my fingers over its

rough wooden surface as I assess its viability as a bomb shelter. It's a beat-up old thing, with a thick base and a top that lifts for storage.

I'm not really sure what a nuclear bomb is. But I know only too well what ordinary bombs can do. For unlike my classmates, I recently moved to the United States from Germany, a country that was reduced to an enormous heap of rubble by the end of World War II.

I think about my best friend in Germany, who was born during the bombing of her family home. Huddled in the basement, her mother screamed the baby into life as the walls crumbled around her. I think of the mutilated men I used to see walking the streets—sad, defeated-looking men without arms, legs, or jaws, men in whose eyes the light seemed to have gone out.

I know there's nothing glorious about war. War is horrifying and traumatic—something no one should have to experience. War means cities in ruins, children screaming, parents wailing. War means ancient cities destroyed forever, along with their priceless art and architecture. War means unimaginable grief and misery—green turning to black.

Fear sits like a hard lump in my chest. Is World War III about to start? What's going on? Why is our favorite teacher lying to us? For in the sure, intuitive way of a child, I know she is lying. If the bombs start falling, our desks will not protect us. She too knows this. And so she fidgets with her necklace and looks out the window as if longing to rush out into the clear golden day and run as fast as her legs will carry her.

What makes matters worse is that I'm not only German but

also Jewish. Deep in my bones I carry the knowledge that my seemingly solid and secure life could crumble to dust in the blink of an eye, as did my father's in 1938 when he, his parents, and his two brothers fled to the United States. Among them, he was the only one who returned to Germany after the war.

A year after we were told to duck under our desks in the event of a nuclear attack, my family moved back to Germany. There, the air still retained the bitter scent of terror, loss, and grief. Now and then, rows of newly constructed apartment buildings gave way to the ruins of bombed-out houses—roped-off reminders of hell. On my long walk to and from school, I often stopped in front of them. Who lived here? I wondered. What was it like when death descended from the skies?

Over the next years, my sense of dread slowly dissipated. But what remained was a troubling awareness of belonging to a strangely warped species. Surely something was very wrong with us.

History class only confirmed my suspicion. I was once again living in Germany, and European history—the only kind we were taught—seemed to consist entirely of long wars punctuated by short interludes of peace—war upon war reaching back into the distant unknown. The very soil of this land was soaked in blood.

Even the sweet lullabies we learned in music class had a dark underbelly. "Sleep baby, sleep," we would sing:

Your daddy's tending the sheep.

Your mama shakes the little tree,

A sweet dream comes floating down.

Sleep baby, sleep.

But there was also another, far darker version from the 17th century:

Fly away baby, fly.

Your daddy's gone to war.

Your mama is in Pommernland (Northern Germany),

Pommernland has burned to the ground.

Fly baby, fly.

At sixteen, I sat on my bed, library books piled around me as I stared at horrific photographs from the concentration camps: Mountains of children's shoes, heaps of naked and emaciated corpses, skeletal survivors with hollow cheeks and haunted eyes.

My heart was aching and my mind spinning with questions for which nobody seemed to have answers—at least none that satisfied me. How did this land of picturesque villages, heart-melting melodies and magical fairy tales spawn such atrocities? How could Nazism have sprung from the same soil that nurtured Bach, Beethoven, and Mozart, Goethe and Rilke?

It would have been comforting if I could have dismissed Nazism as a rare bout of insanity. But I could not. I knew only too well that terrible atrocities were still being committed on every continent. The details varied, but the level of brutality and cruelty did not.

I felt a desperate need to understand what was going on. Was there a curse that periodically turned us into monsters? Were we an evolutionary aberration? What was it that compelled us to choose suffering over joy and turn heaven into hell? Was there any hope for us, and if so, where did it lie?

Many of my friends were Catholics. We're tainted by original sin, they told me. Ever since Eve handed Adam the infamous apple, we've been plagued by their transgression. Flawed and exiled from paradise, our only hope is to be saved through the mercy of Christ.

It was a relief to know I was not the only one who felt that something was amiss with us. Yet my friends' explanation of what that was, and how to right it, struck me as absurd. I'd held newborn babies and seen the light shining through their eyes. I knew they weren't tainted with sin.

Haunted by the need to understand the incomprehensible, I began scouring the world's sacred scriptures. I soon set aside the Old Testament, whose God seemed to embody our own worst qualities: vengefulness and violence, possessiveness and jealousy.

Jesus, on the other hand, comforted me and gave me hope. My Catholic friends claimed he was God's only son. But the impression I got in reading the New Testament was that he didn't want us to perceive him as fundamentally different from ourselves. Both human and divine, he served as a mirror for others to recognize their own essential divinity and their as yet unrealized capacity for compassion.

I felt equally drawn to the teachings of the Gautama Buddha, who sought and found a path from suffering to peace. Evil, he claimed, has no independent existence. We are not innately evil. However, ignorance and unconsciousness cause us to commit acts of evil.

This struck me as true. Still, I kept tripping over the question: If evil is rooted in ignorance, then what exactly are we ignorant of? Why do we so stubbornly cling to our unconsciousness, and what will it take for us to wake up?

Turning to Hinduism, I was told that the culprit responsible for our ignorance and violence was the ego—a teaching I would run into many times. Trapped in an illusory sense of separateness, the ego fails to comprehend our essential oneness and must be shed, transcended or dissolved, if we are to live in peace.

Perhaps this message was meant to convey hope. But to me, it sounded terribly discouraging. I didn't doubt that now and then, some rare individual managed to shed his or her ego. But I personally had never met such a person, and it didn't seem likely that a significant portion of the human population would cast off its ego anytime soon. Egolessness, I concluded, might be an inspiring goal for certain spiritual seekers. But for a species teetering on the edge of self-annihilation, it wasn't a practical solution.

Meanwhile, the Vietnam War had become an ever-present reminder of what was at stake. Though the United States was far away, there were large anti-war demonstrations, and more than once, our entire school was dismissed so that we could participate. Wisely, our teachers realized that with or without permission, many of us were determined to go. Young people are quite capable of telling right from wrong, and the wrongness of what was happening in Vietnam was evident to us.

Clearly, this was a war waged by people who
nessed war close up, and did not understand
doing.

> *Man is the only animal that deals in that atrocity
> of atrocities, War. He is the only one that gathers his
> brethren about him and goes forth in cold blood and calm
> pulse to exterminate his kind. He is the only animal that
> for sordid wages will march out... and help to slaughter
> strangers of his own species who have done him no harm
> and with whom he has no quarrel.... And in the intervals
> between campaigns he washes the blood off his hands and
> works for "the universal brotherhood of man"—with his
> mouth.*
>
> —Mark Twain

We, on the other hand, were still struggling with the aftermath of Hitler's attacks on other nations—nations that had
not threatened Germany, and wanted only to live in peace.
We knew the unspeakable suffering war causes, the danger of
cowing to bad leaders, and the importance of standing up to
say no. Far away though the United States was, we felt a sense
of kinship with the American war resisters and wanted to support them.

Little did I know that someday I myself would be living
in the United States, watching helplessly as it invaded first

Afghanistan, then Iraq, with Iran next on its list—all nations that had never attacked the United States.

By the time I settled in America, I was thirty years old. I'd spent over a decade healing my personal wounds and studying various therapeutic modalities, from gestalt and bioenergetics to massage and acupressure.

Most recently, I'd been learning Indian temple dance in South India. There, I connected with an ancient lineage of priestesses who modeled the integration of spirituality and sexuality that eludes so many of us in the West. Now, I was eager to share some of the gifts I'd received in both Europe and India with my new American friends.

Deeply immersed in the practice of Indian temple dance as I was, I decided to offer a workshop on movement as a spiritual practice. I wanted us to co-create a sanctuary space where we would slow down and listen deeply to our hearts and bodies. Intuitively, I knew that we needed to form a circle. However, I had no idea how strong my passion for circles would grow over the years and how it would deepen.

People often want to know where I learned to lead circle gatherings. "Where did you study this?" they ask. But it wasn't something I studied or absorbed from the outside in. Rather, it was a knowing that emerged from the inside out. I sometimes joke that just as chickens are born knowing how to lay eggs, I was born knowing how to create circles.

Soon, I was leading circles on a regular basis, and gradually, the method I call *Circlework* evolved. Within a few years, I was training other circle leaders. Educators, ministers, social workers, activists, and executives, they all recognized the potency of circle gatherings and wanted to share this ancient medicine with their communities.

Initially I'd been guided by intuition alone. But to teach others, I needed to articulate what I was doing, and why. And so, in the process of developing the Circlework Leadership Training, I began to formulate many of the concepts this book introduces.

One of the fundamental lessons of the circle is that to maintain harmonious relationships, we must learn to open our hearts and, more importantly, *keep* them open, even in the midst of emotional turmoil. When we succeed, the energetic field of the circle becomes palpably charged with love. But if even a single member closes his or her heart, a chill ensues that touches everyone, as if menacing thunderclouds had suddenly swallowed the sun.

More than mere openheartedness, heart-thinking is an ongoing practice that strengthens our ability to keep our hearts open, even under challenging circumstances.

We all know how good open-heartedness feels. But most people experience it only when the conditions are just right. Yet it's when the conditions *aren't* right—for example, in the midst of conflict—that the value of an open heart becomes most apparent. Open-heartedness happens— or not, as the case may be. In contrast, what I call *heart-thinking* is an ongoing practice that strengthens our capacity to keep our hearts open, even under challenging circumstances. Through heart-thinking, we become more effective agents of peace and of the greater evolutionary intelligence that is birthing a new consciousness on our planet today.

Many of my circles consisted of people I barely knew, and who barely knew each other. And yet, at times we experienced a sense of connectedness and unity so profound that many other forms of relationship seemed to pale in comparison. Often I found myself thinking, "This is the only thing I know that's as good as great lovemaking."

As I immersed myself in the practice of Circlework, I began looking forward to those moments in which all sense of separation dissolved. I began to see with increasing clarity that we *weren't* just a bunch of individuals, each working on his or her own healing. We were *one*. Just as people sitting in a circle share a single center, *we* shared a single consciousness that we each accessed from a slightly different angle.

Much as I love circles, I always caution people not to idealize them as havens of unconditional love and acceptance. We all harbor impulses that are fiercely opposed to heart-thinking and jealously guard the boundaries of the small self. Some call them the forces of evil. Others speak of the ego, the shadow or the adversary. Unfortunately, labeling them one way or another doesn't actually give us much insight into their nature. Where do these darker impulses originate? What purpose do they serve?

Once again, I found myself grappling with the same questions that had haunted me decades ago: Why are we so quick to close our heart to others, and what can we do about it? Now, however, I had a new teacher to help me explore these questions: *the circle.*

Previously, regardless of whether I'd approached the issue from a psychological or a spiritual angle, I'd always focused on the journey of *individual* transformation. Some defined its goal as wholeness or happiness; others spoke of individuation, of enlightenment or liberation. Either way, everything seemed to hinge on our personal consciousness.

Of course, there is ultimately nothing personal about the ego. Even though we experience it as intensely personal—after all, the very word means "I"—its strategies, tactics and habits are predictable and common. Nonetheless, I'd always been encouraged to approach the journey of transforming the ego as an entirely personal endeavor.

Most of my teachers agreed that human consciousness needed to evolve, if our species was to survive. But, they would hasten to add, collective change can only occur one individual at a time. Since we can't force others to change, the biggest contribution we can make toward healing the world is to heal *ourselves.* How? Through tools such as therapy, counseling and meditation—all of which rely on individual (and often solitary) effort.

Something about this line of thought had never sat right with me. It sounded reasonable enough, but it didn't *feel* right. However, I had never been able to articulate why. Now, I gradually began to understand my misgivings. For what the circle showed me was that despite our individualism, we have never lost the capacity to experience ourselves as particles within a single overarching intelligence, rather than as separate individuals.

To describe this experience of becoming one with a group to someone who has never experienced it is a lot like trying to describe the taste of a banana to someone who has never eaten one. But perhaps you can get a whiff of what I'm talking about if you imagine that a group of people cease to function as separate individuals and instead fuse into something like a healing chalice—a great bowl capable of holding in compassion whatever needs to be held. On a personal level, this experience is tremendously liberating. At the same time, it gives us access to the evolutionary power that is fueling our collective transformation.

For many, the idea of tapping into our collective consciousness is scary. They immediately think of situations in which people sacrificed their personal integrity to the group or to a corrupt leader. Thankfully, that is not at all what we're talking about here. When moments of oneness occur in my circles, it is never because we have denied our differences and our unique personalities. On the contrary, there's a sense of being so fully seen, respected and honored that we no longer feel the need to assert our personal boundaries. They still exist, but they no longer separate us.

In such moments of true union, I feel that we are truly doing the work we have come together to do. Instead of working from the narrow platform of our personal psyche, we are tapping into the collective consciousness of our species. Ancient wounds begin to break open and heal as we hold them in the vortex of our attentive presence. Millennia old tectonic plates begin to shift, and like a phoenix, a new awareness of who we really are begins to rise out of the ashes of the past.

The Realm of Collective Consciousness

As I continued to work with circles, I began to see that the habits that cause us to close our hearts have both shallow and deep roots. The shallow roots lie in our childhood and up-bringing, and it is here that Western psychology focuses all its attention. But while the exploration of our personal psyche is valuable and important, we will never understand human be-havior unless we also look at its deeper roots. And invariably, these lie in the shadowy realm that C.G. Jung called "the col-lective unconscious."

Jung realized that though our conscious memories are lim-ited to our own lifetime, our psyche also contains images and memories of times long passed. Our conscious mind is after all just one dimension of our being—and, contrary to what we would like to believe, not always the most influential. If we are lakes, then our individual psyche is merely the sun-warmed layer on top. Beneath it lies an infinitely deep reservoir of shared history and memories.

Jung's thesis was that these memories are stored in a realm of the human psyche that we all share in common. Most of the time, we have no access to this dimension. Now and then, however, it surfaces, for example in our dreams. Here, Jung explains his views:

> My thesis then, is as follows: in addition to our im-mediate consciousness, which is of a thoroughly

personal nature and which we believe to be the only empirical psyche (even if we tack on the personal unconscious as an appendix), there exists a second psychic system of a collective, universal, and impersonal nature which is identical in all individuals. This collective unconscious does not develop individually but is inherited.

It is, I believe, within this shadowy realm that has so much power over us, yet of which we know so little, that we'll find the keys to understanding our collective insanity. Here, traces of experience gathered over millions of years are gathered, distilled, and fashioned into the rules, beliefs, habits, and assumptions that guide our ego. In its efforts to protect us, it is this deep reservoir of ancestral memory upon which the ego depends.

Much of spiritual and psychological literature ignores this realm entirely. Even those who do acknowledge its existence generally minimize the extent to which it governs our relationships, shapes our thinking, and impacts our lives. Yet I've come to believe that the keys to understanding and shifting our self-destructive course lie here, in the dimly lit caverns of our collective consciousness.

Jung called the collective realm "the collective unconscious" because he considered it inaccessible to the conscious mind. I would agree that we generally have little or no awareness of the collective realm. However, I believe this can change. If what I've witnessed in my workshops is any indication, we are capable of raising significant chunks of material from the depths of our collective psyche into the light of conscious awareness. Indeed, I believe evolution is demanding in no uncertain terms that we do so. For as we shall see, some of the impulses that arise from those depths have become potentially suicidal liabilities.

Caught up in our individualistic bias, we'll inevitably fail to respond appropriately to expressions of collective pain or negativity. Terrorism is a case in hand. The fundamental strategy in the so-called 'war on terror' has been to identify and disable individuals who are believed to be involved in terrorist activities. Unfortunately, this has not made our world a safer place, because those individuals aren't operating in a vacuum. Rather, they are channels of *collective* feelings and attitudes.

Our habitual response to people who offend or threaten us is to judge them, classify them as enemies and ultimately seek to destroy them. For thousands of years, this was a tenable response, if not an enlightened one. Today, on the other hand, it's suicidal. Every victory won through violence is a boomerang that will sooner or later come back to strike us down.

I am not suggesting that we stop holding each other responsible for our actions. However, we need to understand clearly that we cannot overcome violence with violence. Instead, we need to address the unmet needs that fuel it. All human beings share the need for respect, autonomy, economic security and safety. Disregard any one of needs, and violence is sure to follow. Just as a volcano will break through wherever the earth's crust is thinnest, people's collective rage and frustration will express itself through those individuals whose ego is most vulnerable. Who they are is not the point—if it's not one person, it's another.

Over the years of leading circles with people from all walks of life, my ability to perceive the collective force fields and energies that move through us grew steadily stronger. Gradually, a host of ancient habits began to reveal themselves, like primordial creatures rising out of the mist. Diverse as they are, they all have one important commonality: they cripple our capacity for heart-thinking, and in doing so, contribute to our present state of collective insanity.

It's true, transformation really does happen one individual at a time. But from where does our desire for transformation emanate? From what source do we derive the energy that allows us to complete this great migration? Our individualistic society tells us we're motivated by our desire for personal happiness, freedom, or wisdom. No question, personal desire is an important factor. Yet I believe that a far more powerful stream of energy flows from the collective consciousness of our species. This greater body of intelligence wants us to wake up because it recognizes that our survival depends on it. Sure, collective transformation begins with individual transformation. However, if your final goal is merely personal wholeness, you will fall short, whereas if you approach your own healing as a contribution to the healing of the planet, your own transformation will quicken.

When I first started leading circles, I too shared the individualistic bias of my culture. Had you asked me what the purpose of my circles was, I probably would have said that they provided a much needed source of nurturance and healing and helped us reclaim our wholeness.

This was and still is true. But as the disastrous impact of

unconscious collective conditioning came into view, I began to see Circlework in a new light. I realized that together we are not merely healing our personal wounds and strengthening our capacity to live with wisdom and grace, but we are also contributing to a much larger process of collective evolution. Through us, a new consciousness is emerging that has the potential to heal not only our own lives, but also the planet. For just as we have the capacity to tap into our collective pain, rage, anger and other negative energies, we're also capable of serving as channels of a greater collective wisdom, courage and compassion.

The key to the insanity of the human ego lies within the realm of the collective unconscious. Here, traces of experience gathered over millions of years are gathered, distilled, and fashioned into the rules, beliefs, habits, and assumptions that our ego depends on for guidance.

When a woman gives birth, no amount of Lamaze training can protect her from the experience of physical pain. What it *can* do is prepare her to soften into the pain and to work *with* instead of *against* nature. Along the same lines, the awareness that a new consciousness is birthing itself through us certainly doesn't erase our collective labor pains. But it *does* make it easier for us say 'yes' to the process, scary as it is. This book will, I hope, give you a new understanding of what that new consciousness is, and how by cultivating it, we can become a species capable of living in peace.

After leading circles in the West for many years, I started

wondering how Circlework might serve people in other parts of the world, especially those affected by violence and warfare. If this work could help the participants of my circles cultivate inner and outer peace, then perhaps it could help others do the same. That, at least, was what my intuition told me. But as long as I was exclusively working with Westerners who enjoyed relatively privileged lives, I couldn't know for sure.

Soon, however, life presented me with the perfect opportunity to find out. It was 2001, and the United States had started waging war in Afghanistan. My thoughts kept turning to the women of that country.

In times of crisis, I thought, it's always up to the women to put food on the table and somehow make sure that life goes on. My heart was aching for those women and spontaneously, I offered a prayer: "Please, let me share my work with the people who need it most, and can do most good with it."

Two days later, I got a phone call from two women, both dedicated peacemakers.

"We're calling from Israel," they told me. "We want to come to the Circlework Training."

Nitsan Gordon was Jewish, Mirvat Hamati was Palestinian. Together, they were leading workshops that brought women from both sides together.

I took a deep breath. My prayers had been answered.

Soon after, the Institute for Circlework, a non-profit organization that I founded to support the evolution of Circlework, helped Nitsan and Mirvat attend the Circlework Training. They in turn invited me to Israel, and in 2005, with the help of many supporters from the United States and Canada, I began leading circles in the Middle East for Jewish, Palestinian, Druze, and Bedouin women.

Needless to say, it was a big leap from facilitating gatherings for Americans and Canadians to working with Middle Eastern women who lived in a war zone and typically carried a heavy burden of trauma, grief, and resentment. Yet, to my delight, I found that in the Middle East the benefits of Circlework were even more obvious than in the United States. These women were desperately hungry for effective tools and new insights, for in their eyes, collective transformation was no mere personal luxury but rather a matter of life and death. Trapped as they were in an ancient tribal feud, the power of unconscious collective conditioning was obvious to them. They had personally experienced its devastating effects and were as a result firmly committed to the journey of collective evolution.

It was exhilarating and profoundly satisfying to see Jewish and Palestinian women discovering their sisterhood and coming to understand, respect, and even love one another. Many were peacemakers with years of experience under their belts. Now, however, they began to clearly recognize their role in a much larger process of global transformation. Simultaneously, they recognized the value of Circlework as a potent tool that by its very nature inspires not just personal but above all *collective* healing and transformation.

Today, I lead workshops and trainings for people from around the world, including the Middle East, Afghanistan, and Europe. I've spent thousands of hours observing how we react and interact, what helps us open our hearts and what gets in the way, and why some people get along while others don't.

This book contains the distilled essence of what I've learned along the way. All the concepts and practices I introduce here have been tested in the fires of every kind of relational challenge. I know that, aided by the power of heart-thinking and armed with an understanding of the inner adversaries we're facing, we can resolve even the most bitter conflicts, heal horrendous psychological wounds, and come out the other side whole, radiant, and empowered.

My work has also gifted me with a new love and appreciation for my own species, for which I am infinitely grateful. As a German Jew, I came to the circle burdened by a deep sense of alienation from the human race. Today, I routinely fall in love with total strangers and am consistently amazed and humbled by our capacity for courage, wisdom, compassion, and forgiveness.

I've witnessed transformations I would never have believed possible, and know that if what I witness in my circles could be multiplied by a million, our world would be a very different place. Motivated by a sincere desire for peace, we gain access to a collective wisdom we could never access on our own. Together, we can solve seemingly unsolvable conflicts and heal seemingly incurable wounds.

Today, I know without a doubt that the human psyche wants to evolve, to become wiser, more loving and peaceful. Evolution is not just what the planet is demanding of us. It's also what we ourselves most want, difficult and painful though the process might be.

And so, despite the relentless violence of our species, a huge wave of change is washing over us. We are longing to evolve, ready for it, and capable of it. Having glimpsed what's possible, our souls are straining at the leash like a dog that have caught the scent of a squirrel. "What are you waiting for?" they're crying. "Come on! Let's go already!"

Today, we live in two simultaneous realities. On the one hand, our planet is groaning under an unbearable burden of toxicity, unleashed by the most violent, arrogant, and destructive species that ever was. But at the same time, millions are awakening to a new consciousness. We know, in a way former generations did not, that we live on a small planet where all beings are interconnected. We know how little national boundaries really mean. We know that Earth is not the limitless playground we once believed it to be but rather a beautiful yet alarmingly fragile gem. From the Internet to subatomic physics, from the global economy to the ecological crisis, everything is colluding to expand our sense of who we really are.

Of course, to judge by the media, one would never guess the true magnitude of the birthing that's underway, for in our society, the evolution of consciousness, no matter how momentous, is rarely considered newsworthy. But that doesn't mean it isn't real. It *is*. It's real, it's powerful, and it's growing by leaps and bounds. The shift in human consciousness that our planet needs is not just possible—it's already happening.

Some are likely to dismiss this claim as wishful thinking. I believe they're wrong. What is happening is a very real and powerful movement that seeks the restoration of human sanity and dignity, and the healing of our beloved Mother Earth.

Just how many are involved in this movement? It's hard to say, but one thing we know for sure: their numbers are vast. As author Paul Hawken says, "Describing the breadth of the movement is like trying to hold the ocean in your hand. It is that large."

Paul Ray and Sherry Anderson, co-authors of *The Cultural Creatives*, conducted studies spanning thirteen years and involving over a hundred thousand Americans. Their conclusion is that at least fifty million are what they call "cultural creatives," people who care deeply about ecology, saving the planet, self-actualization, spirituality, and relationships—people, in other words, in whom a new consciousness is awakening.

Perhaps no one says it better than Barbara Marx Hubbard, passionate spokeswoman for what she calls "conscious evolution": "We will either evolve toward a more sustainable, compassionate, and creative global system, or we face the real possibility of devolution and destruction of our life support system and of much of life on Earth within our own or our children's lifetime! This dangerous reality is motivating us to enter into what I call the first age of conscious evolution—that is, evolution by choice and not by chance."

Is everyone capable of embracing the new consciousness that is arising within us? I doubt it. But fortunately, it isn't necessary. For as Malcolm Gladwell points out in his book, *The Tipping Point*, changes made by small numbers of people can ripple outward until a critical mass or "tipping point" is reached. Today, all indicators suggest that the tipping point is now. Any step you take to support the shift this book outlines will have far greater impact today than it would have even ten years ago.

No question, we have a long way to go. We're still governed by ancient habits that cause us to tense up when we need to relax, harden when we need to soften, and close down when we need to open up. To support the birthing of a new consciousness, we'll need to re-educate ourselves. This book will explain what that process of re-education involves. We'll discuss the various types of collective conditioning that are holding us back—how and why they evolved, how they affect us, how we can overcome them and thereby contribute to the healing of our world.

Like a map, this book will show you where we came from, where we stand today, and where we're going. It will reveal a bigger picture and help you see that despite the gravity of the situation, there really is cause for hope. Together, we can move from wounding to healing, from fragmentation to wholeness, from insanity to wisdom, and from violence to peace.

What this book can't do is replace the experiential, hands-on process of grappling with your collective conditioning in the midst of daily life. Just as you can't learn to play the piano by reading about it, the only way to learn the art of heart-thinking is by practicing it. That said, the better you understand the dynamics involved and the obstacles you're likely to face, the better prepared you'll be to deal with them.

I recommend you do not try to absorb whole chapters in a single gulp. Read a section, then put it aside and take some time for contemplation. When you come across new ideas, dwell on them, digest them, and then make them yours. Share your thoughts with friends. Experiment with the questions and exercises provided at the end of this book. If you're interested in forming a discussion group, you can download a set of helpful guidelines from my website. The more time you spend communicating and sharing your ideas and responses, the more clarity and insight you'll gain.

And now, join me as we dive into the deep waters of our collective consciousness.

Part I

Heart-Thinking: Our Key to Peace

CHAPTER 1

THEY SAY THEY THINK WITH THEIR HEADS

Perhaps the heart is not just a sort of valentine. More than a way of loving, the heart may be a way of experiencing life, the capacity to know a fundamental connection to others and see them whole.... When people look at others in this way, the connection they experience makes it a simpler thing to forgive, to have compassion, to serve, and to love.... Perhaps the healing of the world rests on just this sort of shift in our way of seeing, a coming to know that in our suffering and our joy we are connected to one another with unbreakable and compelling human bonds. In that knowing, all of us become less vulnerable and alone. The heart, which can see these connections, may be far more powerful a source of healing than the mind.

—Rachel Naomi Remen, *Kitchen Table Wisdom*

Linda is a beautiful, curly-headed woman with bright blue eyes, an infectious laugh, and a passion for creating healthy, fulfilling relationships. For several years, she's been part of a group of people who are pioneering new ways of connecting and building communities.

"There are about forty of us," she explains, "a mix of Americans and Europeans."

Recently, the group went through an intense process. "It was one of those things you just never forget," Linda says.

It all started when their group leader gave them a most unusual assignment: they were to plan a vacation they would all take together. To make it even more challenging, the rule was that this had to be a vacation every single member of the group could commit to.

Linda throws up her hands up in mock horror and rolls her eyes. "Have you ever tried to get forty busy people to agree to be in the same place at the same time? How on earth would you do such a thing? Just trying to pick a date when forty people all have vacation time is ridiculous."

Somehow, after much discussion, they managed to find dates that worked for everyone. Linda was impressed. "It seemed like a little miracle," she laughs. But agreeing when to go was just the first step. Next, they had to decide where to go. And that, it turned out, was not so easy.

Linda grins at the memory. "A bunch of people stood up and said, 'Well, I don't get much time off, and if I'm going to take a vacation, I want to go to the sea. There's no way I'm going unless it's by the sea.'

"Others said, 'Well, I'm not going unless we go to the mountains.'

"So all these people were taking their stands. We started arguing about it, and this went on for a long time, back and forth, on and on. We wanted to do this, we really did, but it was hopeless. We were getting nowhere; we were stuck in the mud."

"Finally, this woman stands up and says, 'Look here, I'm fed up. I'm sick of this and I'm getting a headache. Let's take a break. Let's put on some music and shake out our bodies. Let's put out big sheets of paper and draw pictures of the vacation we want.'

"So that's what we did. We played music, we danced, and shook out all our stress. Then we sat around on the floor and drew pictures of mountains and cottages and playing in the water, and all these images of our perfect vacation.

"Well, it was amazing, because by the time we sat down again, the whole mood had shifted. There was no tension in the room anymore, none. Instead, we just felt how much we loved each other.

"And suddenly, everyone came to the realization that they would much rather be together, no matter where, than in their favorite place on Earth all by themselves.

"That was it. From that point on, it was easy. I learned so much from that circle. It was a peak experience for me."

"So," I ask Linda, "where did you decide to go?"

Linda's face lights up with a big smile as she says, "We're going to Spain, to a resort by the sea."

Jung and the Pueblo Chief

Wow! What happened here? What was the magic that led to such a dramatic turnaround?

The answer is simple: The group shifted from *head-thinking* to *heart-thinking*. What Linda describes is something I have witnessed many times in my own circles. No matter what the issue at hand and no matter how knotty and intractable a conflict we're dealing with may be, there *is* a way that works. But to find it, we have to stop thinking with our heads and start thinking with our hearts.

Heart-thinking is a term I first encountered in the autobiography of Carl Gustav Jung. There, he tells of a life-changing encounter he had with a Pueblo chief during the 1920s. Perhaps conscious of Jung's interest in mental health, the chief remarked that as the Pueblo saw it, the whites were a bunch of sad, unhappy, tortured souls. What was their problem?

"They are always seeking something," the chief said. "What are they seeking? The whites always want something; they are always uneasy and restless. We do not know what they want. We do not understand them."

Jung was taken aback by this portrayal of his people. The chief not only considered them unhappy and discontent, but also outright insane. And when Jung asked what this conclusion was based on, the chief responded without hesitation.

"They say that they think with their heads."

Jung was startled.

"Why of course. What do you think with?" he asked the

chief.

"We think here," he said, indicating his heart.

Head – and Heart-Thinking

As we shall see, head-thinking can take many forms. However, they all have one thing in common: They split us in two and disconnect our mind from our heart and body.

You know what I'm talking about if you've ever driven somewhere, only to realize upon arrival that you have only the foggiest memory of the actual journey. Your body was driving while your mind was rehashing the past or planning the future. Your body was in one place, your mind in another.

Of course there are times when it's absolutely appropriate to temporarily concentrate all our energy in our brain—for example, when we're trying to figure out a complex mathematical problem. However, this choice to focus completely on a mental process isn't the same thing as head-thinking. Head-thinking is not a conscious choice but an unconscious habit. It's not an option but a *compulsion*.

Anytime you notice that you've become lost in head-thinking, remember that the journey home begins with a simple downward shift of awareness from your head to your heart. With this, you automatically return to your body. And since your body always lives in the present, you also come to rest in this moment.

This doesn't mean that your thoughts will suddenly vanish

into thin air. They might, but more often, the show goes on. Now, however, instead of letting your mind run your life, you can use it in the best possible way—not as a dictator but rather as an ally eager to help you achieve your goals. Faced with a problem, you can seek its advice, much as you might turn to a smart, well-meaning friend. You can appreciate its brilliance without giving it license to run your life. Rather, in all decisions, your heart retains the last word: if it says "no," then no it is.

Obviously, what we're talking about here is not the physical organ but rather that nucleus of emotional and spiritual intelligence we refer to when we describe our heart as open or closed, soft or hard, whole or broken.

Your first step toward heart-thinking is to shift the center of your awareness downwards, from your head to your heart. Centered in your heart, you can use your mind in the best possible way—not as a dictator but rather as an ally eager to help you achieve your goals.

Such expressions are by no means arbitrary but rather founded on the bedrock of embodied experience. Consciously or not, we all know the heart to be something far deeper and far more mysterious than a mere physical organ. No matter what our cultural background might be, we all recognize the heart as a vortex of emotion and consciousness.

And while the heart doesn't speak in words, it certainly *does* speak. Like an inner compass, its needle is always pointing towards love. Love is where it wants to go and where it wants to stay. Move away from love and the heart suffers. Move towards love, and it's happy. We see a child leaping into its mother's arms and our heart floods with warmth. We see a friend suffer and our heart contracts in pain. And as recent research confirms, everything that affects our emotional heart also affects our physical heart.

The Marriage of Heart and Intellect

Please don't think of heart-thinking as the opposite of head-thinking. It's not that at all. We're not trying to replace the tyranny of the mind with that of the heart. I emphasize this, because unfortunately, many New Age teachings suggest we do just that. They idolize the heart and demonize the mind. No doubt the intellect has its limitations. Nonetheless it's a invaluable ally without which we cannot find the path to peace.

I sometimes think of the heart as a bowl that can hold the whole world in its compassionate embrace. The intellect, on the other hand, is like a sharp knife that can analyze our perceptions. Just as a cook needs both a knives and bowls to make a good meal, we too need both an open heart and a keen mind.

To suppress or neglect our intellect doesn't serve us. Rather, we want to use it in ways that *support* rather than obstruct the needs of the heart. When I speak of heart-thinking, I am referring to this harmonious union of an open heart and a clear, supportive mind, the fruits of which are inner peace and wholeness.

Many spiritual seekers view their intellect as a spiritual

hindrance—an obstacle they need to overcome in order to set their hearts free. I believe this is an unfortunate misconception rooted in the realities of a bygone era. As our world has changed, so has the role of the intellect.

A mere thousand years ago, most humans knew nothing about what lay beyond the horizon, nor did they need to. The world was a fascinating mystery around which storytellers wove their wondrous narratives, mingling fact and fiction, truth and fantasy. On the other hand, they knew exactly who had gathered and prepared their food, who had made their clothing and built the shelter under which they slept. Under these conditions, one could maintain peaceful and harmonious relationships without much help from the intellect. It was enough to have an open, generous heart.

Fast forward to our times, and it still holds true that in the realm of personal relationships, open-heartedness is far more valuable than intellectual brilliance. But whereas for millions of years, *all* human relationships were personal, today, the vast majority are *not*. We eat food produced by farmers in countries we've never visited. We drive cars built thousands of miles away and go to war against nations we can barely locate on a map. We'll never meet the truck drivers who delivered our food to the supermarket, the Chinese workers who crafted our shoes, or the Iranian women who knotted the rug on our bedroom floor. Nonetheless they're all part of the great web that sustains us. And while this web might feel like an abstraction, the relationships it's comprised of are every bit as real as those we call "personal."

In recent years, neuroscientists have made an exciting discovery. They've found that the heart has its own independent nervous system—a complex system referred to as "the brain in the heart." There are at least forty thousand neurons (nerve cells) in the heart—as many as are found in various subcortical centers in the brain....

"The heart communicates with the brain and the rest of the body in three ways for which there's solid scientific evidence: neurologically (through the transmission of nerve impulses), biochemically (through hormones and neurotransmitters), and biophysically (through pressure waves).... Through these biological communication systems, the heart has a significant influence on the function of our brains and all our bodily systems...

From a neuroscience perspective, the nervous system within the heart is sufficiently sophisticated to qualify as a little brain in its own right....

The heart's electromagnetic field is by far the most powerful produced by the body; it's approximately five thousand times greater in strength than the field produced by the brain, for example.

—*The HeartMath Solution*, Doc Childre and Howard Martin

Under these conditions, it's no longer enough that we extend our kindness and caring to people whom we personally have met. Rather, the reach of our heart needs to expand to embrace the entire planetary community. Instead of defining ourselves merely as members of a specific nation or group, we need to define ourselves as part of a much greater family.

But how shall we know this family, understand its suffering, or appreciate its needs? Without the help of our intellect, we can't even identify the dangers that threaten our own lives. Who has ever set eyes on global warming or on nuclear contamination? To our heart, such things are mere abstractions. But our mind understands that they're absolutely real, and far more menacing than the tigers that once stalked our ancestors.

It's no longer enough that we extend kindness and compassion to the beings we personally have met. Rather, the reach of our heart needs to expand to embrace the entire planetary community.

Divorced from the heart, our intellect becomes short-sighted and destructive. But the opposite is equally true: On its own, our heart is liable to make foolish choices. To effectively serve our planet, we must unite an open heart with an open mind. This harmonious marriage of heart and mind is, I believe, the very hallmark of heart-thinking in the global era.

The great poet Pablo Neruda expressed it beautifully: "To feel the intimacy of brothers is a marvelous thing in life. To feel the love of people whom we love is a fire that feeds our life. But to feel the affection that comes from those whom we do not know, from those unknown to us, who are watching over our sleep and solitude, over our dangers and our weaknesses   that is something still greater and more beautiful because it widens out the boundaries of our being, and unites all living things."

Some may judge Neruda's words to be overly idealistic. Yet today, more and more people feel the same way, and are weaving this awareness into the fabric of their daily lives. Like a child that can hardly wait to learn and grow, our collective spirit is straining towards a new, more expansive kind of love—a love that melds our heart's capacity for compassion with the mind's understanding of how we're connected to the greater web of life.

Heart-Thinking as a Practice

Open-heartedness is a gift that falls in our lap now and then. Heart-thinking, on the other hand, is an ongoing practice, and one that today, more and more people are embracing. Why? Because they realize that it holds the key to peace. If we want peace—both inner and outer—we must learn to keep our hearts open, even under challenging circumstances.

When our heart opens spontaneously, it feels easy and pleasurable. As a practice, it's far more challenging because it requires that we unravel some complex knots within our collective consciousness. As we'll see, many of these knots formed thousands of years ago, and for a long time, they didn't endanger our survival. Today, they do.

This book will help you understand why, despite our good

intentions, we so often fail to maintain harmonious, peaceful relationships. It will highlight the obstacles that can prevent you from meeting the world with an open heart, explain why they exist and show you how to recognize and dissolve them, thereby setting yourself free to love the world with all the expansiveness and generosity you are capable of.

But is it Practical?

In our world, anyone who suggests that we should follow our heart's lead, not just in private matters but out in public, is likely to be dismissed as a dreamer and an idealist. It's just not practical, people say.

But is that really true? We don't call Christians impractical, even though Christ represents a perfection unattainable to ordinary mortals. Why then is it impractical to honor the will of our heart, which orients itself towards love like a sunflower to the sun? Of course we will never attain perfect love; and, of course, life on Earth will never be paradise. But the minute we stop moving towards that vision, we become agents of death and destruction. If, on the other hand, we can stay true to the deepest desires of our heart, we won't go too far astray.

As I see it, the real issue is not that heart-thinking is impractical but that it's scary as hell. If we open our heart, it can be broken. If we care, we can be hurt. If we trust, we can be betrayed. If we allow ourselves to be visible, we can be judged. No wonder many people refuse to expose their hearts to the so-called real world. As Gandhi often said, it takes great courage to walk the path of love, vulnerable as it makes us. Yet our heart is, to borrow the words of poet Mary Oliver, "a lion of courage." And, to the extent that we follow its guidance, so are we.

Another misconception is that the heart is weak or senti-mental. In fact, nothing is more strong and resilient, not to mention far-sighted and wise, than the human heart. At times, heart-thinkers might appear to be more emotional than head-thinkers, but are they really? I don't think so. It's just that they're more in touch with their feelings and less invested in hiding them.

In fact, in many instances, you can count on heart-thinking to make you *less* rather than more emotional. Just consider what happened in Linda's circle. As long as she and her friends were thinking with their heads, the question of where to go on vaca-tion was emotionally charged. The possibility of not spending their precious time in their ideal environment felt so distressing that it threatened to drive them apart. Entangled in anger and fear, they disconnected from their hearts and lost sight of their love for these men and women with whom they had already shared so much, and to whom they were in some cases closer than they were to their own families. Everyone dug in their heels and refused to compromise. They weren't having any fun nor were they

Only when an open heart unites with an open mind can we effectively serve our planet. This harmonious marriage of heart and mind is the hallmark of heart-thinking in the global era.

achieving their goals.

But as Linda discovered, the world we see through the eyes of our hearts looks radically different from the one we see through the eyes of our mind, and many things that the mind cares passionately about matter little to the heart.

Once Linda and her friends switched to heart-thinking, it no longer seemed all that important where they went, as long as they went there *together*. As they discovered, many things that the mind cares about passionately are of little consequence to the heart. Their mind, they realized, had been mistaken; it had been so focused on their need for control that it had overlooked their far stronger need for connection and community.

Centered in their hearts, the veils of illusion lifted, and everything appeared in a new light. As the preciousness of their connection came into view, they recognized friendship and community as their top priorities. Effortlessly, the entire conflictual tangle dissolved, and what had just minutes earlier seemed impossible became easy.

The Heart is Your Inner Compass

If you ever feel unsure of what you're supposed to do in a situation, here's a good rule of thumb: always do what leads to greater love. Love is your job description—no matter what you do for a living.

—Marci Shimoff in *Love for No Reason: 7 Steps to Creating a Life of Unconditional Love*

Your heart knows what will fulfill you and what won't. Just as it connected Linda's friends with their true needs, it can also help you discover your real goals—not the ready-made ones society offers you, but the ones you've been carrying deep in your soul from long before you were born—the sacred ones that, whether or not you ever achieve them, can imbue your life with meaning and purpose. When you allow your heart to guide you towards these goals, you'll feel it signaling its joy, its pleasure, its *yes*.

Sadly, no society raised its citizens to be so cut off from their hearts as ours. How, then, can we know our true goals?

Many people don't. On the surface, they might appear well-adjusted and successful. But scratch the surface, and you'll find that they feel lost and are wandering through life confused and disoriented, unsure of why they're here and where they're going. Like ships without a compass, they have no way of charting a viable course towards happiness.

The mind is like a parent who *thinks* it knows what we need, but really doesn't. What it assumes we need and what we *really* need may be quite different. And so, the goals it sets for us, well-intended though they might be, often miss the mark. As the Jungian analyst and author Jean Shinoda Bolen points out, "Logic can tell you superficially where a path might lead to, but it cannot judge whether your heart will be in it."

Tragically, some people dedicate their entire lives towards the achievement of goals that their heart feels no real connection to and does not support.

Make sure your heart is really in the work you do! It's okay if it's difficult and challenging. But if your heart is unhappy, no matter how great the financial rewards might be, something is wrong. Don't tell yourself, "It's just a job." It's *not* just a job. It's your life, the most precious gift you've ever received.

Heart-Thinking: A Practice for Body, Emotions, Mind and Spirit

As a physical practice, heart-thinking involves staying present in our body. This enables us to hear the messages of our heart and soul, which are broadcast through the body.

As an emotional practice, heart-thinking invites us to fully experience our feelings, be they joyful or sorrowful. Conscious of our true feelings, we can take better care of ourselves.

As a mental practice, heart-thinking transforms both *how* we think and *what* we think. The process of thinking—the how—changes when we stop identifying with our thoughts and learn to detach from them. The content—the what—transforms as we the discard limiting beliefs that once caused us to close our hearts.

As a spiritual practice, heart-thinking connects us to an inner knowing that recognizes separation as an illusion. Oneness then ceases to be a mental idea and becomes a visceral experience.

Heart-Thinking and Global Peace

What we need now is global coherence, an awakening of the global heart, the feeling of being one interconnected planetary body with a shared purpose of mutual growth for the sake of the whole Earth community.

—Barbara Marx Hubbard in Birth 2012 and Beyond: Humanity's Great Shift to the Age of Conscious Evolution

Now perhaps you're thinking, "Well, this heart-thinking stuff may be fine for a bunch of wealthy folks whose biggest problem is where they're going to spend their next vacation. But in the real world, it just doesn't work."

But you'd be wrong. Over and over, I've seen heart-thinking resolve highly fraught and difficult conflicts. Every circle I've led has helped me understand that the positive impact of heart-thinking on our relationships can hardly be overestimated. Centered in an open heart, we gain access to a wiser, more expansive, and far-sighted consciousness. When our decisions and actions come from that place, we respond to life's challenges in ways that are intelligent, practical, and more likely to meet with success.

Your heart can inform you of your real goals—not the ready-made ones society offers you, but the ones you've been carrying deep in your soul from long before you were born—the sacred ones that, whether or not you ever achieve them, can imbue your life with meaning and purpose.

On the other hand, when we try to communicate *without* centering in our hearts, we merely end up wasting a lot of time and energy. In all matters of human relationship, heart-thinking is not just practical—in my experience, it's our *only* practical option.

Especially in conflicts, head-thinking is totally counterproductive. If you take two groups of people, one stressed and emotionally shut down, the other relaxed and open-hearted, and you present them with a challenging interpersonal problem, you can pretty much predict the outcome. The stressed group is going to hit an impasse. They'll get stuck, just as Linda's group did, because people will lock horns and refuse to compromise.

Meanwhile, the heart-thinkers will experience a surge of creative juice that allows them to recognize possibilities the head-thinkers overlooked. Compromise won't feel like a failure or a defeat because the joy of finding common ground will far outweigh the discomfort of not getting one's way.

Recently, I got together with a friend to watch a documentary called *Ten Questions for the Dalai Lama*. At one point, the interviewer asked the Dalai Lama how to bring peace to Israel. Here's his response, verbatim:

> Too much emotions, I think... Negative emotions, frustrations, hatred, anger. I think that's the greatest obstacle. There's too much emotion, too much negative emotion. This should be cooled down, reduced. I think for the time being... I think more festivals, more picnics. Let them forget these difficult

things, these emotions, and make personal friendships. Then start to talk about these serious matters.

My friend wrinkled her nose in disgust. "Picnics!" she yelled. "Does he really think that you can undo decades of bloodshed and hatred with picnics?"

I, on the other hand, loved the Dalai Lama's answer. The message I heard was not that picnics are the key to peace in the Middle East—the Dalai Lama is, after all, no fool—but that as long as Jews and Palestinians fail to connect through their hearts, they'll never solve their problems.

As someone who leads workshops in Israel and Palestine, I know he's right: As long as we remain trapped in head-thinking, we'll never find a path to peace.

The Arabs, Jews, Bedouins, and Druze who attend my circles typically arrive burdened with distrust, anger, and pain. They're wary, and the wheels of their mind are spinning fast. They're tempted to start arguing about who did what to whom, and which side is more to blame—the tedious kind of debate that goes round and round in circles, leading nowhere.

My task, as the facilitator, is to prevent this from happening and instead guide them into their hearts. Only after this happens can real communication and transformation occur. The outer situation may remain the same, but their perception of it does not.

I shall always remember a moment when a Jewish woman turned to her Arab sisters and said, "I don't know the solution to our problems. But one thing I see clearly: we *must* overcome the illusion of separation. Even though it seems like we're on opposite sides, we're really playing a game. I am you, and you are me."

These are extraordinary words, coming as they do from the mouth of someone embroiled in one of the world's most bitter conflicts, where the pressure to take sides is enormous. Yet wherever people are practicing heart-thinking, a similar awareness is growing.

War, says Pema Chodron, begins when we harden our hearts. Peace, on the other hand, begins when we allow them to soften and open. Where the closed heart rejects the conditions that could lead to peace, there is no conflict the open heart cannot resolve. When the heart's wisdom prevails, doors begin to open where we didn't even know they existed.

Cultivating True Intelligence

Our scientific power has outrun our spiritual power. We have guided missiles and misguided men.

—Martin Luther King

Sometimes I imagine beings from some faraway solar system telling their kids about a species that once roamed the earth and, until they annihilated themselves, prided themselves on being exceptionally intelligent.

The kids will scratch their heads in disbelief: "You're saying they poisoned their own water and air, they couldn't stop slaughtering each other, and they considered themselves super smart? You gotta be kidding!"

Intelligence has been defined in many ways, such as the ability to reason, plan, solve problems, analyze, think strategically, and learn from experience. Different types of intelligence have been identified: logical, linguistic, spatial, musical, interpersonal, and emotional. There's no one definition that satisfies everyone. But one point everyone agrees on: *Intelligence is the key to survival.* It's what helps us make sense of our environment, meet our needs, and achieve our goals.

Are we then an intelligent species? We certainly like to think so. But who can look at the state of our world and still maintain with conviction that we have demonstrated a high level of intelligence?

Given the choice to either face or deny truths that are inconvenient—to borrow Al Gore's word—we keep choosing denial, hardly a sign of superior intelligence. Would intelligent beings kill millions of their own kind? Would they destroy their own habitat, amass vast storehouses of toxic materials, and covet the power to turn the planet into a barren wasteland?

Surely not. If we were truly intelligent, we'd use the formidable powers of our mind towards different ends—to create beauty, ease suffering, and nurture the seeds of peace in our world. But until quite recently, peace wasn't our foremost concern. Presumably, most people would have said they wanted it. Nonetheless it wasn't a top priority.

Today, it is. War has always been synonymous with suffering, but now, it's increasingly synonymous with self-annihilation. Under these circumstances, no action deserves to be called intelligent if it poses a threat to peace.

Some years ago, I interviewed a man named Ben Cohen. Famous as the co-founder of Ben & Jerry's ice cream, Ben later became the president of Business Leaders for Sensible Priorities, an organization dedicated to lowering the US defense budget.

In this capacity, he spent a lot of time meeting and interacting with brilliant and powerful people in the government and the military.

"Smart they may be," Ben said with a shrug. "But intelligent? I don't think so. So many of these high-level politicians and scientists simply don't want to look at the bigger picture. Take the people who are working in nuclear labs to develop more lethal nuclear weapons. They're just looking at their little project. To them, it's just a scientific challenge, a puzzle. They're not thinking about the consequences."

I believe he's right. By the standards of mainstream society, these scientists are no doubt super-intelligent. And yet, if we define intelligence as that which helps a species survive, they don't have it. Disconnected from their hearts as they are, they exemplify the tragic lack of farsightedness that has made us such a menace to the entire planet.

They aren't bad guys, just people who were never taught to think with their hearts. Products of a society that rewards them for being consummate head-thinkers, they have lost touch with the inner wellspring of kindness and compassion.

No doubt they're fully cognizant of both the short – and the long-term consequences of nuclear war. But that awareness evokes no feeling response in them—not because they're unusually callous, but because they're living in their head. The head can provide the heart with important information, but don't expect it to feel. This, it's no more capable of than a lawn mower is of flying.

> *A human being is a part of the whole, called by us "universe," a part limited in time and space. He experiences himself, his thoughts and feelings, as something separate from the rest— a kind of optical delusion of his consciousness. This delusion is a kind of prison for us, restricting us to our personal decisions and to affection for a few persons nearest us. Our task must be to free ourselves from this prison by widening our circle of compassion to embrace all living creatures and the whole of nature in its beauty.*
>
> —Albert Einstein

We've long known that heart-thinking fosters peaceful relationships—spiritual teachers have been telling us so for eons. But in the past, the main benefit of heart-thinking appeared to be an increased sense of personal well-being. Today, our collective survival is at stake. From nuclear proliferation to global warming, all our major challenges can be traced back to the fact that at present, our collective consciousness lacks the heart-centeredness without which humankind can no longer sustain itself.

Can we unite the genius of the mind with the wisdom of the heart? Upon this our future depends. Quite simply, heart-thinking reveals a way that works. Indeed, in our times, I believe it's the *only* way that works.

Suggested Exercises:

1. Five Easy Ways to Connect with Your Heart
2. Where did it Come From?

CHAPTER 2

RE-EDUCATING THE EGO

It is said: Before the world was created, the Holy One kept creating worlds and destroying them. Finally He created this one, and was satisfied. He said to Adam: This is the last world I shall make. I place it in your hands: hold it in trust.

—Jewish Prayer

Astronaut Frank Borman returned from the moon a changed man. "When you're finally up on the moon," he remarked, "looking back at the earth, all these differences and nationalistic possible traits are pretty well going to blend and you're going to get a concept that maybe this is really one world and why the hell can't we learn to live together like decent people?"

Why indeed? It's a question most of us have asked ourselves.

Many people will tell you they know the answer: "It's the ego, stupid!"

Of course, the ego is an entirely fictitious entity. Nobody has ever seen or touched one. Nonetheless it's a central concept, not only in psychology but also in spirituality, which defines it as the part of our being that experiences itself as a separate "I." And because this "I" feels vulnerable, it tends to be self-centered, self-serving and—well—egotistical.

Questioning Our Judgments

It's impossible to read what's been written about the ego without noticing the unrelenting harshness with which it's been judged. We all know that the most effective way of drawing out the best in others is to acknowledge and encourage it. But in regards to our own ego, we've done the very opposite. We've heaped insults and abuse on it and have even plotted to kill it. We've described it as an inner enemy, a terrible burden our species has been singled out to carry, and even as a quasi-demonic force. The ego has been called every name in the book—spiteful, jealous, vengeful, small-minded, mean, tricky, manipulative, shifty, dishonest, untrustworthy. In the minds of many, the ego now seems to occupy the place once reserved for Satan. Spoken or unspoken, the message is clear: Just get rid of it, and all will be well.

It's undeniably true that our ego is wedded to an illusion—the illusion of its own separateness. This renders it incapable of realizing our oneness and interconnectedness. Our ego tends to trust in the evidence of the senses, unreliable though they are. And what they say is that we're vulnerable little sacks of flesh and skin.

But let's not forget where the source of this illusion lies—not in the ego's ignorance but in *nature's goodness*. Nature is in love with life, and wants it to continue. She doesn't want her creatures to fade away into oblivion. So she has given us an ego that's deeply attached to our individual existence and willing to fight for it, tooth and claw. With no incentive to protect ourselves and no drive towards self-preservation, life would long ago have come to an end. Our ego clings to the illusion of separateness because that is exactly what nature wants and *needs* it to do.

I hope the following chapters will give you a new perspective on the ego and a new sense of compassion for it. No question, the ego as we know it is problematic. It's arrogant, greedy, and selfish. Nonetheless it deserves to be honored as a sacred force dedicated to the protection and preservation of life.

Befriending the Ego

Our ego tends to view heart-thinking as dangerous, and as something best avoided. Like an over-protective mom, it wants to keep us out of harm's way, and believes that the best way to achieve this is to keep us tethered to our mind.

Not surprisingly, spiritual seekers have not taken kindly to an inner force that stubbornly advocates for head-thinking and tries to keep our heart under lock and key. Heart-thinking holds the key to both inner and outer peace. Therefore, they conclude, the ego must be their enemy.

It's true that the ego's needs often seem diametrically opposed to those of the heart. Our heart wants to open and dissolve in love, whereas the ego's agenda is not love but survival and success—it's not interested in becoming one with others. In fact, it equates the experience of oneness with death, and resists it with all its might.

How, then, can we reconcile the needs of the ego with those of our heart and soul?

According to many teachers, we *can't*—as long as the ego has a say in the matter, our spirit will never be free. In their eyes, awakening or enlightenment is synonymous with liberation from the ego.

As spiritual teacher Andrew Cohen says: "Ego is the one and only one obstacle to enlightenment. If we want to be free, if we want to be enlightened, we have to pay the price. The great wisdom traditions have always told us that the price is ego death."

Accordingly, many seekers make it their goal to kill their ego—to eradicate, crush, or annihilate it. In essence, they're at war with it. Others say no, we don't actually need to *kill* the ego; we just need to stop identifying with it. As long as we can stay detached from it, it can't tyrannize us.

Here, once again, is Andrew Cohen, this time responding to a student's question about whether ego death is really attainable:

> I do believe that the death of the ego is possible, but I don't think it is an *attainable* goal. If something like that is going to occur, it's beyond our control, and it's extremely unlikely for most of us.... But the point is, it doesn't really matter. If you are willing to face and take responsibility for your ego's self-centered motives, conditioned responses, and often irrational impulses to such a degree that you are able to choose not to act on them, they might as

well not exist.... There won't be any karmic consequences. And that is a reasonable, realizable, attainable goal.

This is good news, given that most of us are as likely to
shed our ego as camels are to shed their humps. But is it true
that the only way to co-exist with our ego is to put in quaran-
tine, like a dangerous virus?

Of course it's crucial that we be able to detach from our ego
and see it for what it is. To be completely identified with it is to
be a slave without even knowing it. Yet keeping it in shackles
doesn't end the internal war that splits us into opposing frac-
tions. Sure, containing the ego may be preferable to giving it
free reign, but it's still a far cry from actually making peace
with it.

Is it possible, then, to actually *befriend* our ego?

I believe it is. I believe we *can* have an ego and at the same
time live in harmony as a global community. We can view ourselves as separate individuals, look out for our own interests,
and yet be good planetary citizens. We don't have to become
enlightened to save the world. However, before our ego can be
a true friend to us, it will need to change. For the ego, as we
know it, is indeed insufferable.

Imagine a teenage delinquent who's just been busted for
dealing drugs. He's arrogant and self-righteous. He refuses to
take responsibility for his actions. He's confused, ignorant, and
misinformed.

Do we put him against a wall and shoot him? I don't think
so. We talk to him. We work with him. We put him in therapy.
We teach him new skills. Maybe it won't work. Maybe he'll refuse to change. But maybe it will. Maybe he'll discover who he

really is and turn into a beautiful young man whom his mother can be proud of.

Right now, we might not want to deal with him. "Just get lost," we might want to say to him. "Go home." But ask him where home is, and he'll point straight at us. For that boy lives within us, and for better or worse, we're stuck with him. So what are we going to do?

I would suggest that we should heal, transform, and re-educate our ego. Unlike its eradication, its re-education is achievable. I'm not saying it's easy. It may well be the hardest thing we'll ever do. Still, I know it's possible because I've seen it done many times.

Of course, this assumes that our ego is capable of change. Many would deny this; in their eyes, it's a static entity with an innately bad character. Yet in my experience, there's nothing static about the ego. It's a complex, fluid structure comprised of many layers that have been shifting and evolving throughout human history.

If the ego were indeed an unchanging entity, we'd have only two options: Submit to its tyranny, or try to get rid of it. But once we realize that our ego is, in fact, a living, evolving psychic structure, new options open up. Now, we can begin to work with it. We can explore its internal architecture and identify the elements it's comprised of. We can get to know it and enter into a real relationship with it. We can heal its wounds, correct its misconceptions, and teach it how to be our friend.

The Ego as We Know It

I believe that the ego is not inherently opposed to heart-thinking. Rather, we've trained it to be that way.

Nature's instructions to the ego are clear: "Protect and defend your human. Look out for his or her interests and make sure he or she survives."

But how does our ego know what it takes to survive?

Personal experience plays a role, no question. But for the most part, the ego's strategies are *not* based on personal experience. Rather, it relies on messages it gets from the outside world. Parents and society teach our ego what's important, what matters, what success means, what will help us get ahead and what won't.

Had you lived in ancient times, you would have learned that the basis of your survival was your tribe. Therefore your ego's top priority would have been to protect and defend the tribe.

In this day and age, our ego is told an entirely different story. From a young age, we're taught to view ourselves as separate entities responsible for our own success and failure. We learn that we must compete and fight our way to the top, and that the mark of success is to acquire wealth and power.

Remember how puzzled Jung's Pueblo friend was by the white people? Most indigenous peoples would have a hard time understanding what makes us tick. Certainly our extreme individualism would be quite alien to them. Tribal peoples didn't base their sense of self on their individual achievements or their unique personality, but rather on their role within the tribe.

This doesn't mean they had no ego. They most certainly did. However, it was structured differently than ours. *Our* ego tends to be strongly invested in advancing our personal interests. Theirs was primarily invested in advancing the interests of the tribe. Why? Because that was what society told them was the key to survival.

The Ego's Inflation

So when did our ego change, and how did it become what it is today? We don't know for sure, but the shift seems to have started roughly five thousand years ago in Europe, at the beginning of what I *call the era of control.*

Our ego loves being in control, or at least *feeling* in control. But for thousands of years, it rarely did. The individual didn't have much power. People were utterly dependent on their tribe, and the tribe itself was utterly dependent on nature's mercy.

But at some point, two simultaneous changes occurred. The first was that in Europe, matriarchy began to give way to patriarchy, a subject we'll return to at a later point. Second, this shift towards patriarchy coincided with a burning desire on the part of certain tribes to acquire greater power, both over other peoples and over nature.

Gradually, the pursuit of control became a driving compulsion that would henceforth define the development of Western civilization. Eventually, it would lead to new technologies, to the industrial revolution, and ultimately to the radical and irreversible transformation of our planet.

In the process, our ego was outfitted with a whole new story about what it takes to survive and succeed. Basically, it was encouraged to indulge its innate taste for power and control to the max. Go ahead, our European ancestors said. See if you can conquer nature. See if you can expand your territory. See if you can dominate other peoples.

From where we stand today, we can recognize this as a tragically misguided move. But obviously, it seemed like a good one at the time. Gradually, all the restrictions and limitations that had formerly kept our ego in check were removed. For eons, it had been our servant. Now, slowly but surely, the ego became our lord and master.

As we all know, power tends to corrupt. As our ego became more dominant, it began molding society to its needs, until greed, brutality, and other symptoms of rampant egoism came to be seen not only as acceptable but *desirable*.

Today, the ego's favorite playgrounds are business and politics. Huge, multi-national corporations have been designed to conform to the ego's exact specifications, and increasingly, they are determined to shape governments and other institutions to their will.

Yet now, once again, nature is reminding us of who's really in charge. Just as she humbled our ego in ancient times, so she is preparing to humble it again. But how many creatures will have to pay the price? How much suffering will we unleash due to the arrogance of our ego?

The ego, as we know it, is indeed destructive and antisocial. It's crippling our capacity for heart-thinking and destroying our planet. This, however, says more about the nature of contemporary society than about the ego itself. In its single-minded pursuit of personal benefits, it is merely acting in accordance with our collective view of ruthless competition as the basis of survival.

The modern ego is basically an ego on steroids. It's not very likeable. It's arrogant, greedy, and aggressive. No wonder we tend to view it in a negative light. Instead of honoring it as an agent of survival, we perceive it as an anti-social, ruthlessly self-serving force. This, we assume, is the basic nature of the ego.

But it's not. It's merely how our ego has adapted to the social environment we live in and to the stories it's been told.

A New Story

The new survival unit is no longer the individual nation; it's the entire human race and its environment. This newfound oneness is only a rediscovery of an ancient religious truth. Unity is not something we are called to create; it's something we are called to recognize.

—William Sloane Coffin

For millions of years, humans were as elusive as snow leopards or wild lynx. Then, over a period of five thousand years—practically overnight, in the bigger picture—our numbers ballooned from a few million to seven billion, with twelve billion projected by the end of the century. Suddenly a species that had always lived in small, isolated tribes coalesced into a single planetary community connected by a tight economic, electronic and ecological web.

Now, we're facing a task as daunting as it is exhilarating.

We, who for millions of years lived in tribal societies, are now trying to create the first global civilization on Earth. But to succeed, we will need our ego to be on our side. Right now, it isn't. As I said before, the problem is not that the ego is inherently bad. The problem is that it's taking its lead from bad stories—stories that tell us why we should think with our heads, not our hearts.

In Parts II and III of this book, we'll explore the two sets of stories that are misleading our ego and creating our current state of collective insanity. One set tells our ego to defend the interests of our "tribe"—however we define it—at all costs. A second set of stories claims that nothing matters more than the acquisition of power and control.

Programmed as our ego is with a bunch of stories that have nothing to do with our present needs, is it any wonder it's failing to serve us well? Strategies that once made sense are now achieving the exact opposite of their intended result: Instead of protecting us, they're endangering our survival and making us a menace to all life on Earth.

Of course, given the radical transformation our world has undergone in less than a century, it's hardly surprising that our ego has lost touch with the present. Externally, our world is nothing like it was even a few decades ago. But internally, our ego still relies on strategies it adopted thousands of years ago. Accustomed to tiny evolutionary micro-movements, it has yet to catch up with the tectonic shifts that have so abruptly and indelibly restructured our lives. As a result, what was supposed to be our best friend has turned into our worst enemy.

Today, the very function designed to ensure our survival is driving us towards extinction. Yet I would repeat that in my opinion, the answer is not to strive for egolessness. Rather, it's to heal our ego and develop a new relationship with it, so that it can more effectively fulfill its mission of protecting us.

To achieve this, we will need to identify and release the obsolete programs and outdated beliefs that have been leading our ego astray. At the same time, we'll need to offer our ego a new story and a new set of instructions that reflect a clear awareness of our present situation and needs.

The good news is that this is already happening. The ego's job description is no different today than it was ten thousand years ago: *Keep your human alive.* But in our day and age, this means something very different than it used to. For eons, the ego's primary allegiance was to a select group of people. Later, it shifted to the solitary individual. Now our ego needs to devote itself to protecting the entire planetary community. For if the planet dies, so shall we. Paul Hawken says it well: "We will either come together as one globalized people, or we will disappear as a civilization."

Once again, then, our ego will have to recalibrate itself. That it's capable of doing so, I have no doubt. Of course it isn't capable of feeling what our heart feels. But it is capable of understanding that, today, heart-thinking is no longer a mere aid to harmonious personal relationships but a crucial key to our survival.

Today, only the heart has the power to unite us in the face of all our differences. Only through the heart can we realize our oneness in visceral, embodied ways—ways that inspire real and lasting change. Only heart-thinking can reveal a viable path from endless violence towards peace, and from hatred to compassion. Only heart-thinking can allow us to connect despite all our differences, so that we might build new, more life-affirming forms of community. The more of us that become dedicated heart-thinkers, the greater our chances will be of healing the collective insanity that is threatening to destroy us.

This being the case, our ego needs to understand that it can serve us far better by encouraging us to think with our heart instead of *dis*couraging us. Once upon a time, that strategy made sense. Today, it no longer does. Now, the ancient habits that are blocking our capacity for heart-thinking have become unsustainable and must be released.

In the next chapters, we're going to shine the light of consciousness into the depths of our collective ego. We'll explore how our ego has been shaped by our collective history, and how we can bring it into alignment with the present. We'll see how tribal and control-era conditioning evolved, how they affect our thoughts, emotions, and relationships, and how we can liberate ourselves from their tyranny.

> ### What the Ego Is and Isn't
>
> It isn't…
> * Evil
> * Irredeemably selfish
> * An insurmountable obstacle to global peace
> * Our enemy
>
> It is…
> * Dedicated to our collective survival
> * Out of touch with the realities of our times
> * In need of education
> * Capable of changing and evolving

Most people don't realize what a heavy load of collective conditioning they carry. This needs to change, for nobody can overcome an obstacle they don't even know exists. Only when we see clearly what we're up against will real change become possible—for you, for me, for all of us.

Whether you and I personally manage to re-educate and heal our ego might seem of little consequence in the larger scheme of things. But multiply that tiny shift by a billion, and our children stand a chance of inheriting a livable Earth. And that, you'll surely agree, is no small thing.

Who would we be were we to cast off the shackles of our collective conditioning? I believe we'd be more peaceful, open and receptive, better able to listen, healthier, and, above all, happier.

Would we be saints? No. But we'd be sane. We'd be the beautiful, amazing species we have the potential to be. This is no mere pipe dream. It's possible, of that I have no doubt, for every day I see men and women casting off old, outworn identities and opening to a new vision of what it means to be human.

You're about to meet some of them—ordinary people involved in a journey of collective healing that is anything but ordinary. If their stories inspire you and help you walk your own path with greater wisdom and joy, then this book will have fulfilled its purpose.

Suggested Exercises (See Appendix II)

Exercise 3. What Do I Really Want?

Exercise 4. Dear Ego

CHAPTER 3

THE RACIST'S TRANSFORMATION

In separateness lies the world's great misery; in compassion lies the world's true strength.

—Gautama Buddha

War, violence, crime, nuclear waste—all our major problems are self-created. They are caused by human behavior, which in turn reflects our habitual ways of thinking and relating. Within our own psyche, then, is where the shift must begin. If we hope to create a more just and peaceful world, we ourselves must change.

Most people will readily concede that our problems are by and large self-created. But suggest that inner work might be an important part of the solution—just as crucial, say, as political strategy—and they're look at you like you like you just dropped in from another galaxy. They simply don't see the connection between challenges like climate change or nuclear proliferation on the one hand and human psychology on the other.

I believe that to a large degree, this has to do with the way we're taught to separate private from public matters, and to classify all forms of inner work as "private." If you ask people what they associate with terms like 'spiritual evolution' or 'psychological growth' you'll hear a barrage of words such as personal growth, self-help, psychotherapy, introspection, meditation, and so on.

So, you might ask, what's wrong with that? Nothing. The problem lies with what's *missing*. What's missing is the association of inner work with global transformation, disarmament, environmental protection, and social justice—not to mention human survival. These are not things that come to mind when we speak of inner work, because that's not how our culture has taught us to connect the dots. In fact, our very language discourages it.

Personal growth, self-help—such terms convey a clear message: "These are private, personal matters. They're of no public concern." Unfortunately, this cultural bias is blinding us to the real urgency of our need for inner healing, growth and transformation. What we're talking about here is not a personal indulgence or a luxury but rather a potentially life-saving medicine for our species. Whether we realize it or not, our personal healing is part of a collective healing; our own awakening benefits the awakening of all beings.

Therefore, I would suggest that much of what is generally called "personal healing and transformation" should actually be described as "collective healing and transformation." For until we recognize the collective importance and value of expanding our consciousness, we will continue to neglect the very practices and programs we need most. I'd like to give you an example of how one such program supported the radical transformation of a man whom many of us would have considered a hopeless case.

Justin is an African American therapist in his 60s who has worked with all kinds of people. And yet, the memory of the encounter you're about to hear of is especially dear to him.

"It's always present in my consciousness," he tells me.

It all began one fine morning when he was sitting at the reception of the counseling agency where he worked at the time. The door opened, and in walked a white man who looked to be in his early forties. His name was Andy, and he'd been referred to Justin's agency after having been convicted on drug-related charges.

Most people in Andy's situation go to jail. But Andy was lucky: he'd been given the option of participating in an intense rehabilitation program that included both individual and group therapy. Though Andy didn't yet realize it, he was, for the first time in his life, looking at a real opportunity to recalibrate his values and turn his life in a new direction.

In Justin's agency, the rule was that whoever did the intake of new clients also took them on for the duration of their treatment. That day, Justin was responsible for intake. So, after gathering the information he needed, he led Andy into his office and offered him a seat.

It didn't take long for Justin to realize that Andy wanted nothing whatsoever to do with him. "I could tell he was extremely uncomfortable. He was really withdrawn, and he was squirming in his seat, making no eye contact. So I asked, 'What's going on? Can you tell me what you're experiencing?'"

"No," he said, "I don't want to talk about it."

"So for what seemed like an eternity, we just sat there in silence. Finally I said to him, 'Well, here we are, you and I, and we've got this hour. Are we just going to sit here and play this game?'"

"I'm just uncomfortable with you," was his answer.

"Do you know me?"

"No," he said.

"Then what do you have against me?"

"You're black."

"Wow!" I said, and I took a deep breath.

As Justin was soon to discover, Andy was not only an ardent racist but also a Ku Klux Klan member. From the get-go, he hated Justin's guts, and told him so in no uncertain terms.

Had we been in Justin's shoes, most of us would have countered Andy's judgments with our own: "How dare he! This is outrageous. How can he be so disrespectful?"

Amazingly, Justin did none of this. He merely listened quietly to what Andy had to say. Then, he gently remarked, "Well, it certainly happens that people have preferences about whom they want to hang out with. That's cool."

Andy then told Justin he'd been raised to view black people as worthless.

Justin grins as he remembers their conversation:

"So you believe that?" I asked him.

"Well, yeah," he said. "Sure I believe it."

"So right now you think I'm worthless and have nothing to

offer you, and that this is a total waste of time?"

"Yes," he said, "you're damn right. That's exactly what I think. I'm not going to talk to you."

"Well," I told him, "I don't want to mess with your beliefs, but you have to talk to someone. So let me see if I can get you transferred to somebody else."

Justin got up and sought out his supervisor, who listened sympathetically. But then, he shrugged. "I'm so sorry," he said, "I understand this must be really uncomfortable for you, but right now, no one else is available."

So Justin had no choice but to go back and tell Andy how things stood. Basically, he had two choices: Work with Justin, or go to jail.

As you can imagine, Andy was not happy about this. But Justin tried to encourage him.

"Look, whatever the differences are between us, I'm here to help you with the courts. I promise you, whatever you think of me, I'll do my best. So why don't you tell me how you got into this felony situation.

"Andy was really, really resistant. But very slowly, he started talking, and I just listened, and validated his feelings. He was angry at a lot of people. He believed that black people were the problem, and that the government was failing to protect white folks like him.

"I assured him that if he cooperated with the system and did what he needed to do, he could get through this ordeal without going to prison.

"In addition to seeing me once a week, he had to participate in a group four times a week. I told him that I would definitely support him and advocate for him throughout the entire process, which lasted a year. When he heard this he started scratching his head.

"You?" he asked, totally incredulous. "You are going to advocate for me?"

"Absolutely," I said. "That's what I'm here for. If for a moment you can put the issue of color aside, then we can work together. Afterwards, if you like, you can pick it up again. But somehow we gotta get you through this thing.

"He accepted this. He didn't like it, but he saw that he had to. And over the next weeks, very slowly, we started talking about the issue of race.

"He told me quite openly that there were Ku Klux Klan groups in our community, and that he belonged to one of them. They weren't burning crosses, but they were very upset about what they perceived as far too many leniencies being given to black people while white men were being disempowered. They held a vision of a world where white people were in control and dominated everyone else.

"We had many dialogues in which I, as a black man, accepted him completely for who he was. I didn't fight him in any way, nor did I feel any sense of defensiveness towards him. And increasingly, he saw that he didn't have to fight me either, because I wasn't present as his enemy. That was a completely new experience for him."

Had Justin felt even the slightest urge to "fix" his client, their relationship would have been doomed to fail. Sensing

Justin's agenda, Andy would have responded by hardening his position all the more.

But Justin never demanded that Andy change. Instead, he simply offered his client a safe place where he could examine his beliefs, without feeling pressured one way or another.

For decades, Justin had been a student of Chinese martial arts. At the heart of this tradition lies the recognition that to be whole, empowered beings, we need to balance the outgoing, active energy known as *yang* with the receptive, yielding force known as *yin. Yang* energy is described as fiery and masculine, *yin* as watery and feminine.

Normally, we counter *yang* with *yang*. If someone judges us, we judge them right back. If they attack us, we attack *them*.

Yet according to the Chinese tradition, the only power capable of overcoming aggression is *yin* energy. This is the receptive, spacious force that the famous Tao Te Ching celebrates as "the Valley Spirit:"

The Valley Spirit never dies,
It is named the Mysterious Female
And the doorway of the Mysterious Female
Is the base from which Heaven and Earth sprang.
It is there within us all the while.
Draw upon it as you will, it never runs dry.

"In our society," Justin tells me, "we don't understand the power of *yin*. We think of it as passive or weak. If you plunge your fist into water, it won't fight you. It will just yield. And yet it carved the Grand Canyon. So actually, water is the most powerful element of all. Just like it yields to your fist, you can disarm an attacker simply by getting out of their way.

This is precisely what Justin was doing in his work with Andy. Instead of fighting him, Justin kept encouraging Andy to speak his truth and express his feelings. And so, his clenched fist plunged into the cool, calm water of Justin's acceptance.

To be effective, acceptance can't be faked, nor can it be conditional. Justin's message was not, "I'll accept you if you stop putting me down and start showing some respect."

No. Over and over, he let Andy know that he accepted him, just as he was.

We've all experienced acceptance. We all know how good it feels. But what exactly *is* it? One thing is clear: It's not just a thought but a felt experience. It's an authentic gesture of the soul that reverberates through our whole being, as if we were bowing to reality. More than a gift to others, acceptance is a gift we give ourselves. Life will always present us with situations and people we dislike. Still, if we can accept them, we can feel at home in this world.

To accept something, we need to expand our sense of self until we are large enough to contain it. How far can we expand? Throughout the ages, great beings like Jesus and the Buddha have reminded us there's no limit. We have the capacity to hold the whole world in the palms of our hands like a flower and look at it with clear, peaceful eyes.

We sometimes think of acceptance as a form of surrender, a kind of giving up or self-betrayal. "To accept this," they think, "would be to say it's okay."

But that's not at all what acceptance means. Acceptance is

not an act of resignation but of self-empowerment. To accept something doesn't mean we condone or excuse it. It simply means that we can be present with it in a non-reactive way, as Justin was present with Andy. We can be whole within a broken world and at peace in the presence of violence. We can stop insisting that darkness should have no place in God's creation and come to terms with the fact that, obviously, it *does*.

In doing so, we reclaim our inner sovereignty. Instead of allowing outer circumstances to dictate how we feel, we make a choice for inner peace. Then, instead of wasting our energy on futile resistance, we can use it to actually address the situation at hand.

Had Justin been attached to his own beliefs, he and Andy would never have found common ground. But Justin understood that war is only possible when you have an enemy. Andy expected to find an enemy in Justin, and to some extent even needed to, since he was so invested in his identity as a Ku Klux Klan member.

We have the capacity to hold the whole world in the palms of our hands like a flower and look at it with the clear, peaceful eyes of a Buddha. This is not an act of resignation but of self-empowerment that allows us to be whole within a broken world and at peace in the presence of violence.

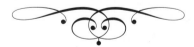

Most of us would have played into Andy's hand by reacting defensively and thus providing the enemy what he was looking for. Yet Justin remained consistently peaceful and receptive. And so, Andy could find no enemy, and a bitter war came to an end.

"Over the next six months, I repeatedly came to his rescue by talking to the probation officers and by acting as a kind of buffer between him and the system. I kept helping and encouraging him as he gave up drugs, and gradually we started forging a close relationship.

"Eventually, he got comfortable enough around me that we could actually laugh together and joke about things that were happening. And in the last months, he told me several times that he felt really good about our relationship.

"At the end of the year, the people who've completed the process and have overcome their substance addiction have a sort of graduation ceremony in court. Normally, they don't say anything; they're not expected to participate in any way. But Andy stood up and said he had something important that he wanted to say. 'I want you all to know that I would never have made it, were it not for Justin,' he began. Then he went on to say a lot of incredibly beautiful and touching things about our relationship that brought tears to my eyes. Six months later, I ran into him again, and he was still clean, and in a positive space."

After hearing Justin's story, I told him how impressed I was that he was able to accept Andy so unconditionally despite his rampant racism.

Justin nodded thoughtfully. "Somewhere, someone has to be non-reactive; otherwise, conflicts just escalate. In the greater scheme of things, who is going to do this? Someone needs to be the one who will keep the peace by saying, 'We are not going to react to this. We are not going to respond to hatred with hatred or meet violence with violence.'

"It's the only sane choice. And it sure doesn't look like our politicians are going to do it. We have to do it ourselves."

I nodded. Then, thinking out loud, I wondered whether perhaps we all have a piece of Andy within us. We might not be racists, but we all know what it feels like to get mired in judgment and to close our hearts. How do we relate to ourselves when that happens?

If we judge ourselves, we'll only turn our inner world into a battlefield. But if we can offer ourselves the same unconditional acceptance that Justin offered Andy, then maybe our judgments will begin to shift.

"Acceptance begins within us, within our own heart," Justin echoed. "The mind always has to react one way or another; that's just what it does. It always has to take a stand. But the heart knows how to receive life and hold it without passing judgment. That's the medicine we need. It's the medicine that can heal our world."

Acceptance, listening, open-heartedness—these are all time-honored and universal spiritual keys, as well as keys to emotional healing. Certainly, then, we could approach Justin's story as a beautiful example of spirituality in action or of skillful psychotherapy.

But as I mentioned before, we have an unfortunate tendency to think of both spirituality and psychotherapy as something private—something we engage in because it makes us feel more centered or more peaceful. But when you consider Justin's story, you'll notice that his objective was not just to turn

Andy's personal life in a more positive direction. Rather, it was to make Andy's community a safer and more peaceful place for *everyone*. What a different world we would live in, were we to acknowledge that our collective well-being depends on each citizen's capacity to maintain harmonious relationships!

Andy was just a petty criminal. Obviously, people in positions of power can have a far greater impact on their communities. Their relational skills, or lack thereof, can set processes in motion that affect millions. Yet tragically, many CEOs and politicians have yet to learn the lessons Andy learned in his year with Justin. The fallout of such relational incompetence has disastrous effects on entire nations and indeed, on our entire planet.

What Justin did, we're all capable of learning. And if we do, our relationships too will transform. There is nothing idealistic or utopian about this. The way of relating that Justin modeled—the way I have described as heart-thinking—is simply a way that *works*. It's practical and effective. In contrast, the harshness and arrogance with which we generally respond to hostile and challenging people is *not*.

Suggested Exercises (See Appendix II)

Exercise 5. Making Space
Exercise 6. Our Children's Children

Part II

Shedding the Shackles of Tribal Conditioning

CHAPTER 4

THE TOXIC LEGACY OF BELIEF ADDICTION

One does not become enlightened by imagining figures of light but by making the darkness conscious.

— C.G. Jung

In 2005, *Time* magazine published an interview with a young Iraqi man named Farwad. At the time, Farwad was being trained as a suicide bomber—or, as he called it, a "martyr."

"I will ask Allah to bless my mission with a high rate of casualties among the Americans," Farwad told the *Time* reporter.

"Then I will ask him to purify my soul so I am fit to see him, and I will ask to see my mujahedin brothers who are already with him."

Farwad went on to explain that according to the Koran, it's the duty of Muslims to bring terror to the enemy. Therefore, he concluded, "being a terrorist makes me a good Muslim." (For the record, the Koran says no such thing.)

Farwad's words are a chilling example of what I call *belief addiction.* At their worst, belief addicts are completely enslaved to their ideology. For its sake, they'll do anything—wipe out entire villages, murder their own children, commit suicide— you name it. Against the loud roar of their beliefs, the quiet voice of the heart has as much chance of being heard as the cry of a tiny bird caught in a raging forest fire.

Belief addiction may well be the most divisive force on Earth. However, it's not the beliefs themselves that are divisive but rather our attachment to them. That our opinions differ isn't a problem. The problem is that we think they *shouldn't.*

How does a young man like Farwad convince himself that blowing up innocent people is good, righteous, and godly? We shudder when we hear about such people. We can't begin to imagine what goes on in them; nor are we sure we want to, for they strike us as instruments of evil, and evil is something most of us would rather keep at arm's length.

But until we learn to understand people like Farwad, we'll remain powerless against the very real challenge they pose. Why are they the way they are? Why do they do what they do?

Analyzing their personality, upbringing, and background may reveal some contributing factors. But to uncover the deeper roots of their insanity, I believe we need to look beyond their personal history to the history of the human ego. For

That our opinions differ isn't a problem. The problem is that we think they shouldn't.

unlike you and me, who have lived for a century at most, our ego has millions of years under its belt.

When geologists look at various strata on a cliff, it's as if they are looking at an open book in which they can read the entire history of our planet. Our psyche, too, contains various layers of residue that correspond to distinct phases in our collective history. The ancient past is not just our past—it's also our present, in that the lessons we learned and the beliefs we internalized eons ago continue to affect how we think, feel and relate now.

For hundreds of thousands of years, all humans lived in small tribal groups. For most of us, this tribal way of life seems as remote and unreal as a half-forgotten dream. Yet compared to our tribal past, the modern era is no more than the sheerest film of ice on an infinitely deep lake. Tribal life was the womb in which our collective ego gestated and where it began to acquire its present shape and form. So to understand who we are today, we must consider who our ancestors were. So let's take a moment to consider their world.

Tribal Conditioning

Today, about 6 percent of the human population still claim some form of tribal heritage. However, thousands of cultures have vanished, and others are disappearing as we speak. With every culture and every language that dies—on average, one every two weeks—another piece of our collective heritage vanishes, along with its music, art, stories, medicinal knowledge, and ancient wisdom—a tragic and irreversible loss.

The tribal peoples that have survived the onslaught of the industrial era are the last representatives of a way of life that goes back to the beginning of time. For hundreds of thousands of years, all humans lived in tribal groups, as had their pre-human ancestors for millions of years before that.

Throughout this period, the pace of change was exceedingly slow. Earthquakes reshaped the contours of the land. Thick sheets of ice advanced and receded. Now and then, a meteor struck or a tsunami gobbled up an island. There were great migrations and some important discoveries, such as how to control fire. But the basic structure of human society barely changed at all.

Leda Cosmides and John Tooby, two of the foremost experts in the field of evolutionary psychology, say that, "our species lived as hunter-gatherers a thousand times longer than as anything else... Each of our ancestors was, in effect, on a camping trip that lasted an entire lifetime, and this way of life endured for the past ten million years."

Tribal conditioning evolved in response to the experience, sustained consistently for hundreds of thousands of years, of depending on the support of a homogenous and often isolated group of people.

Much like a herd of antelope or a group of gorillas, our early ancestors lived in the moment, at one with their environment. Firmly rooted in the land they lived on, they knew its seasons, its plants and animals, its shapes, colors and secrets. We can safely assume that their senses were far more alert than ours, attuned to the slightest variation in the usual forest sounds, the cry of a disturbed owl or a faint rustling in the underbrush.

But what were their dreams and hopes? What did they think about? Despite archeology's best efforts, we know little about how they experienced the world. Still, there a few things we *do* know. One is that their survival depended on belonging to a strong and viable tribe. We, with our rootless, free-wheeling lifestyle, can hardly imagine being part of such a tightly bonded community. Encircled by their tribe from birth to death, each individual knew exactly where he or she belonged and what their role was.

In our world of rapid-fire change and radical insecurity, where all too many people feel lost and alone, the idea of belonging to a rock-solid tribal community has obvious appeal. However, we should also consider the near total state of dependency that bonded individuals to their tribe. Without it, they were nothing. It was the bedrock of their lives and their only reliable source of protection.

If—God forbid—the tribe should reject them, their odds of survival were poor; banishment was generally a death sentence. Alone, their ability to hunt was compromised. Alone, they had no protection against the ravages of injury, sickness, or predators. Alone, they could not procreate and had no future.

There are two other things we know about tribal life in ancient times. The first is that tribes were generally extremely isolated no roads and no means of transport other than one's feet, a hundred miles could separate two tribes far more effectively than the great oceans separate us today. The second thing we know is that tribes were highly homogenous. Each tribe inhabited a world of its own and maintained its own distinct identity. Within the tribe, everyone shared the same race, ancestry, genetic code, language, values and customs.

Over the millennia, the trinity of dependence, isolation, and homogeneity that defined life in the tribal era gave rise to what I call *tribal conditioning*. Tribal conditioning has, I would emphasize, nothing to do with specific tribal cultures. Rather, it's a complex web of habits, instincts, beliefs, and behavioral patterns that evolved in response to the experience, sustained consistently for hundreds of thousands of years, of depending on the support of a homogenous and often isolated group of people.

The single most basic symptom of tribal conditioning is "us-versus-them" thinking. During the tribal era, "us-versus-them" thinking was a natural and inevitable byproduct of isolation. Yet in our increasingly diverse global world, it has become obsolete, and wherever it rears its ugly head, suffering is sure to ensue.

In the film Hotel Rwanda, there's a scene in which an American visitor to Rwanda has a drink with an African friend. The African points to someone sitting at the bar, and remarks, "He's a Tutsi." Then, he points out another man: "That one's a Hutu.

"But they look the same," the Westerner objects. "How can you tell the difference?"

"You can't," his African friend concedes.

This interchange, and the terrible slaughter that ensues,

expose the tragic absurdity of warfare between people who inhabit the same land and are physically undistinguishable. The only difference between them lies in a label their tribe has attached to them—two syllables that determine who is "us" and who is "them," who shall live, and who shall die.

We all inherit tribal conditioning, and it has an enormous impact on how we perceive the world and relate to one another. Our (generally unconscious) yearning for a tribe can attach itself to just about any group, whether it's a nation, a political or religious organization, or just a group of friends.

We sometimes lovingly refer to the people with whom we feel a deep, abiding sense of connection as our "tribe." These are the people we know we can call on and count on in times of need. But let's be clear: This is not a tribe, at least not in

> ## Three Defining Characteristics of Life in the Tribal Era
> - Dependence on the tribe
> - Homogeneity (shared race, ancestry, religion, language, values, customs, etc.)
> - Isolation and separateness of each tribe
>
> ## Three Defining Characteristics of Life in the Global Era
> - Interdependence of the planetary community
> - Diversity (of race, ancestry, religion, language, values, customs, etc.)
> - Merging and mingling of all tribes

the traditional sense. In a tribe, everyone lives together and shares the same heritage, religion and culture. This is rarely the case among friends today. Nonetheless, tribal conditioning still has an enormous impact on how we perceive and relate to each another.

The Evolution of Belief Addiction

Given that our early ancestors needed their tribe in the most existential way, they naturally treasured the attributes that marked them as members of their tribe. But what exactly were those attributes? How did one determine who was "us" and who was "them"? How did one know who belonged and who did not?

This is where a startling fact comes into focus: Unlike ants, who know the members of their colony by their scent, or whales, who recognize the special songs unique to their pod, we know the members of our tribe by their *mental architecture*. This architecture is constructed from elements such as language, stories, and beliefs. From the moment of its birth, every child begins to absorb the mental constructs that will henceforth structure its thinking, perception, and relationships, and that will mark it as a member of a specific society.

In most societies, certain stories, beliefs, and symbols acquire an aura of sanctity. They command the utmost respect and reverence, and are endowed with divine power. Any insult to these stories or symbols is viewed as an insult to the entire tribe, and is in many cases considered a serious crime.

For example, most Americans don't view the American flag as a mere piece of cloth. To them, it's something precious and meaningful. It symbolizes a piece of mental architecture unique to the American people. Similarly, to Christians, the cross is not just a cross but a profoundly meaningful and sacred symbol. Such symbols always represent specific beliefs or belief systems that unite a group of people and define their identity.

So for how long have humans used beliefs to define their identity? My guess would be that we've done this for around 100,000 years. Why? Because this is the estimated age of language. Some researchers believe it developed much earlier, but for our purposes, it really doesn't matter.

Unlike ants, who know the members of their colony by their scent, or whales, who recognize the special songs unique to their pod, we know the members of our tribe by their mental architecture, which is constructed from elements such as language, stories, and beliefs.

The important point is that the evolution of language sparked an enormously important change in the way we defined our identity. Until then, what bonded members of a certain tribe were the same kind of factors that bonded herds of animals, such as shared genes and territory. But once we developed language, stories, values, and beliefs emerged as the defining markers of tribal membership. And with that, the foundation was laid for the evolution of belief addiction.

Like all forms of tribal conditioning, belief addiction once had a positive function: it bonded the tribe and ensured its homogeneity. Like all manifestations of tribal conditioning, it is therefore rooted in goodness, not evil. That said, there can be no question that today, it has become a life-threatening liability. It lies at the root of racism and all other forms of prejudice, and causes us to kill millions of our own kind, something no other animal does.

Wherever belief addiction prevails, the surest way to insult others is to call them non–believers. In doing so, we're not merely expressing our dissent. Rather, we're questioning their right to be part of our tribe and ultimately, their right to exist.

Belief addiction is responsible for many of the worst plagues of our time, including fundamentalism, totalitarianism, terrorism, cults, gangs, military dictatorships, racism, and other forms of prejudice, nationalism, and warfare—to name just a few. As one glance at the daily paper can remind us, there is no end to the problems we create when instead of having beliefs we allow *them* to have *us*. When our identity hinges on a belief system, we're liable to resent those who reject it. At best, we'll consider them ignorant and unenlightened. At worst, we'll declare them to be infidels and enemies.

But let's not forget, when we see someone like Farwad, who clings to his obviously insane beliefs as if his life depended on it, that for untold millennia, it really *did*. The perception of certain ideologies as inherently good, even sacred, is etched deeply into our collective psyche, as is the conviction that someone who dies for that ideology will win the tribe's everlasting approval. In a strange paradox, their deep-seated yearning to serve their tribe in the most heroic way has turned many people into monsters.

Dissociation

To appreciate the true toxicity of unconscious tribal conditioning, you have to consider that in tribal times, people who weren't members of our own tribe were often perceived as potential enemies. They couldn't count on being treated with kindness and compassion. In fact, they couldn't even count on being treated as human. If they spoke a strange language, followed strange customs, or dressed in strange ways, they were liable to be perceived as members of an entirely different species.

According to DNA research, we all share a single foremother. Mitochondrial Eve, as she's called, lived in Africa some 150,000 years ago. So when we speak of the human family, we're not just speaking metaphorically. We really are family. We truly are kin, a word not coincidentally related to *kind* and *kindness*.

The Three Stages of "Us-versus-Them" Thinking

1. Fear and prejudice: They frighten us. We find them strange, alien. We don't understand them. We avoid them.

2. Segregation and dissociation: They're different. The ethical standards that apply to our own people don't apply to them. It's okay to exploit, dominate, and harm them.

3. Hatred and warfare: They're enemies. We're determined to destroy them by any means.

But our ancestors didn't know this. In a number of ancient tribal languages, the word for "human being" also means "member of the tribe." The inference is clear: non-members weren't recognized as human.

Well, you might say, at least that can't happen in our day and age. We might consider someone our enemy, but at least we'll never question their humanity.

But don't be so sure. One of the many ways tribal conditioning affects us is that it predisposes us to dissociating from anyone we label as "not one of us." We're usually not conscious of doing this, but we do it nonetheless, and it completely changes our feelings towards "them."

Dissociation disables our natural inhibition against harming or killing our own kind. Furthermore, it gives us a kind of moral amnesty; we feel that the moral standards that govern our relationships with other humans don't apply here.

Just consider what happened during WWII to thousands of Japanese-American citizens. Suddenly classified as enemies, they were stripped of all their rights. Their property was confiscated and they were sent to concentration camps—right under the nose of their fellow citizens, who acquiesced without a murmur. For once the Japanese had been classified as enemies, people dissociated from them; as a result, outrageous acts of injustice were deemed acceptable.

The single most powerful trigger that activates tribal conditioning is fear. This is why any collective crisis is likely to trigger a surge of tribalism. We need only remember what happened in the weeks and months after 9/11. Suddenly, millions of Americans began to view unquestioning loyalty to their political leaders as a sign of patriotism and submissiveness as a virtue. American flags started showing up everywhere, along with bumper stickers that read, "God Bless America!"

But here and there, sprinkled among them, another bumper sticker started showing up. This one said:

God Bless Everyone!

(No Exceptions)

Here, in a nutshell, we see the difference between the kindness that tribal conditioning allows for and the kindness that heart-thinking inspires. Where tribal conditioning would have us reserve our concern for a select group of people, heart-thinking flings the doors of the heart wide open.

Symptoms of Tribalism in Groups

If you're wondering whether a group has tribalist tendencies, take a look at this list of the most common symptoms of tribalism. If you answer "yes" to any of these questions, the group displays some form of tribalism.

- Is membership considered a sign of superiority?
- Are people pressured to join?
- Is joining touted as the ticket to success, salvation, or liberation?

- Are members forbidden or strongly discouraged from questioning the beliefs of the group?
- Are members forbidden or strongly discouraged from questioning the leadership?
- Are leaders exempt from accountability?
- Is the leader considered divine or superhuman?
- Does the leader make important life decisions on behalf of members?
- Are financial dealings murky or exploitative?
- Are certain people scapegoated?
- Are certain people or groups considered enemies?
- Does the group advocate illegal activities?
- Does the group condone violence in any form?
- Are members ever pressured to have sexual relationships with other members or leaders?
- Are members discouraged from joining other groups, exploring other teachings, or connecting with other people?
- When people want to leave, are they

shamed, attacked, or guilt-tripped?

- Do members or leaders use judgment, guilt, or shame as a means of influence or control?
- Does the group use religion to instill fear?
- Does the group resist learning from other groups?
- Is the group unwilling to connect and collaborate with other groups?
- Does the group have secrets?

Belief Addiction Affects Us All

If you're reading this book, you probably don't consider yourself a belief addict. Yet we should never declare ourselves immune to belief addiction. Most of us have pockets of it—issues we feel so strongly about that we really aren't open to alternative views. It could be the death penalty, abortion, vegetarianism—even something as banal as a pair of sneakers.

Sneakers?

Absolutely—some people have very strong feelings about sneakers. Last week, my friend Krista purchased a pair for her teenage son Matt. Matt, however, adamantly refuses to wear them, because they aren't the right brand.

Krista thinks this is ridiculous. "Why should I pay eighty

bucks for a pair of sneakers when I can get perfectly good ones for twenty-five?" she asks.

But Matt is adamant: He won't touch them.

Of course, this really isn't about sneakers at all— it's about tribe and tribal belonging. Just as mountain lions scent-mark the boundaries of their territory, Matt and his friends are using beliefs to define their identity.

Adolescence is traditionally a time when we cement our bond to the tribe and claim our place in it. This is why many adolescents are attracted to groups that have a tribal flavor.

Of course, Matt and his friends aren't tribesmen. But like all of us, they've inherited tribal conditioning. Trivial as their endorsement of a certain brand of sneakers might seem, the underlying issue is anything but trivial. Naturally, Matt doesn't want to jeopardize his place within his "tribe." So no way is he going to show up with the "wrong" brand of sneakers on his feet.

Compared to the ideologies that motivate cult members and suicide bombers, a boy's belief in the superiority of a certain type of shoe might seem harmless. But if you've ever been the kid that didn't have the right sneakers, and got rejected because of it, you know that even in its less extreme forms, belief addiction can cause a lot of suffering.

Having Beliefs Isn't a Problem

Islamic fundamentalism sounds disturbingly like Christian fundamentalism. They show the same instincts: damn the infidel, reverse modernity, and scour the holy book for justification.

—Tom Enrich

If you're wondering whether all this means you have to get rid of your beliefs, let me assure you that you don't. Our beliefs aren't a problem. Our attachment to them *is*. We all have beliefs, and as long as we keep an open heart and mind towards people who don't share them, they can be useful; they help us navigate the world and organize our perceptions.

We just need to be mindful lest we cross the line into addiction. When this happens, we draw a thick line around our beliefs. "These are the only right ones," we insist. "They define me, and if you don't share them, you're not my friend." With that, we close our hearts and cut ourselves off from the flow of love that reveals our kinship with others.

If you notice yourself becoming agitated, upset, or angry when someone challenges your beliefs, then watch out! They may be perfectly valid, but your attachment to them is driving a wedge between you and others.

As the families of cult members know only too well, trying to relate to a hard-core belief addict can be an extremely frustrating experience. My friend Julie has a son who spent two years in a fundamentalist cult. Pushing her thick glasses up her nose, she frowns as she remembers this period in her life.

"We'd always been so close," she recalls.

"But this was something we just couldn't talk about. There was no way in. It was like trying to talk to a brick wall. It was such a difficult time, and I felt so helpless."

Recognizing the Signs of Belief Addiction

If, when someone disagrees with you, you experience any of the following symptoms, your belief addictions may have been triggered:

- Tension, restlessness, discomfort
- Anxiety or fear
- Irritability
- Anger, hostility, hatred
- Feeling argumentative or combative
- Judgmental thoughts
- Feelings of superiority
- A sense of emotional distance from the other person
- The desire to run away or avoid the other person

Some people equate clinging to their beliefs with holding fast to the truth. But beliefs aren't capable of grasping the ultimate Truth. Beliefs are thoughts, and thoughts are mere brainwave patterns, ever-shifting formations of dancing electrons. How could something as mysterious and multidimensional as reality be grasped by an instrument as primitive—relatively speaking—as the human brain? At best our thoughts can grasp small, relative truths which serve us best when we use them as stepping stones on our journey towards higher levels of understanding and insight. As long as we cling to one step, we can't move on to the next. The more attached we get to a specific belief, the less open our mind becomes to the inflow of a vaster wisdom.

One of the hallmarks of truly great leaders is that they're completely unattached to their beliefs. They're always open to changing their mind, and when they do, they aren't ashamed of admitting it. This is something ego-driven leaders will never do. They care too much about their public image, and in the eyes of the public, changing one's mind is often considered a sign of weakness.

In fact, the capacity to change our mind is a sign of mental health. Healthy minds are not afraid of changing and growing. They're always willing to question old assumptions, look at things in new ways, and abandon old beliefs in the light of new evidence. Whereas the belief-addicted mind is rigid and armored, the healthy mind is always open to new information and insights.

The Dalai Lama is an inspiring example of this. Though he's the head of Tibetan Buddhism, he's repeatedly demonstrated his willingness to reject any religious dogma he deems misguided, no matter how venerable it might be.

Once, during a visit to San Francisco, he was asked about his position on homosexuality.

"Our religion does not approve of it," he replied firmly.

Not surprisingly, San Francisco's gay community was not happy with this answer. So they inquired whether the Dalai Lama would be willing to meet with a delegation of them.

Yes, he said, he would.

The next day, they had a long meeting, and when it was

over, the Dalai Lama publicly announced that he had changed his position on homosexuality.

"I was wrong," he said. "I was speaking in accordance with traditional Buddhist teachings, but I now believe they are misguided."

I've always loved the Dalai Lama, but when I heard this story, my respect for him skyrocketed. How often do we see religious or political leaders who don't hesitate to acknowledge when their beliefs are in need of correction?

No Enemy

We have failed to grasp the fact that mankind is becoming a single unit, and that for a unit to fight against itself is suicide.

—Havelock Ellis

Like all forms of head-thinking, belief addiction is contagious. The more you insist that your opinion is the only right one, the more likely I am to dig in my heels and defend my own position. The more I judge you, the more likely you are to judge me right back. If I insist that my position is the only right one, you'll probably dig in your heels and defend your own beliefs.

Our challenge, then, is to relate to belief addicts without ourselves falling into the trap of belief addiction, and to keep our hearts open to people whose beliefs we not only disagree with but consider dangerous and menacing.

Belief addiction is easily recognized when it shows up in the form of terrorism or fanaticism. But often, it comes shrouded in less obvious forms. Even peace activists aren't immune. Unwittingly, they sometimes fan the very fires they're determined to extinguish.

In the following transcript from a recent Circlework Training, I discuss this issue with Allison, a young environmental activist. Our conversation begins when I remark that in the circle, there is space for all kinds of people, as long as they don't insist that their way is the only right one:

J: For example, if I'm Christian, I need to have equal respect for Jews and Muslims. Their path is equally valid. So Circlework requires a basic attitude of respect.

A: Does that mean we are at war with fundamentalism?

J: No, no.

A: But then how are we going to survive fundamentalism?

Are we divided inside? If we are divided inside, there's no way in hell or heaven that tomorrow we're not going to have a divided world. It doesn't matter if we've got the best intentions in the universe; what really matters is the state from which we act.

—Adyashanti

J: Fundamentalism is rooted in fear and ignorance. If you can see through the rigidity and self-righteousness, you'll probably find someone who wants to feel safe and secure. Once you see their underlying need, you're no longer in a place of reactivity but of compassion.

A: But these people could take us into nuclear war.

J: So?

A: So we have to stop them. They're our enemies.

J: No, they're not our enemies. They scare the shit out of us, is all. We feel vulnerable, so it's tempting to do the same thing they do, which is to say, 'We're right, and you're wrong, and we're going to force you to do it our way.' Instead, can we stay with the simple fact that we're scared?

A: But what about anger? I'm so angry at them.

J: Well, what kind of anger are we talking about? There's violent anger, and then there's what I would call 'peaceful anger.' Peaceful anger is incredibly powerful. It can change the world. But it's never directed against people, only situations. It always asks: What is the most skillful response to this situation? That's the question people like Martin Luther King and Gandhi asked.

Gandhi was outraged when he got kicked off the train in South Africa because of the color of his skin. But he didn't spend the rest of his life being outraged. Instead, he looked at the situation and said, "What needs to happen here?" And then he set out to change things from a place of total centeredness. "Be the change you want to see in the world" was his message. What an amazing teaching! So if we want to see peace, we have to be peace.

A: That's hard!

J: It's terribly hard. I think that's why we need our circles. When we realize our whole world is threatened, we cannot deal with our distress alone. We need community. We need places where we can release our rage in a way that doesn't harm anyone and where we can grieve and be held when we fall into despair. Alone, it's too hard.

You can't overcome fundamentalism by waging war on it. If you try, you'll just strengthen it. This is true in general: whenever you see something you would like to transform, you need to become big enough to hold it in love. This initiates a movement towards transformation. You don't need to push for it; it just starts to happen. Whereas, when you try to force situations or people to move in a certain direction, they're going to resist.

So in the case of fundamentalism, we need to have compassion for them as well as for ourselves. And that means we have to accept the possibility that the planet may die.

A (crying): But I can't accept the death of the planet! I can't bear it. No, no, no!

For a while, Allison sobs while two women hold her. Then she says: I've always tried to avoid grief. It's easier to find someone to blame than to feel the grief. I'm very committed to my work with the environment. But I always believed we could solve all our problems by making everyone else see the truth. Then, we'd all be safe, and there would be no more suffering.

It's scary to face that I can't make suffering go away. I've always known how to fight and how to make space for my anger, but I've never learned how to own my fear and my grief.

Transcending Belief Addiction

I am a veteran of thirty-plus years of protesting in the streets. And I see only too clearly the inadequacy of the old way of trying to bring about change in this culture. I recently read an article that described the real divide in world culture as being between those who recognize the interconnection of all beings and those who don't. As long as we continue to operate as if we don't recognize that interconnection, and create us-against-them paradigms, we can't bring about the changes we want to see. The revolution we envision would be the kind that just pits one power against another. Demonstrating against what we don't like isn't working. Instead, we need to become demonstrations of the positive change we want to see in the world.

— Circlework Graduate

Allison's experience can remind us of why it's hard to release our enemy projections: In the process, we also have to let go of the comforting belief that once we defeat the bad guys, everything will be fine.

But it *won't*, because the bad guys aren't the real problem. The sickness we see manifested in them is actually a sickness of our collective ego. Albert Camus recognized this clearly as he contemplated the nightmare of WWII: "We used to wonder where war lived, what it was that made it so vile. And now we realize that we know where it lives, that it is inside ourselves." Inside ourselves, then, is where the change must begin.

Obviously, habits as ancient and ingrained as us-versus-them thinking, judgment, blame and belief addiction aren't going to dissolve overnight. Yet change is underway. For thousands of years, most people took these relational habits for granted and never questioned them. Today, we *are* questioning them. A host of spiritual teachers such as Adyashanti, Gangaji, Eckhart Tolle are encouraging us to detach from our mind and recognize the limitations of thought. Every belief, they remind us, no matter how sacred it might be in our view, is merely a mental construct, and can only grasp a relative and limited kind of truth.

Science, too, is helping us see our beliefs in a new light. In recent decades, we've learned a lot about how the mind works, how various chemicals and hormones affect it, and how it interacts with our heart and body. Thanks to these new findings, it's becoming easier to recognize the mind for what it is—an extraordinary tool, fine-tuned and honed over eons—but nonetheless just a tool, not the god we've made it out to be.

What our mind presents as solid truth is actually a mere cobweb, a puff of smoke, a firework display staged by neurons. Our beliefs about reality are one thing, reality itself another. As navigational guidelines, our beliefs can serve us well. But to write them in stone is to invest them with a power they are not qualified to hold.

Most of our attachments to certain beliefs seem quite harmless. Yet a straight line leads from belief addiction to violence and warfare. Let us therefore remember that every time we soften our grip on a cherished opinion or belief, we send a healing ripple through our collective consciousness. By holding our convictions lightly, with humility and humor, we contribute to the transformation of an inner adversary that is threatening to destroy us. And while this might seem like a small step, it's an act of self-liberation that will not only improve our personal relationships but can go a long way towards healing our world.

Suggested Exercises (See Appendix II)

Exercise 7. Detachment Practice

Exercise 8. Five Breaths

CHAPTER 5

RELIGION AND SPIRITUALITY

Religion is a candle inside a multicolored lantern. Everyone looks through a particular color, but the candle is always there.

—Mohammed Naguib, Egypt's first president

Approached by Christian missionaries who wanted to build a new church, the Native American Chief Joseph shook his head. "We do not want churches," he said, "because they will teach us to quarrel about God."

He's right, of course. If belief addiction is a weed, then religion is a hothouse where those weeds grow to monstrous proportions. And since religious beliefs are exempt from any kind of rational scrutiny, these weeds often are quite bizarre and outlandish.

Religious beliefs are often extremely specific. Take, for example, the Nicene Creed, also known as the Credo (Latin for "I believe"). With slight variations, the Nicene Creed has been adopted by many Christian denominations, including the Lutheran, Presbyterian, Anglican, and Eastern Orthodox Churches. Here's the Catholic version:

I believe in one God,
the Father Almighty,
maker of Heaven and Earth
and of all things visible and invisible.
And in one Lord Jesus Christ,
the only-begotten Son of God,
begotten of His Father before all worlds,
God of God, Light of Light,
very God of very God,
begotten, not made,
being of one substance with the Father,
by whom all things were made;
who for us men and for our salvation came down
from heaven
and was incarnate by the Holy Spirit of the Virgin
Mary
and was made man;
and was crucified also for us under Pontius Pilate.
He suffered and was buried.
And the third day He rose again according to the
Scriptures
and ascended into heaven
and sits at the right hand of the Father.
And He will come again with glory to judge both
the living and the dead,
whose kingdom will have no end.
And I believe in the Holy Spirit,
the Lord and giver of life,
who proceeds from the Father and the Son,

who with the Father and the Son together is worshipped and glorified,
who spoke by the prophets.
And I believe in one holy Catholic and apostolic
Church,
I acknowledge one Baptism for the remission of
sins,
and I look for the resurrection of the dead
and the life of the world to come. Amen.

I quote this text in its entirety because it shows how we are
taught that to belong to a certain religious tribe, one must embrace a long and detailed list of beliefs. And since none of them
can be verified, they must be taken on faith. In the process,
we learn a very dangerous lesson: To be spiritual, one must
adopt certain beliefs. From here, it's just a skip and a jump to
identifying the ideal spiritual seeker as a hard-core belief addict—someone who never questions their beliefs and will cling
to them even unto death.

So yes, Chief Joseph was right. Religion does incite conflict.
Inconceivable atrocities have been committed in the name of
God, often with the blessing of religious authorities. And tragically, many religious scriptures contain passages that explicitly
sanction violence against non-believers.

Sam Harris, author of *The End of Faith*, quotes a Biblical
passage that tells us to "tear down their altars, smash their
standing stones, cut down their sacred poles, and set fire to
their idols." And here's how we're supposed to respond when
someone tries to convert us to another religion:

"You must show him no pity, you must not spare him or conceal his guilt. No, you must kill him, your hand must strike the first blow in putting him to death and the hands of the rest of the people following. You must stone him to death, since he has tried to divert you from Yahweh your God." (Deuteronomy 13:7–11)

Needless to say, such teachings aren't exactly conducive to peace. And unfortunately, the scriptures of many religions contain similarly violent passages. No wonder many people view religion as a dangerous toxin! The world would be better off without religion, they say. It promotes beliefs that we would reject as crazy were we to encounter them in any other context. Worse still, it poses a serious threat to peace because it condones violence.

Take belief addiction out of the picture and you'll find, as history has borne out many times, that religion need not be an adversary of peace, and that people of diverse faiths are capable of getting along just fine.

I'd have to agree that overall, religion doesn't seem to have made our world a better place. And yet, I don't believe religion itself is the problem. Even if abolishing religion were an option—which it obviously isn't—doing so would be futile; we'd merely be cutting off one head of a many-headed monster.

That monster is, of course, *belief addiction*. As long as we base our sense of identity on specific ideologies, we're bound to fight over them. But take belief addiction out of the picture and you'll find, as history has borne out many times, that religion need not be an adversary of peace, and that people of diverse faiths are capable of getting along just fine.

What is Spirituality?

What is spirituality, if not a belief system? Trying to capture its essence in words is like trying to catch the wind in one's bare hands. That said, a good working definition might be this:

Spirituality is the realization of oneness in mind, heart, and body, and the journey of aligning our lives with that realization.

The realization of oneness is like pure water—simple, clear, potent, and healing. Religion pours it into a wine glass, non-religious spirituality into a water glass. Either way, it's the same water that quenched the thirst of Moses and Mohammed, and that can today quench the fires of violence and warfare on our planet.

Dimensions of Oneness

Earth is one—a single eco-system woven by a vast array of interconnected species, all dependent on the same soil, water, and atmosphere.

Time is one. Real only in a relative way, it has no absolute existence.

Space is one. We can build walls to enclose an area, yet space itself remains unaltered and indivisible.

Consciousness is one. Your consciousness is no more separate from mine than the space within a house is separate from the space that surrounds it.

When we define spirituality in this way, the spiritual signif-icance of heart-thinking becomes obvious. For while the mind can think about oneness, the actual experience is the preroga-tive of the heart. Only through the heart can we access that in-ner sanctuary where all sense of separation dissolves.

For us, who will have no future unless we awaken to our oneness, spirituality is a potential life-saver. Religion is option-al; spirituality is not. We can survive quite well without a set of beliefs about the afterlife or re-incarnation, but not without connection to our innermost self, to nature and to the cosmos. Perhaps this is why today so many people are experiencing spontaneous spiritual awakenings.

The Astronaut's Awakening

On February 5th, 1971, Edgar Mitchell became the sixth human to set foot on the moon. After his moonwalk, he was gazing out the window of his space craft when Earth floated into his field of vision—a beautiful blue gem moving slowly and majesti-cally through the vastness of space.

At that moment, Mitchell entered a state of consciousness he'd never experienced before. By training a consummate head-thinker, he was abruptly catapulted into heart-thinking. An overwhelming sense of love surged through him and si-multaneously he realized, with absolute clarity, that all beings are one. Separation, he realized, is an illusion. Not only that, but it's the illusion that lies at the root of all our problems.

Mitchell was almost certainly the first human to have a

spiritual awakening in space. But the experience itself was by no means unusual: many, if not most, spiritual awakenings involve a sudden shift from head – to heart-thinking. For only through the eyes of the heart can we apprehend life's intrinsic wholeness, as well as its holiness. Whether we're contemplating a plant or a planet, our heart recognizes the mystery that shines through them, and is flooded with gratitude and reverence. Therefore, the heart is universally acknowledged as the gateway to the soul.

Through the eyes of the heart, the intrinsic wholeness and holiness of all beings is revealed. Therefore the heart is universally acknowledged as the gateway to the soul.

The overwhelming love Mitchell felt in the face of Earth's beauty signaled his shift from head-thinking to heart-thinking, and from analytic to holistic vision. As he contemplated our small blue-white planet, he transcended the illusion of separateness and knew himself as a tiny speck within the great interconnected cosmic web.

In Mitchell's biography, we read: "As he hurtled earthward through the abyss between the two worlds, Mitchell became engulfed by a profound sensation "a sense of universal connectedness." He intuitively sensed that his presence, that of his fellow astronauts, and that of the planet in the window were all part of a deliberate, universal process, and that the glittering cosmos itself was in some way conscious. The experience was so overwhelming Mitchell knew his life would never be the same."

Indeed, it never was, for in that moment the hard-edged scientist transformed into a lifelong spiritual seeker and peace activist. Soon after this event, Mitchell founded the Institute of Noetic Sciences, which today serves as an important hub for people dedicated to the transformation of human consciousness.

Few people have actually seen our planet from outer space, but the photographs of that sight have had a profound impact on our collective consciousness. When they first flickered across our television screens, we were awestruck. Of course, we'd long known that our planet is round and blanketed in white clouds. But never before had we actually been able to see it with our own eyes. It was as if Earth had been blind until that moment. Now, through our eyes, she was finally able to contemplate her own form. She'd received the gift of sight and could for the first time regard herself in the mirror.

Not surprisingly, the image of our blue-white planet has in recent decades become the worldwide symbol of global consciousness. Printed on mugs and T-shirts, reusable shopping bags and Earth flags, it broadcasts the most important truth we need to absorb, if we hope to survive: "Earth is one. We are one. Separation is an illusion."

Awakening to Our Interconnection

Buddhists have a name for the insight Mitchell had as he gazed at our small planet: They call it the realization of interconnection. The word *interconnection* is often used as a synonym for *connection*. But strictly speaking, interconnection refers to something far more intriguing and baffling than mere connection. You and I can feel connected without giving up our egoic sense of separateness. But in the experience of interconnection, all sense of separation dissolves: I know myself as a part of you, and you as a part of me.

One of the clearest explanations of interconnection is found in a two-thousand-year-old Buddhist scripture called the *Avatamsaka Sutra*. The cosmos, it says, is a vast web woven from an infinite number of minute pearls. Each pearl is a mirror that not only reflects the other pearls but also contains them within itself. So delicate and sensitive is this web that by touching a single pearl, we set a ripple in motion that spreads to the farthest reaches of the cosmos.

The Sutra then concludes: "In the same way, each person, each object in the world, is not merely itself, but involves every other person and object and, in fact, on one level is every other person and object." Or, as author Jean Houston puts it: "Every part of you is a nexus of all occasions that ever were and ever are. You are therefore the whole and the part.... The structures of your being quite literally reflect the ongoing structures of the universe."

So long as mystical experience was the only way to access this realization, it naturally remained a rare phenomenon. For most people, interconnection was nothing but a highly esoteric theory with no obvious practical significance and no impact on their lives. But once we entered the global era, this changed radically. Suddenly, interconnection became an obvious, inescapable concept with far-reaching practical implications.

Today everything, from climate change to the global economy, is driving home a single message: we truly are interconnected, and will not survive unless we align our lives with this truth.

Fortunately, our interconnectedness has never been easier to realize than it is today. Just consider what is surely the most revolutionary invention of our times: The World Wide Web. More than just an electronic marvel, the Internet reflects our collective awakening to that intricate, multidimensional web of which the ancient Buddhist sages spoke. Having witnessed revolutions launched on Facebook, we're aware of the power of technology to weave a global web of connection. The fact that important information can now circle the planet in mere seconds is making it increasingly easier for us to experience ourselves as a single field of evolving intelligence.

Another important factor is modern science. As it delves ever more deeply into the mysteries of the material world, it's discovering a reality radically different from the one our senses show us. Astoundingly, science is now beginning to embrace what had long been dismissed as a spiritual fiction: the interconnectedness of all that is. Surely, no science fiction writer has ever dreamed up anything quite as wild and weird as the churning subatomic world with its perplexing multidimensionality, where particles appear and disappear, hovering on the threshold between existence and non-existence.

The Newtonian model of the cosmos as a complex piece of machinery is long obsolete. Instead, many scientists now acknowledge that the Buddhist metaphor of the cosmos as an interconnected web of pearls may be closer to the truth than we ever knew. We are enmeshed in ways our mind is incapable of grasping. To realize this intellectually is an important step, but it's not enough. For the realization of our interconnectedness to transform our lives, it must be accompanied by an opening of the heart.

Of course, science does not speak about love. And yet, it seems increasingly likely that the 16th century Indian poet Kabir was on to something when he described the cosmos as "shot through with a single kind of love." Today, millions of people who have never had a mystical experience are nonetheless beginning to understand that although we might appear to be separate, we really aren't. We're all part of a single, tightly knit eco-system.

Ray Anderson's Story

Ray Anderson, a businessman who died in 2011, is an example of someone whose life was transformed as radically as Edgar Mitchell's—not, however, in response to a mystical experience but rather in response to certain facts and ideas. Anderson was the founder of a company called Interface that manufactured synthetic carpeting. Under his leadership, Interface became an enormous and extremely successful corporation.

But at some point, Anderson began to become increasingly aware of the fact that synthetic carpeting was nothing if not an environmental nightmare. The bitter truth was that his company was poisoning the land that the lives of his children and grandchildren depended upon.

One day, Anderson picked up Paul Hawken's book *The*

Ecology of Commerce. In it, Hawken argues that industrial society is destroying the planet, and that the only people capable of turning the situation around are the industry leaders.

Many people would have shrugged off such an inconvenient truth, but Anderson was a heart-centered man, and his heart was aching with a pain he couldn't deny.

"Is there no better way?" he wondered.

After reading Hawken's book, Anderson knew that if there was, it was up to him to find it. The ball was in his court.

And so, he set out on a mission of discovery. No longer content to just make a profit, he insisted that his business should serve rather than destroy the planet. With the launching of "Mission Zero," Interface committed to the ambitious goal of eliminating all negative impact on the environment by the year 2020.

To achieve this, Interface would have to be rebuilt from the ground up. The company started redesigning its products, applying new technologies, and using renewable materials and sources of energy. Slowly but surely, a huge, environmentally toxic corporation began transforming into a model of sustainable business.

By 2009, Interface had half-way reached its goal and Anderson was able to assure his aching heart that, yes, there was indeed a better way.

What had transformed in this process was not just the company, but the man himself. Though heart-thinking was not a term he used, his whole life had become an expression of it. No longer was the circle of his concern limited to his immediate family and community. Instead, he felt a powerful sense of kinship with all forms of life—past, present, and future, human and non-human. No longer were his heart and his mind at war. Rather, he had fused them into a single organ of compassionate wisdom.

When Anderson initiated the transformation of Interface, the very word "spirituality" was noxious to him. It was, he now admits, "a term that, frankly, turned me off, because I associated it with religiosity." Had someone suggested that he might be experiencing a spiritual awakening, he would undoubtedly have pooh-poohed the idea.

In later years, however, he came to see things differently. Having witnessed the transformation of his own consciousness, he declared that "today, the survival of our species depends most of all on changed minds." Spirituality, he realized, doesn't have to involve religious beliefs—or, for that matter, beliefs of any kind. As he said, "The growing field of spirituality in business is a cornerstone of the next industrial revolution, as I see it.... The destiny of our company, its higher calling, and its ultimate strategic purpose have flowed from that wellspring of spiritual awakening."

Religious Pioneers

At present, most religions are like gardens overgrown with the weeds of belief addiction. If religion is to serve as agents of global peace and healing, some intensive weeding will have to be done. Otherwise, instead of helping us birth a new planetary civilization, religion will only deepen the chasms between us.

Fortunately, a growing number of religious pioneers understand this. Reaching out across religious boundaries, they're developing new forms of spiritual practice that inspire a sense of global solidarity.

I think, for example, of a group of Swiss nuns that my friend Sarah has been working with. Last time I saw her, she'd just returned from a week-long workshop with the nuns. The workshop was focused on the Palestinian issue, and the group consisted of Palestinians, Jews, and Arab Israelis, as well as Americans.

Beaming, Sarah declared it had been one of the best weeks of her life. "There were fifty of us, men and women. We sat in circle every day, all day. And every morning began with a prayer or a ritual that was either Muslim, Jewish, or Christian."

Sarah told me she loved the process and the healing it brought. But what had touched and moved her most of all were the nuns themselves. "They're deeply spiritual," she explained, "and they exuded a peacefulness that we all felt. The circle wasn't just this holy place. There was a lot of conflict, too. But it was held in the spirit of peace."

These nuns may be radical, but they're not alone. In every tradition, similar pioneers are showing up to bring a new consciousness to their religious communities. Once again, I would mention the Dalai Lama. Obviously he has the deepest respect for his culture and for the art, scriptures, chants, and rituals that make Tibetan Buddhism such an extraordinary tradition. Yet as a true global citizen, he doesn't hesitate to discard any beliefs, no matter how venerable, that aren't conducive to inner and outer peace.

Unfortunately, not all religious leaders share his enlightened consciousness. Over the centuries, many religious organizations have become increasingly hierarchical and authoritarian. Forgetful of their true purpose, they have turned into a veritable bulwark of belief addiction. Fearful of change, they cling to hierarchical power structures that have outlived their usefulness, rituals that have become predictable and boring, and the shallow comforts of the familiar.

> *I am a Hindu. I am also a Muslim. I am also a Jew and a Christian. Some would even say I'm an atheist. Religion and the color of one's skin—what useless ways to define and establish a nation!*
>
> —Mahatma Gandhi

Stifling the raw power and intimacy of authentic spirituality, religious organizations obstruct the very experience they are meant to facilitate. Instead of encouraging heart-thinking, they discourage it. Their leaders' allegiance is not to the human soul or the global community, but to the organization that has bestowed such power and authority on them.

Years ago, I connected with a group of nuns who were exploring new forms of spiritual practice. The first time I attended one of their services, I had no idea what to expect. I was ushered into a large circular room through which the gentle sound of wooden flutes wafted. To my surprise, there was no altar. In fact, there was no furniture at all, aside from a book-stand. Instead of sitting on chairs, people were sitting on za-fus—meditation cushions used in Zen practice. And instead of sitting in rows, they had formed a circle. Other than the music, there was no sound. Everyone was sitting quietly, and many seemed deep in meditation.

As I sat down in the circle and let the gentle waves of sound wash over me, I felt my body and mind growing quiet. Eventually, the music ended and gave way to a deep, peaceful silence that lasted perhaps ten minutes.

Then, one of the nuns stood up and went to the bookstand. In a sweet, lilting voice, she read a variety of texts from a wide range of traditions—Buddhist and Christian, Hindu and Native American.

The entire service was a beautiful celebration of global spirituality. But as far as I was concerned, the ending was its high point. After a second period of silent meditation, a bell rang. And suddenly, the whole room was pulsing with music—not the gentle, angelic chords we'd heard before, but music that was wild and rhythmic. And this time, instead of listening quietly, the nuns leapt from their seats and threw off their black habits. Gasping in astonishment, I watched them plunge into the center of the circle. And there, dressed now in ordinary street clothes, they started dancing with wild abandon.

"Sweat your prayers!" the dancer Gabrielle Roth says. And so these women were, joy written all over their faces. God, I have no doubt, was smiling.

But the Pope was not. After hearing of their activities, he intervened, and the nuns were forbidden to continue their celebrations. I still feel sad when I think about this. His repressive response reflected a distrust of nature that has for centuries held us back from celebrating our passion. This must change, for in the long run, a species that wages war on nature cannot survive.

Suggested Exercises (See Appendix II)

Exercise 9. Twelve Ways to Align Your Religious Practice with Heart-Thinking

Exercise 10. Gratitude

CHAPTER 6

WHY JUDGMENT IS OBSOLETE

You do not define anyone with your judgment. You only define yourself as someone who needs to judge.

—Wayne Dyer

Many years ago, I led a workshop at a beautiful retreat center overlooking the Pacific Ocean. Our morning session had just ended, and it was a gorgeous, sunny day. A long afternoon break lay ahead—perfect for a drive up the coast.

I grabbed my keys, and off I went, sniffing happily at the fresh, tangy air. The road curved gently, hugging the coastline and revealing one dazzling view after another. Eventually, I pulled over at a small restaurant that overlooked the ocean. I'm in luck, I thought as I walked in. It's empty. I can sit at the window and watch the waves roll in.

As the waiter handed me the menu, I noticed another man who was leaning against the kitchen door. A heavyset fellow with a paunch, he was obviously in no hurry. He must be the owner, I figured.

My coffee arrived, and still he stood there, clearly observing. I wished he would leave, but no. There he remained, hovering like a hawk. A couple of minutes passed as I sipped my coffee and tried to ignore him. But then, alas, he sauntered over and started asking me questions. Was I a tourist? Was I on vacation? What was I doing here? His demeanor wasn't exactly unfriendly, but clearly, I was being checked out, as if my right to enter his territory were under question.

Inwardly, I began to bristle. I don't remember whether the word 'redneck' actually crossed my mind, but I had definitely pegged him as one. Of course it didn't help that, as fate would have it, he quite literally did have a red neck.

Rednecks scared me. I saw them as overweight bullies prone to abusing women, politically conservative, racists, and bigots. Whenever I encountered someone who seemed to fit the bill, I would draw a wide circle around them. And so, though I was answering the café owner's questions, and appeared to be connecting with him, in truth I had already rejected him and wanted nothing to do with him.

My usual strategy would have been to put up walls and discourage any contact. But this time, I couldn't get away with it, the reason being that just before we broke for lunch, I'd given the workshop participants an assignment for the afternoon. It was a practice I call "Seeing with Sacred Eyes." And the instructions were these:

Whenever you encounter someone, mentally greet them as God. Inwardly, bow to them, and honor them as embodiments of Spirit.

"If you're uncomfortable with the word God," I told the

women at the retreat, "no problem. Just use whatever words work for you. You might greet them as sacred beings or as embodiments of the great Mystery."

The practice of inwardly bowing to someone is a wonderful way to evoke the perception of them as unique, special, and sacred. And since only the heart is capable of perceiving others as sacred, this practice automatically leads us to heart-thinking. And is this not what we all long for—to see the sacred all around us, all the time, and to live in a world imbued with mystery?

But sitting in that restaurant, my instructions felt like a tall order. Dismayed, I considered my redneck. Surely the divine Beloved wasn't supposed to look like this! He wasn't supposed to have a beer belly and hairy hands.

But there he stood, not in the least deterred by my lack of encouragement.

"Okay," I sighed, "here goes."

Then, I inwardly began to talk to him.

"No matter who you are," I told him, "I know that God lives within you, and that you are one of His manifestations. Please help me release my judgments, which are rooted in ignorance and fear. The truth is, I know nothing about you. All I know is that you're somewhat overweight and inquisitive. Please forgive me for judging you. I bow to you. I honor you and thank you for your presence."

I continued to talk with the man. Outwardly, nothing had changed. But my inner world felt very different than it had five minutes ago.

> *Then it was as if I suddenly saw the secret be*
> *their hearts, the depth of their hearts where*
> *sin nor knowledge could reach the core of reality, the*
> *person that each one is in the eyes of the divine. If*
> *only they could see themselves as they really are, if*
> *only we could see each other that way all the time,*
> *there would be no more need for war, for hatred, for*
> *greed, for cruelty. I suppose the big problem would*
> *be that we would fall down and worship each other.*
>
> —Thomas Merton

I didn't tell my new friend that I was leading a women's workshop in which we were exploring the archetypal meaning and symbolism of the divine marriage. However, I did tell him that I was leading a retreat for fifteen women. Having gathered this information, he finally appeared to be satisfied and retreated to the kitchen.

I heaved a sigh of relief. Finally, I was free to drink my coffee and enjoy the play of sunlight dancing on the rolling waves. Half an hour later, I asked for the check, paid, and stood up to leave. But as I headed towards the door, my red-necked friend came running out of the kitchen.

"Wait, wait!" he cried.

Surprised, I stopped.

"Just a second," he panted, quite out of breath. So I waited, though for the life of me I couldn't imagine what he wanted ɔw. Turning on his heels, he raced back into the kitchen. A minute passed, then another. I started getting impatient.

Finally, the kitchen doors flew open and he burst out beaming. In his arms, he was cradling three steaming hot pies. Looking at me with a shy grin, he explained, "This one's cherry. This is apple walnut. And that—that's rhubarb strawberry."

Seeing my puzzled look, he added, almost apologetically, "Well… you see, I made them for your women. I thought they might enjoy them."

I was dumbfounded. While I was having my coffee, relieved to be rid of him, he'd been baking up a storm to make a special gift to a bunch of women whom he'd never met. Would he have acted any differently, had I not honored the divine presence in him? Who knows. All I can say for sure is that when we judge people, we go blind to their divinity. But by opening our hearts, we call forth the best in them. And there it was, in his simple gesture of hospitality, kindness, and welcome.

Judgment is Obsolete

War is obsolete, the Dalai Lama says. I would add that so is judgment, one of the most insidious forms of tribal conditioning there is. Just take a closer look at any war in recent history, and you'll see both a long trail of judgment leading up to it and a sorrowful trail of judgment that follows in its wake.

If I were to name the single most important step we can take towards peace, it would be to learn more skillful ways of dealing with judgment—not the kind that informs us whether it's safe to cross the road, but the kind that involves a put-down. The more we judge, the less space we have to breathe, for like a boa constrictor, judgment wraps itself around our heart and squeezes.

Like my judgment of rednecks, most of our everyday judgments seem pretty harmless. But no judgment is truly harmless. Even if it doesn't trigger an act of violence, it reinforces a habit that most certainly does. No matter how much we might claim to want peace, as long as we keep mindlessly indulging in judgment, we'll continue to sow seeds of conflict.

No judgment is truly harmless. No matter how much we might claim to want peace, as long as we keep mindlessly indulging in judgment, we'll continue to sow seeds of conflict and violence.

Judgment is the great iceberg against which so many precious relationships crash and burn. Who has not seen a marriage, a friendship, or a community destroyed by judgment? It inflicts deep emotional wounds that fester and can lead to violent explosions.

What exactly is judgment? It's often equated with the use of pejorative labels: "He's an idiot. She's a liar. He's lazy." The mindful use of language is important. But why do we reach for those negative labels? What purpose do they serve?

As I see it, their true function is to justify why we're closing our hearts and shifting to head-thinking. Simply put, judgment is our excuse for not loving. Here, then, is my definition:

Judgment is the way we rationalize why we're closing our heart and withholding our love from someone.

Most people have a strong, unquestioned faith in the power of judgment to initiate positive change. They don't see judgment as an inner adversary or a threat to peace. In their view, it's crucial to upholding moral standards. Yet if you look closely at your own experience, you're likely to find it doesn't support this view. Just think of

Judgment is how we rationalize why we're closing our heart and withholding our love from someone.

a time when you felt judged. What happened? Probably, you shut down and became defensive, perhaps even hostile. When we reject someone, they push back. Whatever we resist will in turn resist us. And so, our judgments tend to backfire, creating friction and hostility. More often than not, judgment brings out the worst in us.

For many people, it comes as a surprise to discover they're perfectly capable of expressing their needs, wants, and preferences without judgment. We tend to view it as a necessary tool for warding off abuse and upholding social standards. But look more closely, and you'll realize judgment accomplishes neither of these goals. By letting go of it, we can dramatically improve the quality of our personal relationships. At the same time, we contribute to the transformation of an extremely toxic collective habit.

But if judgment is so toxic, how come we think of it as a friend? Why are we so convinced it will lead to positive change?

Just as in the case of us-versus-them thinking and belief addiction, I believe we must look to our distant past for answers.

Previously, I mentioned three elements that defined the nature of most tribal societies: People were utterly dependent on the tribe, most tribes were isolated, and within the tribe, there was no racial, religious or cultural diversity. It's not hard to see how in conjunction, these three factors would have made judgment a highly effective tool for enforcing conformity. In a context where people had no alternative community to turn to, the specter of tribal rejection was terrifying since rejection was tantamount to a death sentence. And since everyone shared much the same values, the judgment of one was likely to reflect the judgment of all. Under these circumstances, even the most rebellious individual would think twice before misbehaving. It's likely, therefore that throughout the tribal era—which is to say for untold millennia—judgment really *did* trigger positive change.

The more tribal a society is, the more power judgment is likely to wield over its citizens. India, for example, with its booming computer business on the one hand and its villages steeped in ancient tribal ways on the other, is typical of many cultures that stand with one foot in the tribal and another in the global era.

When I lived there, I was struck both by the pervasiveness of judgment and by the innocence with which people wielded it. By innocence, I mean that they never questioned its value as an essential tool for upholding moral standards. They would watch each other carefully, stowing away their judgments like jars of pickles and would happily engage in lengthy discussions about the rightness or wrongness of a particular action. There was no question in their mind that there was a right and a wrong way to do everything, from governing the nation to dealing with stray cobras. Family bonds were strong, caste and religious bonds were strong—and judgment was the glue that held it all together.

But around the world, things are changing fast. Like its twin, belief addiction, judgment is a remnant of the past, a legacy we've long accepted without questioning whether it truly serves us. Now, we're beginning to realize that not only does judgment not serve us, it poses a serious threat to peace. Once an ally that helped harmonize the tribe, it has now become an adversary responsible for endless conflict and violence.

The Family as Tribe

On a small scale, we each relive the evolutionary journey of our species. Every child is, after all, born into a tribe of sorts— a small group of people upon whom its survival depends. As long as this state of dependence persists, their judgments are likely to have a fair amount of clout. Most children will do everything within their power to gain approval and avoid rejection.

But though judgment can still be painful, in our day and age it's rarely life-threatening. Moreover, parents' judgments lack the foundation of collective consensus that once endowed them with so much power. Children may get one set of rules from their parents, another from their peers, and yet another from the media. Once they realize that their parents' views are by no means universally shared, the power of judgment tends to wane quickly. No wonder parents and teachers are having such a hard time with discipline! The tool they traditionally relied on—judgment—is like an old lion who has lost his teeth.

Kicking the Habit

Judgment is no easy habit to shed, in part because it's highly addictive. Like cats get high on catnip, our ego gets high on the sense of righteous superiority it enjoys whenever it passes judgment on others.

Of course we want to hold people responsible for their actions. But let's also consider our *own* responsibility, which is to find skillful ways of responding to negative forces. And unfortunately, judgment is *not* a skillful response. Like a corrosive acid, it eats away at the web of our connections, causing bitterness and pain yet never making a dent in greed, corruption, or cruelty.

The only thing that will change the dysfunctional behavior of our species is a shift in our collective consciousness—and that shift must begin with us. A good place to start is with Marshall Rosenberg's book, *Non-Violent Communication*. Rosenberg is a brilliant relational educator and peacemaker who views every judgment as an act of violence. His book describes a simple (though by no means easy) four-step process for expressing oneself in non-violent ways. When I first started practicing non-violent communication, I was shocked to realize how judgmental I really was. Judgment often disguises itself as something else—an innocent observation, a joke, or even a tone of voice.

Containment

Between stimulus and response, there is a space. In that space lies our freedom and power to choose our response. In our response lies our growth and freedom.

— Viktor Frankl

When you notice that you're judging someone, try reminding yourself that they aren't having a problem—*you* are.

"He made me angry," we say.

But others don't "make" us angry. By blaming them, we only widen the gulf between us.

Another useful practice is to internally acknowledge our judgments without speaking them out loud. Since judgment is toxic, we might think of this as the energetic equivalent of environmental protection. Can we, out of respect for others, contain our judgments mindfully, rather than spewing them out? Can we take a careful look at our negative emotions, instead of dumping them on others?

The Buddhist teacher Pema Chodrun calls this patience. "Patience," she says, "has a quality of honesty and it also has the quality of holding our seat. We don't automatically react, even though inside we are reacting. We let all the words go and are just there with the rawness of our experience."

In my circles, we spend a lot of time doing this. The practice of listening quietly to people without responding forces us to sit with our judgments and witness them without discharging the negativity they evoke in us. By noticing where we falter in our ability to accept others, we discover where our edges lie and where our demons live.

Ancient as it is, judgment can feel so right, so natural, so inevitable. Yet in any circle gathering, you can see how differently people respond to the same situation. Where one throws a fit, another feels amused.

In the grips of judgment, it can be difficult to recognize that we're caught up in an ancient habit that has become not just obsolete but dangerous. We're so sure we're right that often, we mistake judgments for facts. Yet when we release our judgments, our perceptions and relationships may transform in seemingly miraculous ways.

Carol, a participant in one of my ongoing circles, talks about this. "At times, my first reaction to some people was: I don't like them. You'd mentioned up front that this might happen, and you told us that even if we disliked someone, we should try to respect their core and look for the essence behind the personality.

"I really took that in, and didn't do what I would have done in the past, which was to just shut them out. In social situations I'd be pleasant, but really, I wasn't open to them.

"This has been an incredible experience of absorbing, listening, being patient, and making space for differences. I have learned that someone who annoyed me half an hour ago might say something truly profound or teach me something extremely valuable. Now, I really love some of the people in the group whom I didn't like at first.

"I used to want certain people to be more spiritual, or different in some way, but now I feel, no, they don't have to change for me. I feel very connected to everyone. I am seeing them differently, and really accepting them and loving them the way they are. That's so new for me. I've watched my criticism turning to understanding and affection, and have discovered that on the other side of every judgment is love."

Doing Our Part

Sometimes we lose sight of the obvious. We talk about peace, as if it were a matter of political negotiation or strategic maneuvering. But peace is first and foremost a matter of *human relationships*. When the relationships between individuals and groups are harmonious, they're at peace.

How then can we separate the art of peace from the art of relationship? If we want to create a more peaceful world, we must hone our skills in the art of maintaining peaceful relationships. I emphasize this because we don't usually draw a connection between our personal judgments and the greater picture of what's going on in the world. We don't think that how skillfully we manage our personal disagreements and conflicts has any impact on world peace.

Yet all wars are the outcome of hundreds of small

interactions that escalate and eventually culminate in outbursts of violence perpetrated by individuals just like us. Since collective transformation can only happen through individuals, each step we take towards overcoming the habit of judgment will help others do the same.

It's inspiring to realize that through our personal evolution, we can contribute to our collective healing. We are, after all, by nature programmed to want the best, not only for ourselves but for our community as well. We derive courage and strength from the knowledge that our personal struggles are part of a larger struggle, and that others

We don't usually draw a connection between our personal judgments and the greater picture of what's going on in the world. Yet all wars are the outcome of hundreds of small interactions that escalate and eventually culminate in outbursts of violence perpetrated by individuals just like us.

will benefit from our victories over judgment and fear. When the going gets hard, this sense of collective solidarity can give us the courage to do what might otherwise feel too scary, whether it's speaking our truth, revealing our vulnerability, or owning up to our judgments.

Every time we judge or blame each other, we're colluding with an inner adversary who pretends to be harmless yet is in reality anything but. Vice versa, every time we recognize our judgments for what they are—defensive tactics born of fear— we strengthen the forces of peace. And no matter how small and insignificant that contribution might be, it is only out of the accumulation of these tiny changes that major changes will come.

Suggested Exercises (See Appendix II)

Exercise 11. Giving Honor

Exercise 12. Listening to the Heart of Humanity

CHAPTER 7

MEDINA'S STORY

Every gun that is made, every warship launched, every rocket fired signifies, in the final sense, a theft from those who are cold and not clothed. This world in arms is not spending money alone. It is spending the sweat of its laborers, the genius of its scientists, the hopes of its children. This is not a way of life at all in its true sense... it is humanity hanging from a cross of iron.

— President Dwight Eisenhower

I f you want to know the true price of tribal conditioning, take a close look at a warzone. From a distance, war can be easy to rationalize. Up close, it's another matter. From a distance, one can count the casualties and tally the financial costs. But up close, it's obvious that the real victim of war is the human heart, which gets trampled underfoot and is left bleeding, shattered, and broken.

We used to believe that after something was over, it was over. If you survived the war, the rape, or the famine, you could get on with your life. Today, we know it isn't so. The true cost of war goes far beyond lives lost and homes destroyed. War leaves in its wake a deeply traumatized population. Such trauma never affects just one individual. Friends, families, and communities all suffer too. They bear the heavy brunt of depression, rage, and addiction—all typical responses to trauma.

People traumatized by violence and war need more than just psychiatric help. Just as a mortally wounded person needs medical assistance, so does the mortally wounded heart. The good news is that we don't need to be physicians or psychologists to provide such assistance. For what the heart needs, most of all, is loving presence, compassionate attention, and caring community.

As physician and psychotherapist Rachel Naomi Remen reminds us, "Healing is not the work of experts. Often we heal others simply because of who we are. Then by some Grace, our very wounds can serve to strengthen the life in others. Although I have witnessed this many times, I still find something mysterious in such occasions, as if something unknown, finding us worthy, has used us just as we are to be an instrument of healing."

Healing happens whenever suffering is held in love; and today, people are gathering in many places around the world to do just that. Conscious of connection as the antidote to prejudice and hatred, they are creating spaces where former enemies can sit face to face, eye to eye, and discover who the other *really* is.

Renate is a group facilitator who has participated in many such circles. She's seen first-hand how easily head-thinking can derail the process, but also how the presence of a single heart-thinker can tip the balance between success and failure.

One circle, in particular, made a deep impression on her. Its members included twelve men and women whose lives had been shattered by the Bosnian war in the 1990s. Six Bosnian-Serbs and six Bosnian-Muslims, they'd been meeting regularly, each time for several days at a stretch, with an intention of healing their wounds, restoring mutual trust, and learning how to follow the path of peace.

People in conflict often need an outsider to guide them. In this circle, the facilitator was an American. Herself a teacher of peace studies, she had brought two of her students with her: a young man and Renate.

The road to reconciliation is often rough, and not all attempts are successful. Like clay pots that crack under the heat of the oven, some circles break. This circle, too, could easily have shattered. For in a moment of crisis, when the healing balm of kindness and compassion was most needed, tribal conditioning rendered some members of the circle incapable of providing it.

Renate nurses her cup of tea as we sit on her comfortable overstuffed sofa, enjoying the soft evening light. Meeting my gaze with clear gray eyes, she smiles and says, "What happened in that circle was really pivotal for me. It allowed me to understand in a deeper way than before the power of circles to bring peace, even under very difficult circumstances."

The incident that affected Renate so profoundly had occurred on the third day of a four-day retreat. That morning, the facilitator had placed a stone in the center of the circle. Each participant, she explained, was to share a story about something they'd experienced during the war. Whoever wanted to speak was to pick up the stone while everyone else listened quietly, without commenting or interrupting.

All morning, people told their stories. After lunch, the first person to pick up the stone was Dino, a tall young Bosnian man. Dino told his brief story in a quiet, peaceful way. One day, he said, when he was still a teenager, he and his mother were riding on a public bus when it suddenly drew to a halt. Serb soldiers boarded, holding machine guns in their hands. Slowly, they scanned the sea of silent, terrified faces. Then, they pointed at certain passengers—all of them males—and ordered them to get off the bus. Everyone knew these men might never be seen again.

If Dino was scared, his mother was terrified. *Her* fear, however, wasn't for herself but for her son. Desperately wanting to shield him from the probing eyes of the soldiers, she shoved her tiny body in front of him. Dino chuckled at the memory. "I'm a big guy," he said, "and back then, I was already twice her size."

Dino was lucky; the soldiers let him go.

"But to this day," he ended his story, "my mother's terror lives on in me."

Falling silent, Dino sat quietly for a minute before gently returning the talking stone to the center.

Within seconds, a middle-aged Serbian woman reached for the stone. Holding it against her heart, she nodded at Dino and said, "I understand just how your mother felt. I didn't experience the war first hand, but my nephew was wounded, and I was so scared for him."

So far, so good.

But then, out of the blue, something happened that abruptly shattered the circle's quiet, reflective mood. Medina, one of the Bosnian members of the circle, was a beautiful, pale-skinned young woman with striking green eyes. Dressed professionally in a suit and high-heeled shoes, she had always exuded a sense of total self-control. Now, an entirely different person emerged. Trembling with rage, Medina started screaming at the Serb woman who'd been speaking.

Renate shakes her head at the memory. "It was like a bomb exploding in our midst. You have to understand, we had a rule that you never, ever interrupted whoever was speaking. Not interrupting was like a sacred element of the circle. I'd never before witnessed that rule being broken and I was totally shocked."

Medina had already told a personal story that morning. Yet she had done so in a quiet, reserved way, without actually revealing much about her personal life. Now, as if a dam had burst, the story she really needed to tell came tumbling out in a rush, propelled by a force she could no longer hold back.

"You don't know how his mother felt!" she screamed. "You have no idea how she felt, no idea at all! You don't know what it's like to be a mother and have the soldiers come into your house and your husband isn't home, and they hear your baby girl crying in the other room, and they pick her up by her feet and hold a knife to her throat, and they scream that you have only two choices: either your baby will die, or you will follow the soldiers into the bedroom. You have no idea what it's like to make the choice to save your baby's life, and never talk about it to anyone, never, never, never, not to a single soul, not even your husband or your mother, never ever mention it to anyone at all."

All the while, Medina was trembling violently, as if the rage, grief, and fear trapped in her small body were shaking at the bars of the cage that had held them captive for so long.

"Of course," Renate said, "we all realized that Medina was talking about herself." The rape had occurred six years earlier, yet until that moment, Medina had never dared talk about it. Even within her own family, she hadn't felt safe.

Medina's experience was by no means unusual—during the war an estimated fifty thousand women were raped. In 1992, the United Nations concluded, "Rape has been reported to have been committed by all sides to the conflict. However, the largest number of reported victims have been Bosnian Muslims, and the largest number of alleged perpetrators have been Bosnian Serbs."

Medina's outburst was followed by a moment of stunned silence. Then, a Serb woman reached for the stone.

But now, a second earthquake shook the circle: The facilitator stood up, walked over to her, and took the stone from her hand. Once again, Renate was shocked. "Another sacred rule was being broken. In all the years I had participated in this work, I had never seen the facilitator take the stone away from someone. I couldn't imagine what was going to happen next, and I have to say I was really scared. I was still in training, and

I remember thinking that if I'd been the leader, I wouldn't have had a clue how to handle this."

Fortunately, the facilitator understood that an opportunity for healing had presented itself that might never return. And so, she stood up and walked around the circle to where Medina was sitting. Standing behind her, she gently laid her hands on the young woman's shoulders.

"Medina just told a very important story," she said. "I want us to stay with this and not move on. And I want you to take in what she said."

Then she said to the Serbs, "I want you to recognize that what she needs to hear from you is, 'Medina, I'm so sorry this happened to you.'"

Renate hugs herself as she remembers the mounting tension in the room. "All the Serbs started talking amongst themselves in Serbian," she recalls.

Minutes passed until the translator explained, "They're talking about your request."

More talk in Serbian followed. Finally, the translator turned to the circle and said, "None of these people have ever raped a woman. They say they cannot apologize for something they did not do."

At this, the facilitator nodded but stood her ground. "Even if you can't apologize, there are ways in which you can acknowledge Medina. For example, you might say, 'I'm sorry that my people did this to you. I'm sorry for the suffering it caused you.'"

But after much discussion, one of the Serbs announced in a

tone of anger and frustration, "We just aren't willing to do this."

> *Peace requires something far more difficult than revenge or merely turning the other cheek; it requires empathizing with the fears and unmet needs that provide the impetus for people to attack each other. Being aware of those feelings and needs, people lose their desires to attack back because they see the human ignorance leading to those attacks. Instead, their goal becomes providing the empathic connection and education that will enable them to transcend their violence and engage in cooperative relationships.*
>
> —Marshall Rosenberg

Medina's circle included another peacemaker in training, an American man who now tried to help by modeling an alternative path. Turning to Medina, he said, "I am a man, and I am sorry on behalf of all men that we could do something so cruel to you."

But the Serbs discounted his example. Because he was an American, they felt that he was not one of them and could not understand their feelings. And so, despite Medina's obvious distress, the Serbs dug in their heels and refused to express any sympathy with her.

When we're thinking with our hearts, we can apologize without feeling the least bit diminished. In fact, it's inspiring to realize we have the power to set right something that was wrong. But as we all know, the ego hates admitting any weakness or failure.

This is especially true for men, who are often taught that it's unmanly to reveal any weakness. The more patriarchal a society, the more prevalent this view tends to be. Serb society is highly patriarchal, so the Serb men most likely felt that if they apologized, they'd suffer a loss of face.

However, I suspect that another, even stronger force was preventing them from opening their hearts to Medina. That force was *tribal conditioning*. The Serbs' rejection of the American as "not one of us," tells us that tribal conditioning had a strong hold on them, for as we said before, us-versus-them thinking is the most basic and primary symptom of tribal conditioning.

Under the influence of tribal conditioning we identify, first and foremost, as members of our tribe. Our personal sense of pride hinges on that of the tribe: when it's powerful and well-respected, we enjoy a strong sense of self-esteem, but when its image gets tarnished, we too feel tarnished. Any insult to our tribe is perceived as an insult to us personally, and should a member of the tribe do something shameful, we too feel ashamed.

This aspect of tribal consciousness is clearly spelled out in the Old Testament, where God warns his people not to provoke his anger, for, "I punish the father's fault in the sons, the grandsons, and the great-grandsons of those who hate me."

This view is common to many tribal cultures, and most likely, the Serbs too had internalized it. Now, its harsh voice was telling them that merely by virtue of being Serbs, they were implicated in Medina's rape.

"Shame on you," it said. "Your people have done a terrible deed, and now you too are disgraced."

Of course, the facilitator had never meant to imply that the Serbs were personally responsible for Medina's suffering. Presumably, she felt that since Medina's rapists had been Serb men, their compassion would carry more weight than that of anyone else in the circle. The Serbs, in other words, had a unique opportunity to heal a deep wound.

Unfortunately, that was not how the Serbs interpreted the facilitator's request. Singled out to apologize, they worried they might be blamed for a crime they had not committed. They wanted to perceive themselves as autonomous individuals, and be perceived as such. Yet the ancient force of tribal conditioning negated their autonomy, and insisted they pay for the sins of their people.

If my interpretation is correct, then what they were primarily resisting was the *inner* voice of tribal conditioning that spoke of shame and blame. When the facilitator asked them to apologize, they began projecting that voice onto her. Digging in their heels and resisting all her suggestions was their way of fighting back against the inner judge who threatened to pronounce them guilty because they belonged to the same tribe as Medina's rapists.

Convinced that their dignity and self-respect had come

under attack, their focus shifted from Medina's need for sympathy to their own need to be treated as individuals, rather than as members of their tribe. And so they became trapped in resistance to what was actually an inner force. No doubt they felt bad about leaving Medina in the lurch. Yet their need to take a stand against the crushing judgment of tribal conditioning was overwhelmingly strong.

Just that morning, the circle had felt like a peaceful, safe haven. Now, suddenly, it seemed in danger of shattering. Needless to say, this would have been a devastating outcome for everyone. Each member of this circle had been watering the seeds of peace and reconciliation for a long time.

But one thing I know from experience is that sometimes, all it takes to turn the situation around is a single individual who dares to switch from head – to heart-thinking, even when no one else seems willing. In Medina's circle, the person with that kind of courage was a Serb woman called Dijana.

The second Dijana stood up, the circle got very quiet. You could have heard a pin drop; the air felt charged with electricity. Drawing her shawl across her shoulders, Dijana slowly walked across the circle and sat down in front of Medina. Then, she took Medina's hands in her own and very gently, very tenderly said, "Medina, I believe you. I believe you completely."

Tears streamed down both women's faces as they looked into one another's eyes. Convinced of Dijana's sincerity, Medina nodded wordlessly.

At this point in her story, Renate stops to grab a tissue, as her own eyes well up.

"They really saw each other in that moment, and we all felt it," she tells me. "The room was totally silent. That moment felt so big, so important. We all felt that something sacred was happening, something vast and liberating and holy."

Gentle as a feather and sharp as a sword, heart-thinking had cut right through the thorny tangle that head-thinking had created. Suddenly, everyone's eyes were opened to the simple truth of what was before their eyes: a fellow human being who was suffering, and in need of compassion.

It didn't surprise me to hear that in the end, it was a woman who led the circle through its impasse. Women often model the path of heart-thinking—not because they are by nature more heartful than men, but because they don't have to contend with the paralyzing ideals of masculinity that may cripple men's capacity for heart-thinking.

"So," I ask Renate cautiously, "was it okay that the other Serbs never said, 'I'm sorry?'"

Renate nods. "Yes, it really was. It was just this moment of one Serb saying 'I see you,' and the healing that came out of that. It was huge, and we all felt it.

"Initially, I had been very scared of what might happen, but in the end, everything unfolded in a way that felt just right. In that moment, I knew that if everyone could do what we were doing here, we could heal the world."

Suggested Exercises (See Appendix II)

Exercise 13. Where Did You Come From?

Exercise 14. I Want You to Feel Safe

PART III

SHEDDING THE SHACKLES OF CONTROL-ERA CONDITIONING

CHAPTER 8

THE TOXIC LEGACY OF CONTROL ADDICTION

In these troubled, uncertain times, we don't need more command and control; we need better means to engage everyone's intelligence in solving challenges and crises as they arise.

— Margaret Wheatley

In 2011, a poorly written, third-rate erotic novel shot to the top of the bestseller list. Since its publication, *Fifty Shades of Grey*, by British author E. L. James, has sold forty million copies worldwide, making it the fastest-selling paperback of all time.

The novel deals with sadism and masochism, torture and humiliation, dominance and submission. I have nothing against such practices between consenting adults. Still, I think it's worth asking ourselves: what has happened to our collective consciousness that has made a book like *Fifty Shades of Grey* so attractive?

I suspect it has a lot to do with what I call *control-era conditioning*, or simply *control addiction*. To enjoy sexual pleasure—or, for that matter, intimacy of any kind—one must be able to let go of control, relax, and surrender. For control addicts, this is hard. They're great at achieving and accomplishing things but not so good at letting go.

We are obsessed with power and control. And since our mind is by far the most effective tool we possess for controlling our environment, we've become enslaved to it.

What's a person to do who wants sexual pleasure but can't surrender to it? The fantasy of being *forced* to surrender can help them bypass the inner blockages that control addiction erects within their body and mind. I suspect this is why today, so many men and women are intrigued by sexual games involving dominance and submission.

But how did we get so addicted to control in the first place? To answer this question, let's cycle back to where our journey began.

Remember the Pueblo chief whom we encountered in Chapter 1? The white Europeans, he said, were discontent, restless, and unhappy. Moreover, they were insane, a fact he chalked up to their habit of thinking with their heads instead of their hearts.

C.G. Jung, who met the chief in the 1930s, was profoundly disturbed by this view of his own race as seen through the eyes of an indigenous man. As Jung reviewed the history of his people, he became painfully aware that since its infancy, the hallmark of European civilization has been its ruthless pursuit of raw power and physical dominance. The white man's view of himself as the pinnacle of human civilization, Jung realized, is a delusion.

"For the first time in my life," Jung noted in his autobiography, "someone had drawn for me a picture of the real white man. It was as though until now I had seen nothing but sentimental, prettified color prints."

Revisiting the history of Western civilization from the Roman legions to the armies of the Crusaders, Jung described what he now perceived as the true face of his own culture: "The face of a bird of prey seeking with cruel intentness for distant quarry—a face worthy of pirates and highwaymen."

It's not a pretty picture, but unfortunately, it's an accurate one. For on a spectrum ranging from remarkably enlightened to extremely violent, the forefathers of Western civilization

---

Common Signs of Control Addiction

- You rarely stop thinking for more than a few seconds.
- Your mind is busier and noisier than you would like.
- It's hard for you to stay present.
- You can't tolerate silence for very long.
- You tend to rush.
- Your benchmark of a successful day is that you achieved a lot.
- You're highly invested in feeling that you

---

have all the details of your life under control.

- You feel ashamed of admitting when you're scared.
- You sometimes pretend not to feel pain when, in fact, you do.
- You tend to be too busy.
- You worry excessively.
- Dancing in public makes you feel self-conscious and awkward.
- You hide big chunks of yourself. There's a big gap between who you really are, and how you present yourself to the world.
- You often feel lonely and yearn for greater intimacy.
- Your relationship to money is stressful.
- You use shopping as a way to satisfy a vague inner craving.
- You like men to be tough.
- You tend to be cynical.
- You feel uncomfortable or embarrassed when people express intense passions and emotions.
- You rarely feel totally content.
- You rarely do nothing at all.
- Taking time to nourish yourself feels like a luxury.

gravitated towards the more violent end. They were warriors, to whom the quest for dominance was a way of life, and wherever they went, they brought their violent ways with them. Later, through brutal force and trickery, their descendants would wrest North America from its indigenous inhabitants and proceed to found an immensely powerful and violent empire.

Of course the ego's voracious appetite for power was no more new than was tribal violence. Yet until now, no tribe had ever possessed the military power to consistently assert its dominance over others or to unreservedly indulge its ego.

For a long time, control-era conditioning remained a primarily European phenomenon. Even well into the twentieth century, many non-European peoples remained untouched by it. This is why the Pueblo chief, for example was able to look at Jung's people with clear, unbiased eyes and recognize their addiction to control as the mental illness it is. Yet as industrial society spread around the world, so did control addiction. Today, it's a global epidemic that few manage to escape. One way or another, it touches us all; our pursuit of control has mushroomed into an overarching compulsion that affects every aspect of our lives. And as the Pueblo chief recognized, it has turned us into a race of people who have forgotten how to think with our hearts.

Compared to tribal conditioning, which has governed us for hundreds of thousands of years, control addiction is a fairly young phenomenon. And yet, it's immensely powerful, for the simple reason that our society continuously reinforces and affirms it. Having grown up with it, we take control addiction for granted and consider it a natural byproduct of the human condition. In fact, it's both unnatural and unsustainable.

The most powerful instrument of control we possess is not our military might or the nuclear bomb. Rather, it's *our mind*. Presumably, humans have long valued their mind. We can't run like gazelles, fly like birds, or produce the venom of rattlesnakes, but we sure can think. Thinking has long been the ace in our cap, the magic bullet that has allowed us to beat the odds. Thanks to our superior mind, we've been able to thrive under the most challenging circumstances, in ice and snow, heat and drought, jungles and high mountain ranges.

Nonetheless, for hundreds of thousands of years, we remained at the mercy of nature's fickle moods. Only quite recently did we turn our collective will towards the conquest of nature. Instead of submitting to her will, we wanted *her* to submit to ours. Instead of being controlled, *we* wanted to be the ones in control. And since we recognized our mind as the key to success, we created a civilization that worships the mind and views head-thinking as a great asset.

In fact, if I were to encapsulate the essence of the era of control in a single core belief, it would be this: *The most important mark of success in life is to acquire power and control, and the mind is our key to doing so.*

Descartes' famous statement, "I think, therefore I am," reflects this new perspective. How alien such ideas would have been to our indigenous ancestors! We can only imagine how puzzling Jung's Pueblo friends would have found Descartes' claim, and how it would have confirmed their diagnosis of the white man's insanity.

Facing Our Failure

In our society, we rarely view control addiction as a problem. In fact, we often consider it an asset. Most control addicts will tell you they're just taking care of business, and that without them things would fall apart in no time.

Yet if we take a step back, it's easy to see that our addiction to control has created a world that is increasingly complicated, stressful, and busy. As we scramble to stay on top of our ever more complex lives, we stop looking at the bigger picture. What is this prize we're fighting so hard to win? Why are we depriving ourselves of the simple pleasures that make life sweet and meaningful? What destination, other than our own death, are we racing towards?

I've been told that the Chinese character for "busyness" literally signifies "killing the heart." I believe it's true—our heart is being stifled by our incessant busyness, which leaves it no space to breathe, enjoy life, and simply be.

If our intention is to truly connect with others, rather than dominate them, then love is the way, not control.

Of course we need to have some degree of control over ourselves and our environment in order to survive. But control addiction makes us want to control everything, all the time. We've become locked in an endless war against life itself and against our own existential vulnerability. Instead of making peace with the inherently uncomfortable and risky nature of life, we keep trying to make everything comfortable and safe.

Especially in the realm of relationships, control addiction is bound to backfire, for any creature, whether it's a beetle, a cat, or a human, would much rather be loved than controlled. So, if our intention is to truly connect with others, rather than dominate them, then love is the way, not control.

From control addiction, a straight line leads to violence and warfare, and we have indeed created what is possibly the most violent society that ever was. Yet our violence is threatening to backfire, for as Martin Luther King said, "The choice today is no longer between violence and nonviolence. It is either non-violence or nonexistence."

Yet it's hard to let go of control when one doesn't trust God, Spirit, Life—whatever we call that ultimate source of control. And most of us *don't* trust it. Instead of feeling that the great-er powers are on our side and want to cooperate with us, we believe that we're on our own, pitted against a universe that is at best indifferent and at worst hostile. Given that Spirit is likely to goof up, we feel we had better take things into our own hands.

For a while we actually thought we *could*. We believed that with every day, we were progressing towards a more ideal world, and that eventually all aspects of nature would come under our control. Yet now, we're starting to realize this was a delusion born of ignorance and arrogance. Overpopulation, poverty, environmental degradation, climate change—clearly, things are not working out according to plan. Paradoxically, our addiction to control has created a situation in which everything seems to be spinning out of control. The harder we fight for control, the more it seems to elude us.

Over two and a half millennia ago, the great Chinese sage Lao Tsu gently pointed out the futile and ultimately self-destructive nature of the course we've been following with such blind confidence:

> Do you think you can take over the universe and improve it?
>
> I do not believe it can be done.
>
> The universe is sacred.
>
> You cannot improve it.
>
> If you try to change it, you will ruin it.
>
> If you try to hold it, you will lose it.

Suggested Exercises (See Appendix II)

Exercise 15. Moving at the Speed of Your Body

Exercise 16. Being Peace

CHAPTER 9

THOUGHT ADDICTION

The white people think too much. Then they do many things, and the more they do, the more they think. They make money, and when they have a lot, they worry that they might lose it and have none. So they think even harder and make even more money, but it's never enough. Then, they lose their inner peace. And this is why they aren't happy.

— Dogon tribal chief, West Africa

You know the science fiction scenario where robots take charge and force humans into servitude?

Well, it's already happened.

Can you silence your mind for even sixty seconds? If so, you're a rare bird. Most of us can't stop thinking any more than an alcoholic can stop drinking. For us, thinking is not an option but a compulsion. All day—sometimes all night, too—we wade through a morass of memories, complaints, worries, and plans.

What a strange irony: in the process of gaining so much control over nature, we've lost all control over our own mind.

It evolved to help us survive, and overall, it's done a great job. But it was supposed to serve, not tyrannize us. We, however, have enthroned the mind and authorized it to run our lives. Now, we live in an upside down world where it's the master and we're the slaves.

"The essence of the human dilemma," declared the Buddhist teacher Chögyam Trungpa, "is to be stuck in a huge traffic jam of discursive thought."

This is certainly true today, but was it always? I doubt our tribal ancestors had overcrowded minds any more than they lived on an overcrowded planet. Spacious and slow, their lives reflected the rhythms of nature. Yet along with the explosion of the human population has come an explosion of thought.

In the process of gaining so much control over nature, we seem to have lost all control over our own mind. Now, we live in an upside down world where it's the master and we're the slaves.

Just as today the number of humans on the planet far exceeds the limit of what is healthy and sustainable, so does the number of our thoughts, which proliferate like mice under the influence of stress. They can't help it; the ego's job description is, after all, to take care of us, and the more complicated this task becomes, the faster the mind keeps churning out thoughts.

Of course, if you've ever observed your mind for any length of time, you know that ninety percent of your thoughts are repetitive and unproductive. Like a grinder that keeps running even when there's nothing left to grind, the wheels of the mind keep spinning.

Today, what I call thought addiction has become so common and all-pervasive that it generally flies under the radar undiagnosed. Unless we have a nervous breakdown, or follow a spiritual path that calls for inner silence, we usually don't consider thought addiction a problem. On the contrary, we encourage it. Instead of being sent to treatment centers, thought addicts are rewarded with big paychecks.

> **The Three Core Beliefs of the Ego:**
>
> - I am my body.
> - I am my tribe.
> - I am my mind.

Yet thought addiction will disconnect you from your heart as surely as clouds will block the light of the sun. If the heart is your inner sun, then each passing thought is a cloud that sails across the sky of your consciousness. Nothing wrong with clouds, but when thought addiction takes over, they form a blanket so dense that the sun appears to vanish.

Life is bleak and gray without sunshine. But over the years, many people forget what it feels like to bask in that golden warmth. Habituated to the darkness, they take their state of emotional and spiritual deprivation for granted.

As thought addicts, we don't *want* to lose touch with our hearts. We might even feel a strong commitment to heart-centered values such as kindness and compassion. Yet our thoughts absorb all our attention. So, like a mother too busy to pay attention to her child, we forget about our heart and fail to do the things that would please it: walking through the fall leaves, making music, or hanging out with our cat.

In the grips of thought addiction, we become trapped in a cycle of incessant busyness. Both mentally and physically, we're constantly on the run. There's always one more thing to do, one more chore to complete. Instead of giving ourselves permission to rest, we drive ourselves to exhaustion.

But don't kid yourself—incessant thinking won't make you more productive or more effective. The brain is a physical organ, and like any organ, it can't function optimally without periods of rest. Every time you allow yourself to detach from thought and move into inner silence, you're giving your brain a chance to regenerate. At the same time, you're opening to the inflow of true creativity and fresh inspiration, which always come from a source beyond the mind. Therefore, the secret to thinking more produc-

How Tribal and Control-Era Conditioning Prevent Us from Thinking with Our Hearts

- Tribal conditioning tells us to close our hearts to people whose conduct we perceive as threatening the social order.

- Control-era conditioning teaches us to perceive other beings as objects of control and to replace a sense of connectedness with a sense of separateness.

- Control-era conditioning tells us that the mind is a more competent guide than the heart; therefore, we should disempower our hearts and instead empower our minds.

tively and creatively is not to think more but to think *less*.

> *The rush and pressure of modern life are a form, perhaps the most common form, of its innate violence. To allow oneself to be carried away by a multitude of conflicting concerns, to commit oneself to too many projects, to want to help everyone with everything is to succumb to violence. More than that, it is cooperation with violence. The frenzy of the activist neutralizes his or her work for peace. It destroys her or his capacity for peace. It destroys the fruitfulness of the work because it kills the root of inner wisdom, which makes the work fruitful.*
>
> —Thomas Merton

Don't get me wrong—there's nothing wrong with thinking. The capacity to think is an amazing gift, and as we've seen, effective heart-thinking relies on the support of a keen intellect.

But what we're talking about here is *compulsive* thinking. Just as compulsive overeaters have a warped relationship with food, thought addicts have a warped relationship with their mind. And just as our body suffers when we stuff too much food into it, our brain suffers when we force it to think incessantly.

Some of the harmful effects of thought addiction are easy to spot. Others are less obvious. Consider, for example, the way many people use loud music to pound their noisy mind into pulp. We usually don't put such habits in the same category as alcoholism or drug addiction. But in recent years, I've been encountering more and more people who have irreparably damaged their hearing in this way, and are as a result feeling isolated and cut off from the world.

Breaking Free

As long as we're trapped in thought addiction, we can't quiet our mind. And when we can't quiet our mind, it's hard to connect with our soul, our spirit, our Self—whatever you call that inner light that is the source of our happiness and joy. The great Indian philosopher Krishnamurti speaks of this:

> The mind has the power to do the most extraordinary things.... But the mind cannot create truth.... To find out what is true, the mind must be without any movement, completely still. That stillness is the act of worship—not your going to the temple to offer flowers and pushing aside the beggar on the way.... When you understand the mind and the mind is completely still, not made still, then that stillness is the act of worship; and in that stillness there comes into being that which is true, that which is beautiful, that which is God.

In the grips of thought addiction, we have no access to this realm of blessed stillness. Some people don't care. But for others, being stuck in their busy mind feels like being trapped in a torture chamber.

"That used to be me," says my friend Tony. He isn't religious, nor is he interested in enlightenment. Nonetheless, he meditates every morning. The practice of meditation, he tells me, has shown him that there *is* an alternative to compulsive head-thinking. There *is* a path to freedom. Even when he feels trapped in his mind, he actually isn't. Hence the bumper sticker on his beat-up old truck that reads, "Out of my mind. Back in five minutes!"

> *Whenever we listen with our whole being, thinking stops, and for a brief moment the mind falls perfectly silent. Like a womb, like a chalice, like a secret cave, our heart then becomes the sanctuary where a new sense of wholeness begins to gestate.*

Meditation is a word that some people find intimidating. But actually, it's very simple, because, in essence, it simply means that we start *listening*. Have you ever watched a doe grazing at the forest's edge? Suddenly wary, she freezes, while her ears scan the surroundings. Her jaws stop moving, and the grass hangs unchewed from her soft lips until, reassured, she flicks her tail and returns to grazing. Whenever we listen like that, with our whole being, thinking stops, and for a brief moment the mind falls perfectly silent. Like a womb, like a chalice, like a secret cave, our heart then becomes the sanctuary where a new sense of wholeness begins to gestate.

This kind of listening is a powerful antidote to thought addiction. And best of all, it's something we can all do anywhere, anytime. Try it out right now, if you like. Stop reading and for just one minute, listen to your environment, as if your life depended on it. Listen with your whole being, like that doe.

If you're a serious thought addict, your mind may balk. "We'll do it later," it will say, knowing full well you probably won't. But if you can gently bypass its resistance, you'll find that in any moment of true listening, your mind falls silent.

"Sometimes," Tony says, "when I meditate, I really do get out of my mind. It just stops, like a broken radio, and for a little while, everything goes silent. God, I love it when that happens!"

"For how long does your mind stop?" I ask.

Tony grins. "Half a second? One second? Maybe three, if I'm lucky."

That may not sound like much, but inner silence is a medicine so potent that just a few drops can transform our whole life. How amazing to discover that the prison door is unlocked, and that all we need to do is turn the handle and walk out!

Go on, Rilke urges us in one of his poems, *do* it:

> Whoever you are, as evening falls,
> Let go of those familiar walls
> And enter the vastness beyond.

Many centuries earlier, Rilke's Persian colleague Rumi gave us much the same advice:

> Become the sky.
> Take an axe to the prison wall.
> Escape.
> Walk out like someone suddenly born into color.

Do it now.
You're covered with a thick cloud.
Slide out the side.
Die, and be quiet.
Quietness is the surest sign that you've died.
Your old life was a frantic running from silence
The speechless full moon comes out now.

Detachment from thought is...

- A symptom of awakening
- A practice that inspires awakening
- A medicine for the disease of thought addiction
- A key to overcoming tribalism
- A key to inner and outer peace

Today, millions of people are following Rumi's advice and are "sliding out the side" of their mind into the vastness beyond. For even as our society seems determined to lure us ever deeper into thought addiction, a powerful movement is flowing in the opposite direction—away from mental complexity and towards inner spaciousness and silence.

Our Ally the Body

Jill Bolte Taylor is a Harvard-trained neuro-anatomist. About a decade ago, she suffered a severe stroke that temporarily disabled the left hemisphere of her brain. Since this hemisphere is responsible for rational, analytic thought, she abruptly lost all capacity for any form of head-thinking. No longer could she think in words, let alone speak.

Instead, she plummeted into a realm where there was no mental chatter, no running commentary on life, no possibility of making plans or having inner conversations. There was nothing but deep, deep silence.

Bolte Taylor looked pitiful indeed as she lay mute and pale in her hospital bed, hooked up to various machines. But appearances can be deceiving. For as bad as things looked from the outside, internally, she was basking in complete, unadulterated bliss.

Today, Bolte Taylor has made a full recovery. Better yet, in addition to regaining all her mental faculties, she has acquired a new skill: she can return at will to that state of silent, wordless ecstasy that her stroke initiated.

But how does she do it? How does she prevent the busy mind from taking over once again? When Terry Gross, hostess of "Fresh Air," asked Bolte Taylor this question, her answer was simple: she follows the pleasure principle. After she lost her capacity for cognitive thinking, what remained was a crystal clear awareness of her bodily experience. To her body, inner silence felt incredibly blissful. In contrast, head-thinking felt horribly unpleasant and painful.

Most of us are only dimly aware of how thought addiction affects our physical body. In her case, however, the blinders had been removed. She knew, without a doubt, that head-thinking wasn't her friend.

"When that worrying voice wanted to come back on-line," she says, "I didn't like the way that it felt inside of my body." So whenever head-thinking tries to entice her, she simply says no. "It's very easy for me," she repeats, "because I don't like the way that it feels inside of my body."

She's absolutely right: thought addiction doesn't feel good. In fact, compared to heart-thinking, it's outright painful.

Just consider what it involves: First, we have to dislodge our energy and consciousness from our torso and push it up into our brain. This displacement creates an imbalance that leaves us energetically top-heavy, like cartoon figures with tiny bodies and huge heads. Next, we have to silence the voice of our heart. How? By disconnecting from the right side of our brain, which is where the heart's messages enter our conscious awareness. So to think with our heads, we first have to sever our body from our head, and then disconnect one side of our brain from the other. Is it any wonder our body doesn't like this?

> **Head-thinking** shifts the center of our consciousness upward, from the heart to the head, causing a misalignment of our energy body.
>
> **Heart-thinking** fuses head and heart into a single organ of compassionate wisdom.

On the other hand, it *loves* the experience of heart-thinking. For nature, in her wisdom, has made sure that all life-giving activities are enjoyable. That includes heart-thinking, which awakens love, affection, and connection, all of which are essential to our survival. Naturally, therefore, heart-thinking feels not just good but *great*. Much like eating or making love, heart-thinking is satisfying and deeply pleasurable in that full-bodied way that reaches all the way down into our bellies.

So if you want to overcome thought addiction, remember that you have a great ally: your body. It loves pleasure and recoils from pain. And no matter how much your mind insists on the necessity of head-thinking, your body knows better.

Eckhart Tolle's Story

Like my friend Tony, most of us rarely stop thinking for more than a few seconds. But some rare individuals manage to let go of head-thinking once and for all. Like an alcoholic might walk out of his favorite bar, never to return, they break free from thought addiction.

One such person is the spiritual teacher Eckhart Tolle. Quite suddenly and unintentionally, he stepped out of thought addiction, and has been free of it ever since. Tolle was twenty-nine years old at the time, and utterly miserable. For years, he'd been racked by depression and anxiety and had frequently contemplated suicide. Now, his mental state seemed to be deteriorating even further.

He recalls: "The fear, anxiety, and heaviness of depression were becoming so intense, it was almost unbearable. And it is hard to describe that 'state' where the world is felt to be so alien.... Everything was totally alien and almost hostile. I later saw a book written by Jean-Paul Sartre called *Nausea*. That was the state that I was in, nausea of the world."

One night, Tolle woke up in a state of terrible dread and fear. It was so bad that he said to himself, "I simply can't live with myself any longer."

Immediately, another thought followed: "Who is this person that I cannot live with? Are there two of me?" Miraculously, this question triggered the death of his old consciousness and his rebirth into an entirely new state. Like a derelict house ready to collapse, his old sense of self began to implode. For a brief moment, fear arose as he felt himself being sucked into an inner vortex. But then, an inner voice told him to, "Resist nothing." And so, he surrendered.

He has no memory of what happened after that. He only recalls waking up the next morning and feeling as if he had died in hell and been reborn in paradise:

> I woke up in a state of incredible inner peace, bliss in fact. With my eyes still closed, I heard the sound of a bird and realized how precious that was. And then I opened my eyes and saw the sunlight coming through the curtains and felt: There is far more to that than we realize. It felt like love coming through the curtains. And then as I walked around the old familiar objects in the room I realized I had never really seen them before. It was as if I had just been born into this world; a state of wonder. And then I went for a walk in the city. I was still in London. Everything was miraculous, deeply peaceful.

The phenomenal success of Tolle's books and teachings is an indicator of just how strong our collective yearning for a new relationship with our mind has become. His story also highlights an important point: while thought addiction can be excruciating, it's by no means stopping the collective awakening that is underway. Rather, in some cases, it's actually *fueling* it.

"It's driving me crazy!" some of my clients say of their mind, as if some kind of alien creature has taken up residence within them. Like alcoholics, they're hitting bottom. Simultaneously, they're becoming more receptive to the message of hope that echoes through all spiritual traditions: there *is* a path to inner peace. Enslavement to the mind is not a life sentence. Freedom *is* possible. As our suffering intensifies, our yearning for relief can become the launching pad that catapults us into a new state of consciousness.

> *Be still, and know that I am God.*
>
> — Psalm 46:10

What is that new state? First and foremost, it's one of inner peace. There's less mental traffic and more inner space. When Tolle compares his present state of mind with his former one, the main difference he sees is that he's thinking less—much, much less:

My thought processes after waking up that

morning had been reduced by about eighty to ninety percent. So a lot of the time I was walking around in a state of inner stillness, and perceiving the world through inner stillness. And that is the peace, the deep peace that comes when there is no longer anybody commenting on sense perceptions or anything that happens. No labeling, no need to interpret what is happening, it just is as it is and it is fine.

A Wave of Awakening

Eckhart Tolle's story reads like a fairy tale. One day, he's a miserable, desperately unhappy young man. The next (quite literally), he's a vast presence, deliriously happy and totally in love with life. Once terribly alone and isolated, thousands now flock to him, drawn by his peaceful presence.

Such stories are inspiring. We love hearing them. And yet, we tend to view such people as the lucky winners of the consciousness lottery. "That will never happen to me," we think. And it's true—most of us will never experience the kind of miraculous transformation that overnight turned a suicidal young man into an embodiment of infinite peace.

But this way of thinking misses the point. People like Tolle are merely the crest of a huge wave of collective awakening that is pushing up into our collective consciousness and surfacing wherever it finds an opening. Whether you and I awaken overnight really doesn't matter. But what matters very much is that we make ourselves available to this new consciousness.

For Eckhart Tolle, liberation from thought addiction came as a sudden and permanent stroke of grace. For most of us, it's a more gradual process. Either way, once we get a whiff of inner peace, we're drawn to it like bees to honey. Just as recovering alcoholics come to appreciate sobriety, we begin to develop a taste for the spaciousness of the present moment.

We realize, then, that contrary to what our thought-addicted mind tells us, simple presence is not boring at all. On the contrary, it's delicious, delightful, and deeply pleasurable. Sometimes, it's ecstatic—even orgasmic. The more we taste it, the more we want it. And best of all, as we open to this experience of joy, happiness, and true sanity, we are joining millions of people who are shaking off the collective insanity that is causing us to destroy our beautiful planet. In healing ourselves, we are healing our world.

Suggested Exercises (See Appendix II)

Exercise 17. Five Minutes of Presence

Exercise 18. Breaking the Computer Trance

CHAPTER 10

SAMANTHA'S STORY

The most beautiful experience we can have is the mysterious. It is the fundamental emotion which stands at the cradle of true art and true science. Whoever does not know it and can no longer wonder, no longer marvel, is as good as dead, and his eyes are dimmed.

— Albert Einstein

S amantha is a beautiful woman in her early forties with the pale face, clear gray eyes and blond curls of a Botticelli angel. She's a social worker, as well as a self-confessed perfectionist who likes everything to be neat, tidy, and well-ordered. Her boss knows he can count on her to follow protocol precisely, and to dot all her i's and cross her t's.

"I'm a control freak," Samantha admits with a shrug. "But I'm getting better. I'm starting to understand that when I let go of trying to control things and just become receptive, miracles can happen."

A while ago, Samantha tells me, a miracle *did* happen— at least that's what it felt like. Samantha works at an agency that specializes in helping people cope with trauma. "Because of that," she explained, "my job frequently takes me to communities that have witnessed a death or a crime, and need help in dealing with the aftermath."

One morning, Samantha got a call: her agency wanted her to visit a home for developmentally disabled adults. Apparently, a resident had passed away. She wasn't given any details. However, her understanding was that the staff was in turmoil, and that her job would be to debrief them. But when Samantha pulled up in front of the dilapidated old building and knocked on the door, the housekeeper informed her that the staff had basically fled, and that she was to work with the residents, who had the mental capacity of five – or six-year-olds. The person who had died, a woman named Rose, was their friend, and they were very upset about her death.

Stunned, Samantha sat down on the chair the housekeeper offered her. Samantha is a careful, conscientious person who likes to do a good job at all times. So the idea of working with a population she knew absolutely nothing about was terrifying to her.

The housekeeper, however, was entirely oblivious to Samantha's distress. "Where is everyone?" she scolded as she rushed off to round up the residents.

Fifteen minutes later, all ten of them were gathered in the large living room. They appeared to be anywhere between twenty and sixty-five years old, but as the housekeeper had said, they had the mindset of young children—children who were clearly unhappy and as restless as fish out of water.

"I didn't have a clue what to do," Samantha recalls. "I felt way out of my league. But seeing as I was enrolled in the

Circlework training, I decided to form a circle. I figured at least it couldn't do any harm."

Samantha's agency had given her detailed guidelines on how to proceed in situations where someone had died. There was a set protocol, and Samantha was expected to adhere precisely to it. For starters, she was supposed to give a talk about how sudden loss can affect people and what to expect in its aftermath.

So, with a sigh, Samantha launched bravely into her talk—or at least, she tried. But she might as well have been speaking Chinese, as far as the residents were concerned. Nobody was paying attention. The women were fidgeting and clearly bored. Three men kept whispering to each other and became more and more agitated until one of them started yelling, "I told you so, I told you so!"

"Please, keep it down, folks!" Samantha called out. But hardly a minute had passed before another crescendo of whispers escalated into a shouting match. Frustrated, Samantha repeatedly tried to discipline them.

"Quiet, please!" she pleaded, trying to mask her growing sense of irritation. "Calm down, everybody!"

And so they did. But no sooner had she resumed her talk than a woman interrupted her in mid-sentence. "Miss," she said, "Are you married? The other woman who came to see us was married. Do you know her?"

Samantha felt uncomfortably like a school mistress with disciplinary problems.

"There are rules to this process," she announced, rather

more sternly than she would have wished. They were not to interrupt. But even as she spoke, she knew it was useless; they didn't give a hoot about her rules. One woman had pulled off her shoes and socks and was frowning as she examined her toes. Another was rocking back and forth, muttering to herself in an angry tone.

Samantha grins as she remembers the scene.

"I was starting to panic. I kept thinking, I have to do something. I have to do something! I have to get this situation under control. But I couldn't figure out how. My mind was racing. There just didn't seem to be any way to move ahead according to plan.

"Finally, I took a deep breath and said to myself: 'This simply isn't working.'" At that moment, I panicked for real.

Oh shit. I'm in deep trouble. That was my only thought. *What the heck shall I do? What shall I do, what shall I do?*

"But as soon as that question popped into my mind, I heard a voice, as clearly as if someone were standing right next to me. Believe me, I'm not someone who hears voices. But in that moment, I swear I did.

"Just stop," it said. "Don't do anything. Just let go. Be quiet, open and receptive."

What was this voice? Was it Samantha's unconscious, her soul, her spirit guide, her true self?

All we can say for sure is that within us lie realms inaccessible to the conscious mind. Perhaps you too have experienced moments when thought ceased and some other source of guidance took over. Perhaps, in the midst of a very ordinary situation, someone made a life-changing comment. Maybe a sudden knowing burst out of nowhere or an amazing insight appeared in a dream. Maybe a total stranger gave you some vital piece of information. Maybe you turned on the radio, and there was the answer you'd been looking for.

The more our mind tries to understand, define, or describe such events, the further away we get. We all have access to guidance; that much, my work has taught me. We may receive it in different ways, but it's always available if we're willing to stop and listen.

Letting go and listening were skills Samantha had been practicing for years. She knew that when we stop and listen, we tap into sources of intelligence inaccessible to our conscious mind. So, desperate as she was, she decided to do exactly what her guidance had suggested: Stop. Let go. Just listen.

Samantha gave up her attempts to come up with a plan. Instead, she shifted her attention from her head to her heart. Breathing deeply, she began to relax into a state of quiet, receptive presence.

What happened next showed Samantha, in an unforgettable way, how our own consciousness affects others. One moment she was desperately trying to keep things under control by thinking harder and faster. The next, she was resting in a pool of inner stillness and peace. And as her inner world shifted, everything around her shifted as well.

"It was amazing," she remembers. "The minute I gave up my agenda, and become totally present and receptive, the residents sensed my openness. And suddenly, they started to sob.

One moment, they were yelling and creating total chaos, and the next, they were totally focused and present. It was as if we had suddenly walked from a battlefield into a beautiful sanctuary. Really, it blew my mind. I just couldn't believe what was happening."

Samantha was fortunate. These men and women had not only the intellectual capacity of young children, but also their total authenticity. They weren't interested in hiding their true feelings, or in pleasing and appeasing her. Like clear mirrors, they showed her exactly how her own state was affecting them.

Until that point, Samantha had been determined to stick to her protocol. But now, she realized that her heart had an entirely different need. What it wanted was to simply be with these people and offer them compassionate support.

As long as Samantha had been thinking with her head, she'd defined herself in ways that split the group into two camps: she and her agency on one side, the residents on the other. She had, in other words, unwittingly fallen into "us-versus-them" thinking, which lies at the root of all warfare. As a result, she felt very separate from the residents, and they from her. Unable to hear, accept, or contain their emotions, she was more intent on controlling them than serving them.

But the harder she tried, the more they resisted. What was intended to be a healing environment had become a battleground. Instead of showing them a path to peace, she was at war with them. Yet now, as Samantha entered a state of quiet spaciousness and allowed her heart to open to these men and women, she stopped labeling them as "abnormal" and instead began to notice how special and unique each of them was.

Suddenly, their battle came to an end.

Samantha had brought crayons and paper, and after a while, she started writing down what the residents were saying: "Rose was just beautiful. We loved Rose so much. Rose had beautiful eyes."

They were simple statements, yet imbued with deep emotion and a profound sense of caring. Samantha helped her new friends compile a long list of everything they'd said, written in large multicolored letters. Once they decided it was done, they hung it up on the wall.

"It felt like the perfect ritual," Samantha remembers with a smile. "And yet it wasn't planned; it evolved naturally once I stopped trying to 'do' anything and just listened. The sense of separation between us had dissolved completely. I was no longer seeing them as 'retarded people' and they were no longer seeing me as an authority figure. We'd become friends who were sharing our grief and sorrow."

Samantha left the residence feeling great. But that evening, she started second-guessing the choices she'd made. At the time, they'd felt right, but were they really? The housekeeper had told her that the night before her arrival had been terrible. Some of the residents had nightmares. Others got into fights and broke some windows.

"What's it going to be like tonight?" Samantha worried.

The next day, someone called from the residence and said, "Thank you! I don't know what you did, but they were so different after you left. They had a completely peaceful night.

Nobody acted out at all."

Samantha sighed with relief.

"That experience was pivotal for me," she says. "It gave me a whole new appreciation for the power of not doing, not fixing, not trying to control others. Letting go of my agenda and simply listening was what made an unworkable situation workable."

Open Your Heart and Quiet Your Mind

We must be willing to let go of the life we have planned, so as to accept the life that is waiting for us.

— Joseph Campbell

Collectively, we're facing a predicament not unlike Samantha's. We, too, are running into challenges we never anticipated and feel ill equipped to handle. A crisis has arisen, things are spinning out of control, and we have no clue how to respond. The situation is unprecedented and the old guidelines are obsolete. We feel lost, overwhelmed, and scared. We recognize the danger we're in and the importance of not sticking our heads in the sand. But what can we do?

It sounds paradoxical, but I believe we need to do exactly what Samantha did: *stop, quiet our busy minds, and listen.*

To receive guidance, we don't need to subscribe to any spiritual belief system. We do, however, need to acknowledge the limitations of our mind. In the context of a society that idolizes thought, we need to remember that all the best things in life—love, passion, creativity, inspiration—come from a realm far beyond the mind. Though they may come through it, they originate elsewhere. As the mystic poet Rumi says, "This drunkenness began in another tavern."

"I know now," Samantha says, "that to live in a state of balance and harmony, I need to open my heart and quiet my mind."

Open your heart and quiet your mind—these seven words summarize the central message of many great spiritual traditions. Some, like Buddhism, focus more on silencing the mind. Others, like the Indian Bhakti tradition, celebrate the open heart.

Yet ultimately, the silencing of the mind and the opening of the heart are not separate. Rather, like the setting sun and the rising moon, they're movements of a single dance—the dance of awakening.

Today, untold millions are practicing this dance, a fact all the more remarkable considering that we're continually bombarded with messages that tell us to do the exact opposite: "Stimulate your mind as much as possible, and always stay in control of everything in your life." Why is this happening? Perhaps because intuitively we understand that in our times, opening the hearts and stilling our minds are more than just emotionally and spiritually beneficial practices. Rather, they're essential steps towards rectifying the heart-mind misalignment that is driving us insane and causing us to self-destruct.

Suggested Exercises (See Appendix II)

Exercise 8. Five Breaths

Exercise 19. Heart-Centering in Daily Life

CHAPTER 11

THE FEMININE: OUR KEY TO GLOBAL HEALING

Another world is not only possible, she is on her way. On a quiet day, I can hear her breathing.

— Arundhati Roy

Though scholars continue to argue about the origins of patriarchy, it's generally agreed that in Europe and the Middle East, the reign of men and male gods became the norm about five thousand years ago. Before that, female deities are believed to have predominated, a theory supported by the fact that the overwhelming majority of prehistoric statues, some of which date back thirty thousand years, are female.

But about five millennia ago, the old matriarchal traditions began to weaken or disappear. The Great Mother, long worshipped as the source of life, went underground to enter a long period of hibernation. And slowly but surely, women were forced into subordination.

Patriarchy and control-addiction emerged simultaneously,

hand in hand. In fact, what I've been calling the era of control is more commonly known as the patriarchal era. Yet in my opinion, this is a somewhat misleading term. No doubt patriarchy has to no small degree defined the course of Western civilization. Yet was the driving force behind its evolution really men's need to dominate women? I doubt it. I believe what we were really after was *dominance over nature*. Be that as it may, it's clear that for the past five thousand years, Western civilization has been defined by three elements: Control addiction, head-thinking, and patriarchy.

Some have suggested that the reason patriarchy and control addiction evolved hand in hand is that men are innately more desirous of control over women. Personally, I don't buy this theory. Having led thousands of women's circles, I know how controlling the female ego can be. In my experience, men and women are equally interested in control.

However, they want *different types of control*. Women tend to want control over their relationships. And how could they not, considering the immense vulnerability that pregnancy and motherhood inflicts on women? As long as a woman is raising children—which not so long ago was her entire adult life—she depends on the support of her community. So no wonder women have developed a high level of intuitive and emotional intelligence, along with a genius for building and maintaining community. Of course, this gift also has a shadow side. When a woman feels the need to get her relationships under control, she's liable to pull out all the stops—much to her partner's chagrin. Nobody is more relentless than a woman determined to mold her partner to her needs.

In contrast, men's need for control tends to manifest in relationship to the physical world. Typically, they want to figure out how things work and how they might be put to use. If you were God and you wanted to create a highly intuitive and emotionally sophisticated civilization, you'd do well to women in charge. But what if you wanted to shift humans from the stone age to the space age? In that case, you'd want men to take over the helm—as they have indeed done.

As a global phenomenon, patriarchy is nearing its end; its time has passed. Today, those who insist on male domination are clinging to a belief system that has run out of steam and is destined to dissolve, as all repressive regimes eventually do.

To a woman who is trying to control her relationships, head-thinking is of little value. But to someone who is trying to control their environment, it can be extremely helpful. After all, to gain dominance over nature, what you need is not intuition or emotional intelligence but rather a keen analytic mind. It makes sense, then that patriarchy, control addiction, and head-thinking evolved simultaneously. For the past five millennia, men have been spearheading the conquest of nature, and their intellect has been the indispensible tool they've relied upon.

Presumable, men didn't initially set out to subjugate women. Yet because women bring forth and nurture new life, they have since time immemorial been perceived as nature's emissaries. So when men stopped revering nature as a goddess, and instead began approaching her as an object to be controlled and dominated, it was inevitable that women would eventually share her fate.

Today, patriarchy is still firmly entrenched in many parts of the world. Nonetheless, I believe that as a global phenomenon, it's nearing its end; its time has passed. Today, those who insist on male domination are clinging to a belief system that has run out of steam and is destined to dissolve, as all repressive regimes eventually do.

Meanwhile, however, sexual slavery, rape, and violence against women remain commonplace. All too many women are forced to hide their faces behind veils and their lives behind walls. That this is a recipe for strife is obvious, for how can we hope to live in peace when one half of the human population is at odds with the other? Only when harmony prevails between men and women will we live in peace.

> *The global statistics on the abuse of girls are numbing. It appears that more girls have been killed in the past fifty years, precisely because they were girls, than men were killed in all the battles of the twentieth century. More girls are killed in this routine "gendercide" in any one decade than people were slaughtered in all the genocides of the twentieth century.*
>
> — Nicholas Kristof and Sheryl WuDunn
> in Half *the Sky: Turning Oppression into*
> *Opportunity for Women Worldwide*

There is no way to reconcile the abuse of women with the practice of heart-thinking. And since heart-thinkers are emerging everywhere like crocuses in spring, we're beginning to look at male-female relationships in a new light. Admittedly, the process is unfolding more slowly in some parts of the world than others, but everywhere, women are asserting their value and demanding to be treated as equals.

In the West, we are rightfully proud of having rejected the barbaric forms of abuse that women in many parts of the world still endure on a daily basis. But have we defeated patriarchy? No, we haven't.

While women have indeed gained an enormous amount of power in the West, the feminine has not. In fact, few cultures afford the feminine less respect than does mainstream America.

We need to understand that the empowerment of women is one issue, the empowerment of the feminine another. While women have indeed gained an enormous amount of power in the West, the feminine has not. In fact, few cultures afford the feminine less respect than does mainstream America.

When I speak of the feminine, here, I'm not referring to something universal or essential. I'm simply talking about the feminine, as our culture defines it. For example, our culture considers certain objects feminine that clearly have no gender, such as the earth, the moon, the body, and the heart. Furthermore, there's a wide range of qualities it considers feminine: softness, gentleness, receptivity, to name just a few.

Of course, there is nothing intrinsically feminine about these qualities. Yet, tragically, patriarchy views them as feminine and, therefore, as unmanly and weak. I say tragically, because these supposedly "feminine" attributes are the very ones we need to sustain peaceful, harmonious relationships, both within our personal lives and on a global scale.

That patriarchy slices the body of humanity in half, pitting men against women, is obvious. But we often overlook the fact that it also slices each one of us in half by defining mind and spirit as masculine, heart and body as feminine. As patriarchy pits men against women so too does it pit the mind against the heart. We might be opposed to the oppression of women, believe in the equality of the sexes, and support women's empowerment. But as long as we allow our mind to oppress our heart, we have not cast off the chains of patriarchy.

> *Patriarchy slices the body of humanity in half, pitting men against women. Furthermore, it cuts each one of us in half by defining mind and spirit as masculine, heart and body as feminine. As it pits men against women so too does it pit mind against heart.*

Anna's Dream

No one knows this better than Anna, a vibrant woman in her early sixties. As a successful corporate executive, Anna was once every bit as driven, ambitious, and competitive as any of her male colleagues. But some years ago, she walked out of her old life into a new, radically different one. Walking into her home today is like entering a temple filled with exotic deities, exquisite fabrics, and beautiful objects—a pageant of texture, color, and fragrance designed to delight the senses and awaken the soul.

I never knew Anna before her transformation. So one day, I ask, "What were you like?"

In response, Anna describes a woman who, despite her impressive façade, was profoundly disconnected from her true nature. Like many women in the early stages of feminism, Anna had defined women's empowerment as the right to compete with men. And so, she'd entered the rat race and become a hardcore head-thinker who'd lost all connection to her heart and her femininity.

"I was not at all in touch with the feminine," Anna says.

"In fact, I was in a macho phase that was a reaction against the suppression of women. I was impatient with any woman whom I perceived as weak and unassertive, and very judgmental and ashamed of those aspects of myself that I considered too tender, vulnerable, or feminine to withstand the competitive world."

For many years, Anna wore the straightjacket of patriarchal repression. Outwardly, she seemed strong, free, and successful. She had attained all the privileges that a powerful man might enjoy. The fact that her femininity was shackled remained hidden even to her own eyes, masked as it was by a shiny veneer of success. As long as Anna was competing and winning, she saw no reason to question the game itself.

But then, something happened that would turn her life up-side down and make her the woman she is today: a Yoga teacher, a lover of the goddess, a spiritual seeker who has chosen to live a slow, spacious life and who values inner peace more than outer achievement.

What happened was that Anna had a dream—not an ordinary dream, but one of those rare gifts we treasure for the rest of our lives. As our personal psyche comes into perfect alignment with a higher consciousness, a portal appears through which the great Mystery can touch us. Potent and numinous, ablaze with an otherworldly light, such dreams convey messages from beyond that can benefit us all.

Here, then, is Anna's dream:

> I'm aboard a small ship that feels to me like the ship of my life. I am its captain and only crew member, and everything is going very well. The ship is making good progress through the sea; it's a beautiful day, and I feel exhilarated.

> Then I go to the front, to the stern of the ship. And as I lean over, I see that the masthead is actually a goddess. You know how ships in olden times had mastheads that were carved goddess figures, usually bare-breasted and beautiful? Well, she looks just like one of them.

> But then, as I look down, I realize that this goddess is actually alive, and that she's making magical

gestures with her arms and fingers, which I later learn are called *mudras*.

Two things happened in that moment. One was that I fell immediately and irrevocably in love with her and was filled with a burning sense of passionate desire for her. The other was that I felt deeply humiliated because I realized that I was not the captain of the ship after all, as I had thought. In fact, all the progress I had made through the ocean of my life was actually her doing, not mine.

Overwhelmed by my passionate need to connect with her, I took the lifeboat, got off of the ship, and paddled out in front of the ship to where I could see her. I now found that I had a bow and arrow with me. And without a moment's thought, completely driven by my desire to possess her, I pulled back the bow and shot an arrow that instantly killed her. But in that moment of her death, I became she. I myself died, and as I died, I rose up above my body.

Filled with grief, I hovered above the ship. And without the slightest judgment or blame, I said out loud to the woman below who had just shot me, "It would have been better for me to have lived, and for you to have died.

Listening to Anna's dream, I felt the goose bumps that always let me know when I'm in the presence of sacred power. Never had I heard our collective dysfunction described so clearly, not in the language of the intellect but of the soul, which speaks through images and symbols.

Anna is heterosexual, but in her dream, she embodies the perverse masculinity of the patriarchal, control-addicted ego. She's strong, confident, and determined, but also arrogant, competitive, and determined to possess the beautiful deity who is guiding the ship of her life.

In the same way, we have tried to possess nature, the primordial goddess, and in doing so have brought her to death's door. Now, we too are facing the humbling realization that our sense of dominion over the planet was an illusion: we aren't and never were the true captain of this ship—nature is. We, too, seem destined to learn the hard way that we can never own what is sacred, and that when we try, we condemn ourselves to lose what we most love.

Thankfully, consciousness brings the option of changing course. Anna's response to her dream can serve as a model for how we might collectively respond to the global crisis.

Reflecting on her journey, Anna says, "This dream came out of the blue. It was life-changing, because it awakened me to the fact that my life had been governed by my ego needs, especially my need to make money and be successful. But in the process, I'd been abusing everything about me that was sacred, and killing what was most precious to me. I was off track, and suffering, and this dream showed me the cause of my suffering.

"I woke up filled with grief, but also with gratitude that I had been told in time, and that it wasn't too late to cherish the unknown goddess aspect of my nature, and let her lead me. I'd been attempting to prove myself in an arrogant and ambitious way. Now, I dropped all that, and started embracing the softness of the feminine, her mystery, her tender-heartedness, and her intuition."

Might it be that Anna's dream is *our* dream—yours, mine, everyone's? Might it be addressed to all of us? If so, we had better listen up, for its message is strong and uncompromising. By denying the sanctity of nature and trying to forcefully possess her, we are condemning ourselves to a fate worse than death.

Clearly, it is not enough that we end the oppression of women. We also need to end the equally tragic though less visible oppression of the human heart. Our denial of the heart's needs is causing us to act in unsustainable and murderous ways. Moreover, it's draining our lives of the beauty, grace, laughter, play, sweetness, and sensuality we long for. Disconnected from our hearts, we have become a species that seems intent on destroying the foundation of its own existence.

> *A peaceful revolution is going on, a women's spirituality movement, hidden in plain sight.*
> *Through circles of women, healing women,*
> *Might the culture come around?*
>
> — Jean Shinoda Bolen

Can we recognize and embrace the tremendous strength and power of the feminine? By inviting the spirit of gentleness, beauty, and fierce compassion into our lives, we not only heal ourselves and our relationships—we also illuminate our path towards a more peaceful world.

Shedding Heart-Shame

Rebecca is not your average college teacher. You might call her a closet revolutionary who uses her job to open up her students to new ways of thinking.

One day, she asked the male members of her class what messages their family had given them concerning emotional self-expression. Without exception, every one of them said he'd been shamed when he tried to express "soft" emotions like fear and sadness, and had at an early age learned to hide them.

Heart-shame is one of the most overlooked and least understood strategies that control-era conditioning uses to keep us locked out of our hearts.

At some point in the discussion, a young man named Tyler began to talk about an incident that happened after one of their classmates died in a tragic car accident. Tyler grimaced at the memory.

"We were devastated," he said. "But at the funeral, not one of us cried, even though we were just about shaking with the effort of holding back our tears."

Tears are nature's way of helping us release pain, and to compulsively suppress them is not only difficult but physically and emotionally unhealthy. If Tyler and his friends did so nonetheless, it was because control-era conditioning had taught them to view tears as unmanly and as a sign of weakness.

Usually, this aspect of control-era conditioning operates well below the threshold of our conscious awareness. Tyler and his friends didn't ask themselves why they didn't want to cry in public. They just knew it wasn't cool. So they struggled to keep their grief at bay by making their bodies rigid and their breath shallow.

Though they didn't realize it, they were suffering from something I call *heart-shame*. Heart-shame is one of the most overlooked and least understood strategies that control-era conditioning uses to keep us locked out of our hearts. Like an armed guard who stands at the entrance to the heart, heart-shame effectively banishes us into our heads.

Shame has since time immemorial been used to discourage socially unacceptable behavior. But heart-shame is a uniquely patriarchal phenomenon. Vulnerability, emotionality, sensitivity, forgiveness, you name it—if patriarchy associates it with the feminine and the heart, it's likely to elicit heart-shame.

Heart-shame is a huge obstacle to our collective healing. Rooted in patriarchal disdain of the feminine as it is, it naturally affects men more than women. In fact, it's one of the main reasons why some men avoid heart-centered practices. Like Rebecca's students, men are often humiliated when they display signs of sensitivity or tenderness. At a young age, they learn the dangers of revealing "feminine" attributes.

> *Vulnerability is what we share as human beings: our openness to being affected by one another, for better and for worse, is at the core of our interconnectedness. Because we are vulnerable, we feel pain—not only our own pain, but the pain of others. What we do to others we also do to ourselves. Vulnerability is at the heart of our human capacity for empathy; for suffering but also for joy; for hurt but also for compassion; for loneliness but also for connection. It is the open heart, fragile but strong, easily wounded but capable of great mercy and love. When we are most vulnerable, we are most alive, most open to all the dimensions of existence. In our vulnerability is our power.*
>
> — Miriam Greenspan, Healing Through the Dark Emotions

But as we saw in Anna's story, heart-shame is by no means just a male problem—many women absorb the same repressive values. Let me remind you of how Anna described her former self: "I was impatient with any woman whom I perceived as weak and unassertive, and very judgmental and ashamed of those aspects of myself that I considered too tender, vulnerable, or feminine to withstand the competitive world."

This is a perfect portrait of someone who, because she herself is suffering from heart-shame, seeks to inflict it on others. To free yourself from heart-shame, you need to recognize its symptoms, both in ourselves and others. For example, it's always present when emotional authenticity, or even the threat of it, elicits judgment, ridicule, cynicism, or nervous laughter and jokes.

You also know heart-shame is at work if, after revealing yourself in a way that takes you out of your comfort zone, you find yourself felled by an overwhelming sense of shame. All you want to do is crawl into a hole. "I wish I hadn't said that," you think. "I wish I hadn't done that. I made a fool of myself."

Next time this happens to you—and if you're on a path of inner growth, it most likely will—know that you're experiencing what I call a "shame-attack." Shame attacks are never rational. You didn't do anything wrong; and yet, shame insists that your fundamental worthlessness has been exposed for all to see.

In Rebecca's class, it was inevitable that Tyler's emotional authenticity would trigger a reaction in other students who still held the old patriarchal view of emotional authenticity as unmanly. One of them was a young woman called Margaret. After hearing Tyler speak about how he and his classmates suppressed their tears, she announced, "I gotta tell you it would weird me out to see a man cry. I want him to be strong."

Is emotionality really unattractive in a man? Obviously, some women would agree with Margaret. But a growing number would say the opposite: the most attractive man is one who can express his emotional truth without inhibitions.

The good news is that education has the power to dismantle and transform heart-shame. Rebecca's class is a case in point. In its wake, her students began to see things in a new light. Margaret, in particular, completely let go of her former judgment of tears as unmanly. In the report she handed in a few days later, she wrote:

"This was a great class. Tyler really opened up, and I'm so grateful to him for being so brave. Until then, I really believed that men didn't have emotions like us girls. But after hearing him speak I realized that, wow, they can feel emotions just as powerfully as we do! It really opened my eyes to the fact that it's okay for guys to cry, that they shouldn't bottle things up, and that it hurts them when they do."

Heart-Shame and Violence

A few years ago, I was talking with my Israeli friend Nitsan Gordon. As a woman dedicated to healing Jewish-Palestinian relationships, Nitsan has given a lot of thought to the underlying sources of conflict in her country.

At one point in our conversation, she commented, "The only real problem in the Middle East is emotional." Startled, I asked her what she meant by that. She explained:

There are external problems, of course, but nothing that could not be resolved with some willingness to compromise and cooperate. The real problem is that people are emotionally stuck. They are feeling tremendous pain, and the only way they know how to deal with their pain is by turning it into rage.

This is true of the men, especially. Grief is for women, they think. Grief is weak. So they get stuck in anger and revenge. It's an endless cycle, and there will be no way out until they learn to deal differently with their emotions. Only when the pain has a place where it can be expressed and accepted will it no longer be the major force that drives and controls our actions and reactions as it does now. When that happens, it will no longer cloud our vision and we will begin to see that our problems do have solutions.

Fear of the Feminine Can Manifest as Fear of...

- Intimacy
- Vulnerability
- Communication
- Feeling
- Movement and dance
- Playfulness
- Sexuality
- Ecstasy
- Loss of control
- The unknown
- Death

Take a closer look at any long-standing conflict on the planet, and you'll see that what Nitsan says of the Middle East holds true across the board. The real obstacles to peace are not external but internal, not factual but emotional. And among them, a major one is our habit of using heart-shame to keep men trapped in a prison of fake strength, and all of us in a tragic cycle of violence and revenge.

Look at any region embroiled in violence and warfare, and you'll find men who resolutely repress "feminine" qualities in themselves—men who don't know how to grieve and are ashamed of their tears, men who hide their vulnerability, men who equate violence with strength and compassion with weakness.

Collective Healing

I'm always grateful when people attend my circles who, like Tyler, have the courage to challenge the tyranny of heart-shame. By their example, they reveal new possibilities that may encourage others to step forward and share their own authentic truth.

Shame tells us that there's something wrong with us. And even though we might know this to be a lie, there may still be some place in us where we *don't* know it, and suffer as a result. Feeling defective, we then try to keep certain parts of ourselves under wraps lest they lead to rejection.

Heart-shame is a repressive mechanism that we can only overcome in community. We can't address it in isolation; instead of hiding, we need to connect with people who support us when we reveal vulnerable feelings and respect us more, rather than less, for doing so.

In our society, heart-shame wields tremendous power. Our first step in dismantling it is to recognize it for what it is. Next time you see a public figure putting others down or mocking and ridiculing them, remember that what you're really looking at is the face of fear—the same fear that prevented the young men in Tyler's class from crying at their classmate's funeral—and that is keeping men around the world imprisoned in a tragic cycle of bloodshed and revenge.

Six Groups Vulnerable to Heart-shame

Boys and men: Patriarchy defines all the qualities that signal the heart's opening as feminine, and when males display them, they are often shamed. These qualities include gentleness, tenderness, receptivity, sensitivity, and vulnerability, to name just a few.

Teenagers: Teenagers are highly sensitive to the values of their culture. They want to be perceived as "cool," and since our culture tells them that toughness and invulnerability are cool, that's what many of them try to be.

Corporate executives: Corporate executives are typically expected to be warriors—well armored, competitive, and tough. Judging by their dress code, you might assume they lived in a different galaxy than teenagers. Yet both groups share the same susceptibility to heart-shame.

Activists: Many activists view themselves as warriors in a battle of good against evil. They want to appear strong, and sometimes adopt a tough, combative mask, without realizing that in doing so, they are actually perpetuating a collective sickness.

Feminists: Since heart-shame is an instrument of patriarchal repression, you might not expect to encounter it among feminists. Yet as Anna's story shows, many women have internalized patriarchal attitudes. In order to avoid being stereotyped as weak and submissive, they often suppress their softer side in favor of a tough, competitive façade.

Ministers, clergy, and other religious people: Having worked with many members of the Christian clergy, I have seen the deep sense of shame that results when people are taught that it's wrong to want pleasure, sensuality, and intimacy; wrong to be human and vulnerable; wrong to have the wants and needs they have. However, this problem is by no means unique to Christianity. All religions that have internalized patriarchal values are plagued by heart-shame, including Judaism, Islam, Hinduism, and Buddhism.

Once we clearly recognize the toxic nature of heart-shame, its grip on us begins to loosen. We start noticing when it tries to hold us back. We're less quick to believe it when it says it's only trying to protect us. We know it's lying. In fact, it's nothing but a bully who wants to scare us out of our hearts.

Can we drop our tough façade? Can we rise above our internalized patriarchy and embrace our softness and sensitivity? Can we allow ourselves to be who we truly are, without shame or apology?

Shame has only as much power over us as we give it. When we say no to it, it shrivels and shrinks. Then, we realize that nothing and no one has the power to stop us from embodying the nobility of our wise and generous heart.

Suggested Exercises (See Appendix II)

Exercise 20. Creating Beauty

Exercise 21. Invoking the Feminine

CHAPTER·12

UNDERSTANDING THE ROOTS OF GREED

Blessed are the man and the woman
who have grown beyond their greed
and have put an end to their hatred
and no longer nourish illusions.
But they delight in the way things are
and keep their hearts open, day and night.

— Psalm 1

We are a nation of shoppers. We love looking at beautiful things and being out amongst other people. We enjoy buying gifts for ourselves and others. For us, shopping is a form of entertainment and a way of having fun with friends.

Of course, we *do* need to be around other people. We *do* need beauty, love, fun, and entertainment. Our needs are perfectly valid, but the way we're trying to fulfill them is destroying the planet. Meanwhile, consumer society goes to great lengths to divert our attention from the dark underbelly of all the glossy products it wants us to buy. We aren't supposed to think about the children of the Amazon who are dying because the oil companies have polluted their water. We're not supposed to worry about the Texas-sized island of plastic trash floating in the Pacific Ocean.

In my workshops, I often invite people to ask their heart what makes it happy. "Imagine your heart has a voice." I tell them. "Write down whatever it says. Don't question or edit, just listen and write."

The writings that pour forth whenever we do this exercise never fail to remind us how little the human heart cares for money and possessions. The world over, it wants the same things: love, joy, beauty, peace, kindness, freedom, friendship, connection, and community. Our heart wants to feel full, generous, and expansive, and to experience life as sweet, sacred, and meaningful.

Yet many of us don't.

"You in the West have the spiritually poorest of the poor," Mother Theresa once said. "I find it easy to give a plate of rice to a hungry person, to furnish a bed to a person who has no bed, but to console or remove the bitterness, anger, and loneliness that comes from being spiritually deprived, that takes a long time."

I think she's right; we're suffering from a form of starvation that is less obvious than physical malnutrition yet equally painful. Nothing can replace the joy of feeling our heart lit up with love. Banished from that honeycomb of sweetness, we're haunted by a persistent sense of lack that can't be assuaged by Ferraris or fat portfolios.

Remember the Pueblo chief who gave C.G. Jung a radically new perspective on Western civilization? The white people were strange, he said; he couldn't make sense of them. They seemed so unhappy and restless. They were always searching for something—but what?

We are all too familiar with that painful state of chronic dissatisfaction. Something, we feel, is missing from our life. And indeed, something *is* missing. Because we're stuck in our heads, our fundamental need for communion with our wise, loving heart is going unmet. The result is a nagging sense of deprivation— no matter what our bank statement says, we feel poor.

Deprived of communion with our heart, we feel a nagging sense of deprivation. Sadly, this is exactly how consumer society wants us to feel. Why? Because nobody makes a better consumer than someone who feels deprived.

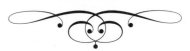

Sadly, this is exactly how consumer society *wants* us to feel. Why? Because nobody makes a better consumer than someone who feels deprived. Literally as well as metaphorically, our economy banks on our feelings of lack. Naturally, therefore, it's highly invested in making sure we never feel content or satisfied for very long. Just turn on your TV, and you'll see how masterfully it reinforces the message that who we are and what we have is not enough.

Nobody likes feeling deprived. We want relief. And so, our ego-mind starts looking for a way to satisfy our vague but persistent hunger. It wants to help, it truly does. But introspection is not its forte; it prefers to look outward. And so, we begin scanning our environment for potential sources of pleasure. Of these, there is no lack—the world is full of desirable objects—gorgeous women and attractive men, luxurious homes and prestigious jobs.

But what exactly are we looking for? What is that special something that will make us happy? Unsure, we're easy prey to those who insist they know exactly what we need. "You're absolutely right," they say cheerfully, "there is a hole in your life. But don't worry, we're here to help you fill it!" Then, they proceed to tell us that what we need is a new kind of wrinkle remover, a new cell phone, or cruise vacation.

Like masterful fishermen, they keep casting their lines until—finally! They find the right lure—something so yummy-looking that we bite. If the new car or the sure-to-make-you-lose-twenty-pounds diet pill won't do the job, then how about a remote-controlled shark for your swimming pool?

"Wow!" we think. "Cool! I want one!"

And lo and behold, we're in luck: it's on sale!

A starving person is easily manipulated, and before we even know what hit us, we've signed over a wad of hard-earned bucks. For a couple of weeks, we have fun with our shark. But soon, it loses its appeal and begins its slow downward spiral towards the basement, where it will stand, nose down, gathering dust amidst other discarded toys and ailing appliances.

Greed and Desire

As I write this, the so-called holiday season is beginning—an annual ordeal comedian Dave Barry describes as "a deeply religious time that each of us observes, in his own way, by going to the mall of his choice."

For many, the darkest days of the year have become the busiest. What nature intended as a season of rest and renewal has become a time of intense collective stress. Diving into a feeding frenzy of enforced consumerism, we turn our backs on the stillness and peace that is winter's greatest gift.

According to Christian theology, greed is one of the seven deadly sins. "Reckless and untrammeled greed," writes the journalist and priest Andrew Greely, "is the most serious spiritual problem in the country today."

Insofar as greed is a moral fault, it's one that humans have always been susceptible to. But in our times, it has proliferated to the point that it's suffocating the global heart of humanity. The ravenous desire for control that has defined the nature of Western civilization is, of course, itself a form of greed; and by sanctioning it, we left the door wide open for others to take hold.

The problem, I would emphasize, is not the fact that we have strong desires. Desire is a healthy, life-enhancing force. Quite simply, it's nature's way of guiding us towards what we need. If we had no desire for food, we would starve. If we had no desire for sex, our species would go extinct.

Greed, on the other hand, is problematic not because it

urges us to pursue pleasure, but because it sends us chasing after the *wrong* pleasures—ones that entice the mind yet fail to satisfy our hearts. Greed makes us, as the famous song puts it, "look for love in all the wrong places." It is, in other words a form of ignorance.

Of course, there are forces within every one of us that resist love and connection, that want us to remain separate and closed-hearted, and that advocate for ignorance. Such impulses are like weeds. Every garden has its share of weeds, but if the garden is well tended then those weeds are kept in check. This is one of the main functions of society: To prevent greed, violence, and other dark impulses from proliferating.

The problem with greed is not that it makes us pursue pleasure but that it makes us pursue the wrong pleasures—ones that entice the mind yet fail to satisfy the heart.

Unfortunately, consumer society has no interest in fulfilling its responsibility in this regard. Not only does it fail to keep our greed in check but it encourages it at every turn. If greed is a moral fault, it's one that our society intentionally amplifies by feeding us a daily diet of lies. We, like all sentient beings, want happiness and contentment. But we are disconnected from our hearts and therefore clueless as to where to look for it. That we're looking for the jewel of happiness is only natural. But greed sends us on a quest that is doomed to fail because we keep looking in all the wrong places.

As the saying goes, nobody can get enough of what they

never really wanted in the first place. So, like the hungry ghosts of Tibetan mythology, we eat and eat yet remain eternally famished, trapped on an endless wheel of unsatisfied craving.

Nazruddin's Diamond

In the Sufi tradition, many stories revolve around a lovable fool called Nazruddin, whose antics make us laugh, even as they highlight our own foibles. One such story gently mocks our habit of looking for fulfillment in places where it can't be found.

Night is falling. And suddenly Nazruddin discovers, to his dismay, that he's lost his greatest treasure: a priceless diamond. Nazruddin's friends find him under a street light by the side of the road, frantically scrambling in the dust.

"My diamond!" he cries. "I've lost my diamond!"

His friends toss their bags aside and get down on their hands and knees to join him in the search. "Was it a real diamond?" they ask.

"Yes," Nazruddin wails, "a real diamond, a perfect, big, round, sparkling diamond."

They scan every inch of ground, leaving no stone unturned. Nothing. Nazruddin's friends love him, and they want to help. But time is passing and it's getting late. Finally, after searching in silence for what feels like a small eternity, one of them says, "Nazruddin, are you one hundred percent sure this is the spot where you lost your diamond?"

Nazruddin lifts his head. "Oh no," he says. "No, it wasn't here. Definitely not. It was over there, in that field."

Furious, Nazruddin's friends leap up. "What? So why the heck have you been wasting our time, making us look here, if you lost your diamond over there?"

"Well..." Nazruddin waggles his head apologetically. "I thought... You see... If you look over there, you'll notice it's quite dark. Really dark, actually. The light is so much better here. When you're trying to find a small object, good light can be really helpful, you know..."

Like Nazruddin, we too insist on looking for the lost jewel of inner peace and contentment where we'll never find it. The only difference is that where Nazruddin is seduced by the bright street lights, we are drawn like moths to brightly lit malls, to sleek sexy bodies, glossy images, and shiny new toys.

Seven Ways in which Consumer Society Obstructs our Awakening

1. Consumer society doesn't allow us to rest. Instead, it pressures us into continuous busyness. This is contributing to a collective state of chronic exhaustion that presents a very real impediment to our awakening.

2. Music is a potent drug, and consumer society continually bombards us with poor-quality music.

3. Consumer society can't tolerate silence, stillness, or darkness, all of which serve as refuges to our soul and as

essential wombs of awakening consciousness. They are medicines that have a potent healing, purifying effect on our energy field and prevent the channels of our awareness from getting clogged.

4. Consumer society pays lip service to the physical body yet abuses it incessantly. Today, even young children suffer from problems like obesity and spinal degeneration.

5. Our environment serves as a mirror to who we are. Instead of reflecting the best in us, the multi-national corporations typically create environments that affirm the worst, ugliest sides of our being.

6. By bombarding us with images of violence, consumer society renders us numb to the suffering of others.

7. Consumer society forces us to eat polluted food, drink polluted water, and breathe polluted air, thereby lowering the chances of our awakening. For though awakening can occur anytime and anywhere, it's more likely to do so in a healthy organism than a polluted one.

Ugliness and Beauty

Our greed has not only devastated the planet but also leeched a tremendous amount of beauty from our daily lives. Just consider the hideous structures— insults to the human spirit, really—that dominate most North American towns.

What a sad irony that the wealthiest society in the world feels it cannot afford to build gracefully appointed buildings! Most industrial and commercial buildings reflect a blatant sense of inner poverty. In no uncertain terms, their ugliness informs us that we matter only insofar as we can serve as cash cows. When people get that message day and night, they can't help but feel they aren't worth much. And when people feel worthless, they begin to behave accordingly.

Of course, we have exported a great deal of the ugliness that is the byproduct of greed to poorer nations, where millions of lives are sacrificed to our voracious appetites. But in wealthy countries, too, ugliness has spread like a blight. Wendell Berry says it well:

> We haven't accepted—we really can't believe— that the most characteristic product of our age of scientific miracles is junk, but that is so. And we still think and behave as though we face an un- spoiled continent, with thousands of acres of liv- ing space for every man. We still sing "America the Beautiful" as though we had not created in it, by strenuous effort, at great expense, and with daunt- less self-praise, an unprecedented ugliness.

Is beauty important? Does it matter? Seen through eyes clouded by greed, it matters only insofar as it boosts our ego or helps us turn a profit.

But the fact that we don't hold beauty sacred doesn't mean we've stopped yearning for it. We can't, because to our soul, beauty is not optional—it's a necessity. As plants need to flower, birds need to sing, and as the sun needs to shine, our souls need beauty.

Beauty gives us far more than pleasure. It gives us a glimpse of paradise and assures us that we have not been abandoned in a barren wasteland. As the 8th century mystic Raba says, "Beauty is my teacher, helping me to know God cares for me."

How Greed Makes Us Stupid

As if it weren't enough that greed is destroying our planet, replacing beauty with ugliness and peace with stress, it's also making us stupid. We can be greedy and clever, yes. But greed and intelligence can't coexist, for whereas true intelligence is farsighted, greed is myopic. What could be more short-sighted than to destroy the planet we depend upon for the sake of money, which is after all a mere abstraction?

Many indigenous peoples have recognized our folly and have tried to warn us. The Cree people, for example, have sent us the following message: *Only after the last tree has been cut down, only after the last river has been poisoned, only after the last fish has been caught, only then will you find that money cannot be eaten.*

That money can't quench our thirst or satisfy our hunger seems so obvious it need hardly be pointed out. But as the Cree realized, they were speaking to people whom greed had rendered stupid.

Apparently, greed has the same stupefying effect on

animals. Just take a look at the old documentary called *Animals are Beautiful People*. In one scene, you'll see an African tribesman who's walking through a dry, arid landscape. He's thirsty and needs to find water. To our eyes, the situation looks pretty hopeless. If you or I were in his shoes—or rather, his bare feet—we might as well just lie down and wait for the vultures to arrive. But this guy has thousands of years of ancestral experience to draw on and knows exactly what to do.

First, he needs to find some baboons, because apparently, baboons know of watering holes no human has ever set eyes on. Since the tribesman is familiar with all their favorite hangouts, finding them isn't too difficult. The problem is, they have no interest in sharing their knowledge, and who can blame them? In this part of the world, water is way more precious than gold.

There's only one way to find out their secrets: you have to outwit them. But how?

Well, first you have to catch yourself a baboon—preferably an old, experienced one. Then, offer him a block of salt—an incredible delicacy in his eyes. Watch him feast, wait a couple of hours, and voila—you have an extremely thirsty baboon who, when released, will race to the nearest watering hole, oblivious to the human in close pursuit. Ingenious, isn't it?

There's just one little problem: baboons are large and strong. Smart, too. Catching them without some form of trap is no easy feat.

So here's what our hero does. At the foot of some cliffs, he spots a group of baboons. Curious yet unconcerned, they observe him as he quietly approaches. He calmly walks up to a large anthill, pulls a small tool out of the satchel around his waist and begins carving a hole.

Within short order, the baboons settle down to watch, all eyes and ears. As far as they're concerned, the entertainment of the day has arrived. One large male, in particular, draws near to check out what his strange relative is doing.

The man, fully aware of the attention he's attracted, carefully bores a little tunnel into the anthill. It takes awhile until it has just the right length and shape. But once he's satisfied with the results, he reaches into his pouch, pulls out a handful of seeds, and deposits them at the very end of the tunnel. Then, he backs off and waits.

At first, the large baboon plays indifferent. Clear as day, his body language says, "I don't give a hoot about your stupid tunnel or whatever is in it." But he's lying. He does care, very much so, and with every passing second, his curiosity keeps growing. Finally, he just can't stand it. He has to investigate.

Cool and casual as can be, he saunters over, sticks his arm in the hole, and grabs a fistful of seeds.

What happens next is amazing.

The second that the baboon's fist closes around those seeds, our man leaps up and grabs hold of him. Now in theory, there's no reason the baboon couldn't escape. He is, after all, much stronger than any human. And yet, he doesn't. Like an idiot, he just sits there and allows himself to be captured and tied up.

The thing is, that hole in the rock is just big enough for the baboon's open hand to get in, but too small for his closed fist to come out. And since he really, *really* wants those seeds, he absolutely refuses to let go—until it's too late.

You'd think such an intelligent animal would realize that to save himself, he needed to let go of the seeds and run. Yet greed blinds him to the obvious. He's quite literally stuck in tunnel vision—that seed-filled tunnel is all he can see. And so, he is trapped by his own greed.

Greed is an issue that concerns us all, for the writing is on the wall. An economic system predicated on force-feeding consumers like caged geese has no future; the planet can no longer sustain our addiction to consumption.

Let's fast-forward to the 21st century. Now, we're looking at a scene in another documentary: Al Gore's *An Inconvenient Truth*. Here, we see an animated cartoon man who's standing in front of two objects. On one side, there's an enormous bar of gold. On the other, planet Earth. The man is supposed to choose between them. The gold or the planet—which is it going to be? Stumped, he stands there scratching his head.

Naturally, the audience erupts in laughter. How stupid can he be? Surely it's obvious that without a livable planet, the gold would be worthless? Apparently, it's not as obvious as one might think. Just as the baboon chose the seeds over his freedom, we keep choosing the bar of gold over the planet. Possessing things has become more important to us than staying connected with life, attuned to it, and aligned with it.

Prison or Ashram?

Simplicity has always been dear to monastics. Today, it's equally dear to those who want to lessen their ecological footprint. It's good for the heart and good for the planet. It protects nature by decreasing our consumption while at the same time fostering serenity and ease.

Bo and Sita Lozoff, co-founders of the Prison-Ashram Project, have been exploring the path of voluntary simplicity for years. Besides teaching prisoners how to meditate and do yoga, they also help them recognize the toxicity of greed, which is in many cases what brought them to where they are.

As Bo and Sita point out, "Prisoners have the opportunity to dedicate themselves to this inward journey without the distractions and luxuries which occupy many people in the 'free world.'"

How the Prison-Ashram Project came about is an intriguing story. Many years ago, the couple's search for inner peace led them to an ashram—the Hindu equivalent of a monastery. This ashram welcomed people who were not lifelong monastics but who wanted to live a monastic life for a period of time.

Life in the ashram was hard. The day began with meditation at 4 a.m. There was no television, no entertainment. Sex was forbidden. All the creature comforts we habitually reach for were unavailable. Nonetheless, Bo and Sita felt happy and content. They appreciated the simplicity of their lifestyle and the freedom it gave them to nurture their spirituality.

Around the same time, Bo's brother Pete was jailed on

drug-related charges. When Bo and Sita visited him, they found him miserable and depressed. As far as he was concerned, he'd landed in hell. Bo and Sita, on the other hand, were struck by an astonishing fact: point by point, life in the ashram matched life in prison.

"We were waking up at four in the morning, wearing all white, working hard on a farm all day without getting paid and eating meals in groups and not having sex, and we visit Pete on the prison farm and he comes out in all white, and he tells us how he has to get up at five in the morning, and he has to work hard on a farm all day, and he doesn't get paid..."

Pete was, in other words, living much the same way as Bo and Sita, with one big difference: Pete hated it, whereas Bo and Sita loved it. The couple went home obsessed with the question of how they could help Pete discover the potential blessings within the apparent curse of imprisonment. They themselves had become disenchanted with the materialism of our society. Instead of more, they wanted less—less obligations, commitments, responsibilities, possessions, worries, and plans. What they wanted more of was free time and inner peace.

Time, they realized, was something Bo's brother had plenty of, but inner peace was not. Thus was born the idea of offering prisoners a new perspective that might allow them to use their confinement as an opportunity to reconnect with their hearts and souls.

Becoming a monk or going to prison—these may not sound like appealing alternatives, and most of us, thankfully, have other options. Yet in a sense, we *don't*. The writing is on the wall: An economic system predicated on force-feeding consumers like caged geese has no future; the planet can no longer sustain our addiction to consumption. So every time we feed our addiction to consumption, even though we know it's unsustainable and is sure to lead to places we'd rather avoid, we're choosing the equivalent of prison. On the other hand, we chose the ashram when we recognize greed for what it is—an inner adversary that keeps us stuck in a constant state of unsatisfied craving—and start nourishing our hungry heart.

> *I now begin every day with the practice of meditation, seated on the cold morning floor, cushioned only by my neatly folded blanket. Welcoming the morning light, I realize, like seeing through clouds, that home is wherever the heart can be found.*
>
> —Jarvis Jay Masters in Finding Freedom:
> Writings from Death Row

Please don't think of an ashram as a place of deprivation. Think of it as a sanctuary that's dedicated to the presence of the sacred. Think of it as a haven of peace. In this sense, our homes can be ashrams, too; simple rather than ostentatious places that foster in us a sense of inner peace and contentment.

Compared to the excesses of the supremely wealthy and powerful, our own greed might seem insignificant. Yet to some degree, we're all participating in the rape of our planet. There are only two things that will make us stop. One is some form of disaster, such as the collapse of the global economy (or, for that matter, of the Internet). The other is a voluntary choice, born of the clear awareness that our ship, like the Titanic, is heading towards an enormous iceberg.

Understandably, we're reluctant to sacrifice the comforts we've become accustomed to. Yet what our ego perceives as a path of diminishment and loss may in fact lead to true happiness. By simplifying our lives, what we stand to gain is not just a livable planet but also liberation from the slavery that greed has sold us into. Let us therefore wake up and remember what, deep down, we already know: The jewel of happiness awaits us within our own heart. As the 15th century mystic Kabir said:

> The small ruby everyone wants has fallen out on the road.
> Some think it is east of us, others west of us.
> Some say, "among primitive earth rocks," others, "in the deep waters."
> Kabir's instinct told him it was inside, and what it was worth,
>
> And he wrapped it up carefully in his heart cloth.

Suggested Exercises (See Appendix II)

Exercise 3. What Do I Really Want?
Exercise 22. Plastic Bags

PART IV

PATHWAYS TO HEALING

CHAPTER 13

WORKING WITH THE MAGIC OF CONNECTION

In the Pacific Northwest, where masks are often used in ceremonies, there is a special type called a Transformation Mask. When a hidden string is pulled, the mask will split open and reveal a hidden face within....

Just so, when we meet people different than we are, we first see them through a mask of otherness. When we get to know them better, that mask of otherness splits open and reveals the essential humanity that unites us all.

—Allison M. Cox and David H. Albert in *The Healing Heart for Communities: Storytelling for Strong and Healthy Communities*

Layla was a young Jewish woman who attended one of my weekend workshops for Jewish and Palestinian women in Israel. As our weekend drew to an end, Layla started talking about what the experience had meant to her.

In the past, she told us, her gut used to contract in fear whenever she heard the Muslim call to prayer wafting over from the neighboring Arab village. To understand what she was talking about, you have to know that in many parts of Israel, segregation remains a stark reality. An Arab village might sit atop one hill, a Jewish village atop the next. And while the inhabitants of the two villages might cross paths now and then, they rarely interact in meaningful ways.

After telling us about the visceral fear she used to feel whenever she heard the Muezzin's call to prayer, Layla shook her head. "It won't be like that anymore," she said as she smiled at the Arab women in the circle. "Now, when I hear that sound, I will think of you, my beautiful Arab sisters. I will remember your sweet voices, your faces and your stories, and when I hear the Muezzin, I'll feel not fear but love."

What had brought about this shift was a medicine as simple and readily available as it is powerful: *Connection*. Tribal conditioning doesn't want us to connect with strangers. There are only two kinds of people, it tells us: *Us* and *them*. *Us* equals safety. *Them* equals danger.

"Steer clear of *them*," it warns us. "Stick with *us*."

For hundreds of thousands of years, this was actually sound advice. It made good sense to keep a safe distance from strangers. How could our initial response to them not have been tinged with fear and distrust? The anxiety we felt as we ventured out of our comfort zone was a valid warning signal: "Stop! Danger! Get back to your tribe."

But today, when our ego warns us not to trust strangers, it's giving us bad advice—*very* bad advice, in fact. Indeed, our unquestioning acceptance of the ego's bad advice is one of the main reasons our world is in such bad shame. If we want to live in peace, then baring our hearts to people of other cultures, races, and religions is *exactly* what we need to do.

Unfortunately, people like Layla are still a minority. Most people instinctively avoid those they perceive as "different" or alien, choosing to socialize exclusively with those who share their religious and political views, race, and social class.

Well, you might say, what's wrong with that? Why shouldn't we seek out the company we're most comfortable with?

Naturally, this is our right. Not everyone has the desire or willingness to expose themselves to radically unfamiliar ways of thinking or being.

But considering how much suffering "us-versus-them" thinking is responsible for, it seems important that we venture out of our comfort zone. As long as we submit to the instinct that tells us to seek safety in distance, we have no chance of mending our deeply fragmented communities.

Of course, connection is not automatically healing. For it to become so, we must approach one another in a spirit of friendship and cooperation, rather than hostility and rivalry. We must learn to speak in ways that foster respect and mutual understanding, and be capable of listening to people whose views run contrary to our own without closing our hearts to them.

In the United States, tribal conditioning is currently blocking that kind of communication. Mired in us-versus-them thinking, belief addiction and judgment, different factions have withdrawn into their separate worlds. The result is a dire lack of fertile exchange that is fast eroding the very principles and ideals upon which the nation was founded.

Looking back over the stories we've heard, you'll see how important a role personal connection plays. Connection was what allowed the Bosnians and Serbs in Medina's circle to find a path to reconciliation. Connection was what taught Samantha the power of inner silence and receptivity. Or consider the encounter between Justin and his racist client. Never in a million years would Andy have agreed to work with a black counselor, had he not been forced to do so by circumstances. And yet, the outcome of their encounters was nothing less than miraculous.

We, who rely so heavily on phones and e-mails, need to remember that while there are many things we can do electronically, nothing rivals the power of personal contact to help us overcome prejudice and hatred. To transform negative relationships, we need to connect face to face and find out who the "other" really is.

Us-versus-them thinking traps us in an insidious web of prejudice and misunderstandings. Connection, on the other hand, is like a sharp sword that cuts through the web and allows us to see that "they" are no different from us. Connection between strangers has always been valuable, but in our times, it's more essential than ever before. Otherwise, how shall we come to know our oneness? Only direct personal contact can replace falsehood and misconceptions with understanding and respect.

Honoring the Stranger

In the tribal era, us-versus-them thinking was an inevitable by-product of the human condition. Yet even then, it often had devastating consequences. All too easily, one fear-based encounter between strangers could trigger an escalating spiral of bloodshed that might lead to the demise of entire tribes.

To lessen the likelihood of such calamities, our ancestors developed a number of strategies designed to bridge the abyss between "us" and "them." Connection, they understood, is a key to peace. One such strategy was to send out peace emissaries to befriend alien tribes. Malidoma Some, a teacher from the West African Dagara tribe who now lives in the United States, is a modern-day example of such an emissary.

In many tribal languages, the word for "stranger" also means "enemy"—a fact that tells us a lot about the tribal roots of us-versus-them thinking, prejudice, and warfare. In the Dagara language, too, the same word signifies both stranger and enemy. Malidoma's name, in turn, means "he who is to be friends with the stranger/enemy." By giving him this name and sending him to the West, the elders of his tribe entrusted him with the task of turning potential enemies (the "white people") into friends.

Another ancient strategy for cultivating peace is the custom of welcoming and honoring any stranger who shows up in one's community with the utmost courtesy, no matter who they may be. The Bible speaks of this: "Remember always to welcome strangers, for by doing this some people have entertained angels without knowing it." (Hebrews 13:2)

Today, this tradition still retains its power to bridge deep cultural chasms. I was reminded of this recently, when two

American friends returned from a month-long trip to Iran. Given the hostilities between Iran and the United States, I was curious about their experience. How, I asked, had the anti-American sentiment affected them? For the most part, they said, they'd been pleasantly surprised at the openness and hospitality they encountered. But then, they told me about Saeed, an engineer who'd hosted them for five days.

Saeed treated them with unfailing courtesy, yet his demeanor was extremely formal and reserved. One evening, as the sky blushed crimson and the heat of the day gave way to a pleasant breeze, Saeed and his guests were sitting on the veranda of Saeed's apartment, chatting about this and that. Eventually, the talk turned to life in America. And suddenly, Saeed got very quiet.

"What's the matter, Saeed?" they asked.

"Nothing," he mumbled.

But they knew something was up, so they kept encouraging him to speak his truth.

Finally, he blurted out, "I have to tell you, I can't stand Americans. They're so arrogant! I hate them."

Seeing the shocked expression on his guests' faces, Saeed hastened to add, "But not you. You are different. You are my friends." And with a dash of Oriental hyperbole, he added, "You are like family to me. Whatever you want, just tell me!"

Saeed's sincerity was evident. But why, my friends probed cautiously, had he taken them in, if his feelings about Americans were so negative?

Saeed shrugged apologetically. He'd acted out of a sense of

obligation. His boss had asked him to host the Americans, and as Saeed saw it, saying no was not an option. Not only did he not want to offend his boss, but he'd been raised to consider offering hospitality a sacred duty.

Then, however, his guests arrived, and the magic of personal connection began to go to work. Slowly but surely, Saeed started shifting out of his head, where all forms of prejudice reside, and into his heart. And with this, *us versus them* gave way to *we*: We, the members of a single human family. We who share the same desire for happiness. We who love music, good food, and good stories. We who bleed when we are cut and grieve when our loved ones suffer.

Eventually Saeed had to admit that he actually liked his guests and had grown quite fond of them. Though his mind still harbored the belief that Americans were evil, his heart was now telling him otherwise.

"After that evening," my friends told me, "things were different. The formality was gone. We had many long conversations and a real sense of trust and friendship developed. In fact, we're looking forward to seeing Saeed again next year.

"Another thing that's changed is our own attitude to strangers. In the past, we would never have opened our home to someone from a totally alien culture whom we didn't know. But after returning from Iran, we took one look at our big house and decided to sign up for a program that hooks up hosts and guests from around the world. Last month, a young fellow from Nigeria stayed with us, and what an interesting man he was! It's great to feel that we have family all around the world."

Heart-Courage

If we want to bridge cross-cultural barriers, meeting face to face is a crucial first step. But let's not forget that the relationship between Saeed and his guests only shifted after Saeed expressed his true feelings. So once we've connected, we also need to speak openly and honestly about the barriers that separate us.

This calls for what I call *heart courage*. Unlike the courage of the warrior, who picks up his arms and goes to battle, heart courage allows us to *dis*arm, lay down our defenses, and face each other in unshielded openness. Heart courage is essential in any relationship, but nowhere more so than in cross-cultural connections where there's a good chance that sooner or later someone will unknowingly offend another. Even when nobody means to give offense, it's likely to happen nonetheless, simply because our cultural norms and expectations may be quite different. What's normal in one culture may be rude in the next. What we take to be hostility may only be shyness.

If we avoid speaking about the issues that are driving a wedge between us, our relationships will remain superficial at best. But if we can muster the courage to communicate authentically, then trust, respect, and friendship can blossom.

I always feel a surge of hope when I hear of people who have the courage to speak up when no one else dares. That's why I loved the story my friend Tonya told me about Lule, a fourteen-year-old Albanian girl whom Tonya met at a summer camp for Albanian and Macedonian children. All of the children had been orphaned during the Yugoslav Wars of 1991–1995.

At the camp, Tonya taught the children circle dances. The children loved dancing, and Tonya in turn loved hearing their joyful laughter. One day, she decided to take a risk.

"I wanted to teach this beautiful dance," she told me. "But there was a problem. You see, it was a Muslim dance. In it, you raise your arms up in the air and say, 'La Illaha Il Allah' which means 'There is no God but God.' To Muslims, this prayer is very sacred. I wasn't worried about the Albanian children. They are Muslims, so this prayer is part of their culture. But what about the Macedonians? The Macedonian kids were Christian. How would they feel about dancing a Muslim prayer? I wasn't sure, but I decided to go ahead and do it.

"Well, I taught the dance, and the kids all did it. Nobody said a word, nobody complained. But I could tell something was amiss. There was tension in the air; the joy was missing.

"But when I asked the children how they were feeling, nobody was willing to open up. It wasn't until the next day that I learned what was going on. That's when I discovered my assumptions had been all wrong.

"That morning, Lule came looking for me. She was a beautiful girl, really shy, with soulful dark eyes and long, silky hair. At first, she wouldn't look at me. But then, she gathered her courage to say what she had to say. 'I need to tell you something,' she began. 'You have to understand this is hard for me because you are my teacher and I was always taught never to criticize my elders. But I am going to tell you this anyway because I love you and I want to be your friend.'

"Then, looking me straight in the eye, she said, 'When you told us to dance and say La Illaha Il Allah, that wasn't okay. You should not have asked us to do that.'

"I was surprised. I looked at her and said, 'Really? Why not?'

"She said, 'Because there is a right way to say that prayer. You're supposed to stand still with your palms turned up. You aren't supposed to move. Doing it like we did, in a dance, is against Islam.'"

A big smile appeared on Tonya's face as she remembered her young friend. "I admired that girl so much," she said. "I was so grateful to her for stepping forward and explaining what was going on. You have to understand that Muslims have a very strict code of manners. You just don't criticize your elders. It's considered extremely disrespectful. That's why none of the other kids dared say anything. Nobody had the guts.

"That girl was so precious. She came and mustered every bit of her strength and courage to tell a woman old enough to be her grandmother what was going on, just so I could better understand her and her culture. After that, we all talked about what had happened, and about our cultural differences. We learned so much from that incident."

To extend a hand to our enemies, to speak our truth without knowing how we'll be received, to take a step that makes us feel vulnerable and exposed—these are probably the scariest things we'll ever do. But they're also the most worthwhile. For as people like Martin Luther King and Gandhi remind us, heart courage is a force that can shake the very foundations of our world.

Gate 4-A

Now and then, we all have the opportunity to connect with someone whom we would ordinarily not meet. If we can embrace such opportunities, instead of turning away, we may discover how easy it can be to dismantle the walls that separate us, and how quickly alienation can give way to a sweet experience of shared humanity.

In one of her story-poems, the Palestinian-American poet Naomi Shihab Nye tells a beautiful story about such an encounter. It's called "Wandering Around an Albuquerque Airport Terminal," and it goes like this:

> After learning my flight was detained four hours,
> I heard the announcement:
> If anyone in the vicinity of Gate 4-A understands
> any Arabic,
> Please come to the gate immediately.
> Well—one pauses these days. Gate 4-A was my
> own gate. I went there.
> An older woman in full traditional Palestinian
> dress,
> Just like my grandma wore, was crumpled to the
> floor, wailing loudly.
> Help, said the flight service person. Talk to her.
> What is her problem? We told her the flight was
> going to be four
> hours late and she did this.
> I put my arm around her and spoke to her haltingly.

Shadow-a, shoo – biduck habibti, stanistanischway, min fadlick, sho bit se-wee?

The minute she heard any words she knew—however poorly used—she stopped crying.

She thought our flight had been cancelled entirely. She needed to be in El Paso for some major medical treatment the following day. I said no, no, we're fine, you'll get there, just late, who is picking you up? Let's call him and tell him.

We called her son and I spoke with him in English. I told him I would stay with his mother till we got on the plane and would ride next to her—Southwest.

She talked to him. Then we called her other sons just for the fun of it.

Then we called my dad and he and she spoke for a while in Arabic and found out, of course, they had ten shared friends.

Then I thought just for the heck of it why not call some Palestinian

poets I know and let them chat with her. This all took up about two hours.

She was laughing a lot by then. Telling about her life. Answering questions.

She had pulled a sack of homemade mamool cookies—little powdered sugar crumbly mounds stuffed with dates and nuts—out of her bag and was offering them to all the women at the gate. To my amazement, not a single woman declined one. It was like a sacrament. The traveler from Argentina, the traveler from California, the lovely woman from Laredo—we were all covered with the same powdered sugar. And smiling. There are no better cookies.

And then the airline broke out the free beverages from huge coolers—non-alcoholic—and the two little girls for our flight, one African American, one Mexican American, ran around serving us all apple juice and lemonade and they were covered with powdered sugar too.

And I noticed my new best friend—by now we were holding hands—had a potted plant poking out of her bag, some medicinal thing, with green furry leaves. Such an old country traveling tradition. Always carry a plant. Always stay rooted to somewhere.

And I looked around that gate of late and weary ones and thought, this is the world I want to live in. The shared world.

Not a single person in this gate—once the crying of confusion stopped—seemed apprehensive about any other person. They took the cookies. I wanted to hug all those other women too.

This can still happen anywhere.

Not everything is lost.

No, not everything is lost. As long as our heart still longs for connection and community, and as long as some of us have the courage to honor that desire, not everything is lost.

Tracy's Circle

Encounters like the one Naomi Nihab Nye describes are gifts of grace. The bad news is, they're all too rare. The good news is that it's not difficult to intentionally create opportunities for people to connect who might otherwise never do so. To provide safe, protected spaces where people of diverse religions, races, and cultures can meet and where deep-seated preconceptions can shift—that is one of the main functions of the circles I lead.

Many years ago, a young African American woman called Tracy joined one of my ongoing women's circles. As she sat down in the circle, I became keenly aware of how her ebony black skin stood out against the pale skin of the other women, all of whom were either Caucasian or Hispanic.

How did Tracy feel about this, I wondered. Was she uncomfortable? Scared? Angry? I was tempted to ask her, but my intuition counseled me to wait until she herself broached the subject. Several months passed before Tracy felt comfortable enough to do so. Only then did we learn just how strong her initial resistance to joining this circle had been:

"For me, the hardest part was that I, as a black American, didn't want to hang out with a bunch of white women. It scared me; part of me just balked at the idea. In fact, I had already decided I wasn't going to come.

"But somehow, I knew this was important. It's taken me a while to grow enough trust in you all to even be able to talk about this. But I'm so glad I stuck it out. I've been just astounded at the possibility of people understanding each other despite the worlds that separate us."

Tracy told us that many of her friends were vehemently opposed to her participation in a "white" circle. As they saw it, black people had only two options: either they could integrate into white society, which meant betraying their own people, or they could keep their distance and try to maintain their separate identity.

"What are you doing with a bunch of white folks?" her friends asked.

Tracy used to share their view. But today, she sees things differently. Like a snake shedding an old, too-tight skin, she's let go of old defenses and is meeting life with open curiosity. No longer is she willing to submit to any belief system that would control or limit her options:

"As a black American, I listen to people in my community who say it's better for black people to live separately, and not even try to integrate into the white world. Others say integration is the key to success.

"I listen to both sides of that argument, and yet I know that there is a totally different way. What this circle has taught me is that if our intention is to live together in peace, then taking sides is not the answer, and neither is choosing an ideology to live by. Instead, I want to live out of the power within me, the Spirit within, and trust it to guide me.

"I tell you, this takes a lot of courage! But when I look back at who I once was, and who I am now, I know it's the right choice. If people around the world could do what we're doing here, war would be a thing of the past."

Connection Changes Us

When we connect with former strangers, what changes is not just our mind. Our physical body changes too. Not only do we begin to think differently about them, we begin to *feel* differently about them.

Feelings like resentment, blame, and hatred are sourced in visceral survival instincts and have a strong physiological component. They affect our blood pressure, our immune system, our heart rate, and so on. But the same can be said for positive feelings like love and compassion. They too are crucial to our survival, and they too trigger visceral physiological reactions.

Whenever we share a heart-warming experience with someone whom we formerly feared or distrusted, we recondition our body to respond to them in a positive way—that is to say, in a way that causes our body to produce positive, pleasure-enhancing chemicals instead of negative, disease-producing ones.

Next time you meet a stranger, whether it's the shrouded mother of your son's classmate or a neighbor who recently immigrated from some distant nation, remember: you're looking at an opportunity to erase a toxic residue of ancient conditioning from the cellular memory of your body, so that we might begin to build a new global civilization built on love and respect.

Suggested Exercises (See Appendix II)

Exercise 19. Heart-Centering in Daily Life

Exercise 23. Cash Flow

CHAPTER 14

WHY WE NEED RELATIONAL EDUCATION

Educators, long disturbed by schoolchildren's lagging scores in math and reading, are realizing there is a different and more alarming deficiency: emotional literacy. And while laudable efforts are being made to raise academic standards, this new and troubling deficiency is not being addressed in the standard school curriculum. As one Brooklyn teacher put it, the present emphasis in schools suggests that "we care more about how well schoolchildren can read and write than whether they'll be alive next week."

— Daniel Goleman

"Profession?" demands the application form that will, I hope, lead to the renewal of my Green Card. I hesitate. I could say that I'm a Circlework leader, but who has ever heard of such a thing? No, that won't do.

I call my friend Margot. "What should I say?" I know I can always count on her for a laugh. And indeed, without missing a beat, she says, "Tell them you're a high priestess."

Hearing my merriment, she relents.

"Okay, okay, maybe that's not such a great idea. Tell them you're a counselor. Tell them you're a public speaker or a leadership trainer."

But in the end, I pick up my pen and write, in big bold letters: "Relational Educator."

Whoever processes my application probably won't know what that means any more than they know what Circlework is. Perhaps, though, they'll get the general idea that I help people create healthy, fulfilling relationships—with themselves, with others, and with the planet.

The cliché has it that outer peace flows from inner peace. This is true, but I don't think it's the whole truth. Some people are perfectly peaceful as long as you leave them to their own devices. But ask them to maintain peaceful relationships with others, and they flounder—not because they're innately incapable of relating well, but because they never received the relational education they need.

I didn't use to think of my work as educational, because it bears so little resemblance to what typically goes on in our schools. In my circles, we never sit at desks and we rarely work with books. You're more likely to find us dancing, meditating, telling stories, or walking through the woods.

This isn't what education typically looks like in our society. But at some point, I realized that part of my job was to help fill a huge hole—a crater, really—left behind by our society's failure to provide a certain type of education, the kind that enables us to relate in peaceful, harmonious ways. Right now, the majority of the human population is relationally illiterate, and as a result, our relationships are blighted with shame, blame, projection, and judgment.

I've never met anyone who didn't *want* to think with their heart. But most of us don't know how because we were never taught. We didn't learn how to take care of ourselves when we felt hurt or how to reconcile our own wants and needs with those of others. Relational education gives us a flashlight that allows us to look within, get to know our true feelings and take better care of ourselves.

Relational education gives us the tools to translate our longing for a more peaceful world into a tangible reality. Without it, we're like birds without wings.

It's telling that we don't even have a name for the study of interpersonal relationships. We can identify a number of contributing fields—psychology, spirituality, sociology, biology, and so on—but we have no name for the art of creating compassionate and peaceful relationships.

My job is to help people look within, identify their true needs and desires, and weave a web of fulfilling, nurturing connections. Over the years, I've been privileged to witness how, as they bring heart and mind into alignment, their lives become more free and joyful. They become more tolerant, more comfortable with differences, more accepting of life's imperfections and more compassionate. Because they themselves are more at peace, they can better serve as agents of peace in the world.

After participating in my circles for a few years, a young

woman commented: "I see for the first time in my life the possibility of learning to communicate in a way that really works. I've always wanted love, but I never learned how to communicate in a way that allowed me to get it. But now I know it's really possible."

What Relational Education Involves

What we know about relationships is not limited to what we learned in this lifetime. As we've seen, the consciousness of our foremothers and forefathers lives on in us, affecting how we relate to our neighbors, how we deal with conflict, how we define our identity, and where we stand politically. So if we hope to create a more peaceful world, it's crucial that we look at the inner obstacles that ensnare us in destructive ways of thinking and relating. We need to better understand why we behave the way we do and what we can do to reclaim our collective sanity.

We are, after all, not powerless against the collective programming we inherit. We *can* deconstruct walls that were once designed to protect us, but are now imprisoning us. A new consciousness is stirring that knows what freedom feels like and won't settle for less. An irrepressible force is pushing at our edges, insisting that the time has come for us to grow and expand.

I believe we *are* capable of healing our collective insanity, and of overcoming habits such as us-versus-them thinking, judgment and control addiction. However, I don't believe it can be done without a major dose of relational education. Relational education gives us the tools to translate our longing for a more peaceful world into a tangible reality. Without it, we're like birds without wings.

What exactly does relational education involve? What skills does it impart? In a nutshell, it teaches us how to think with our hearts. As we've seen, heart-thinking is a complex, multi-faceted art. The following list is by no means comprehensive, but it will give you a sense of what elements a good relational education should include:

- Identifying and transforming tribal-era conditioning
- Identifying and transforming control-era conditioning
- Deep listening
- Locating feelings in the physical body
- Naming feelings precisely
- Identifying wants and needs
- Staying connected with the body
- Understanding what projection is, and how it works
- Maintaining healthy boundaries
- Relating skillfully to anger, grief, and fear
- Communicating in non-violent ways
- Overcoming cultural and religious barriers
- Expressing strong emotions in constructive ways
- Techniques for conflict resolution
- Understanding group dynamics
- Understanding the difference between connecting and merging

- Working with altered states of consciousness
- Developing good leadership skills

Why We Need It

At a talk I gave for a group of business people, one woman asked me, "Why do you say relational skills are so important? Our parents and grandparents did okay without them. So why can't we?"

In response, I pointed out that her grandparents didn't need computer skills, either. Yet to her, they're indispensable. As times have changed, so have our needs.

Then, I asked her whether she was married. Yes, she said, I am.

In that case, I told her, you already know how much relational skill life in the modern world calls for. In the past, men and women had clearly defined responsibilities. When they got married, they didn't have to argue about who would do the housework, make money, or take care of the children, because tradition had already settled such questions. Our relationships, on the other hand, generally begin with a more or less blank slate. Nothing can be taken for granted; everything needs to be negotiated. If so many marriages don't work out, it's to no small degree because our relational skills simply aren't up to the task.

Community is another area where we need a far more sophisticated relational skills than any prior generation did. Our ancestors never had to create their own community. For better or worse, they were born into it. We, on the other hand, must painstakingly build and maintain our own community. Without good relational skills, we can easily find ourselves isolated and alone—a harsh reality increasing numbers of people are running up against. According to a recent study, one quarter of all Americans have not a single close friend—a shocking figure, perhaps, yet hardly surprising in a society that fails to give us the relational skills we need.

And as if having to single-handedly create our own relationships and communities weren't enough, we also inhabit a world far more diverse than that of our grandparents. No longer can we assume that our neighbors will speak the same language as we do, or that they will share our own moral values, religious beliefs, or social expectations.

We can barely manage to get along with our loved ones. How then shall we live harmoniously with people whom we don't understand, and who may not understand us? Without relational education, we don't stand a chance.

Why We're in Trouble

We are convinced, that you mean to do us Good by your Proposal; and we thank you heartily. But you, who are wise must know that different Nations have different Conceptions of things and you will therefore not take it amiss, if our Ideas of this kind of Education happen not to be the same as yours. We have had some Experience of it. Several of our young People were formerly brought up at the Colleges of the Northern Provinces; they were instructed in all your Sciences; but, when they came back to us, they were bad Runners, ignorant of every means of living in the woods… neither fit for Hunters, Warriors, nor Counselors, they were totally good for nothing.

—Written in 1744 by Native American chiefs in response to the white commissioners' offer to send a number of Native American boys to a prestigious white college.

The Latin word *educare* means "to draw out." Education is, in other words, supposed to draw out our innate wisdom and talents. Sadly, much of what we call education has the opposite effect. By the time they're done with school or college, many young people feel thoroughly confused, lost, and alienated. They might know lots of facts, but they lack the relational skills they'll need to lead happy lives. The result is an epidemic of hopelessness and despair that has made suicide the third leading cause of death among 10 – to 24-year-olds.

We will never heal our world as long as we only teach our children trigonometry and chemistry but not how to express themselves respectfully or how to resolve a conflict.

No doubt the world can be a cruel place. Yet I suspect this tidal wave of despair is caused by internal more than external challenges. When you deprive people of the heart-food they need and keep them locked up in a mental prison, you can pretty much guarantee they'll experience life as barren and meaningless.

Our children will never thrive as long as we only teach them trigonometry and chemistry but not how to express themselves respectfully or how to resolve a conflict. Most of them will do just fine without a grasp of trigonometry. But if they can't maintain harmonious relationships, they're going to be in deep trouble.

And, indeed, they *are* in trouble. According to the Center for Disease Control and Prevention, more teenagers currently die of gunshot wounds than of all natural diseases combined. Daniel Goleman remarks:

> In 1990, compared to the previous two decades, the United States saw the highest juvenile arrest rate for violent crimes ever; teen arrests for forcible rape had doubled; teen murder rates quadrupled, mostly due to an increase in shootings. During those same two decades, the suicide rate for teenagers tripled, as did the number of children under fourteen who were murder victims.... Heroin and cocaine use among white youth climbed about 300 percent over the two decades before the 1990s; for African-American youth it jumped to a staggering thirteen times the rate of twenty years before.

The Elephants of Pilanesberg Park

Domestic violence, child abuse, hate crimes, and racism— these are just some of the consequences of relational illiteracy.

Given its tragic impact on our communities, you would expect relational education to be a top priority in our society. Yet it isn't. Why not?

One fact may be the common belief that in the process of growing up, people will automatically develop the social skills they need.

In fact, nothing could be further from the truth. All species that live in complex societies spend a great deal of time, effort, and energy educating their young and teaching them how to relate well to their own kind. Wolves do it. Gorillas do it. Lions and tigers do it, and so should we.

What happens when animals *don't* educate their young became apparent some years ago when a group of young elephants in South Africa's Pilanesberg Park became wildly aggressive and began wreaking havoc on the park. The rangers were particularly concerned by the elephants' attacks on a group of white rhinos that the park had been carefully protecting for years. By the time CBS reported on the problem, the rogue elephants had already killed thirty-nine rhinos—10 percent of the park's total population.

It turned out that the delinquent elephants were transplants from another park. In the process of being moved, they'd been separated from their elders. As the field ecologist at Pilanesberg Park explained, their violent behavior reflected their lack of social guidance. Like thugs who terrorize their neighborhood, they were unleashing their destructive potential on other inhabitants of the park.

"Everyone needs a role model," he said, "and these

elephants that left the herd had no role model and no idea of what appropriate elephant behavior was." In the absence of elders to socialize and discipline them, the young males, in particular, became the elephant equivalent of gang members.

The solution was a Big Brother program of sorts. Large bull elephants were imported, and in short order, they curbed the rambunctiousness of the young ones. Since then, they've apparently been behaving very well, and no more rhinos have lost their lives.

Unfortunately, we are failing to do what elephants, wolves, lions, and gorillas do as a matter of course. It shouldn't surprise us, therefore, that many young humans behave just like those young

Imagine...

Imagine a world where relational education is a major part of every child's schooling. Educators have a mandate to help children enter adulthood well prepared to live peacefully with other humans and other species.

In Relational Studies Class, children use their own relationships as grist for the mill. They learn alternatives to judging, blaming, and shaming. They study non-violent communication and conflict resolution techniques. They learn about human evolution and their own role in it.

Every school has listening circles where, guided by skilled facilitators, children have regular opportunities to talk honestly about their thoughts and feelings. They acquire tools for wise decision-making and effective conflict resolution. They learn to center in their hearts, to understand why others behave as they do, and how to hold others in compassion.

elephants. They are causing tremendous suffering—not because they want to, but because they haven't been taught how to avoid it.

Nobody blamed the young elephants in Pilanesberg Park for their aggression, nor should we blame our own youth. Instead, just as the park rangers took responsibility for re-educating the elephants, we need to recognize our own need for relational education, as well as take responsibility for giving the next generation the relational skills they need. If we hope to evolve from a violent and potentially suicidal species into one capable of living peacefully on this planet, relational education is a must.

Heart-Thinking Can Be Taught

Where do we get our relational skills? Where do we learn what it means to be part of a social group? Obviously, home is one place. School is another. And then, there's the playground, which is unfortunately all too often a place of lawless brutality. Many children are scarred for life by the rejection and exclusion they experienced on the playground.

Vivian Gussin Paley is a teacher who felt concerned about this and decided to do something about it. In her delightful book, *You Can't Say You Can't Play*, she describes an experiment she launched with twenty-five kindergarten children.

As long as the children were in class, they were expected to be "nice" to each other—no hitting, no biting, no verbal abuse. But much of their life unfolded outside of the classroom. And there, they tended to behave like the orphaned elephants of Pilanesberg Park. With nothing to curb their budding ego, the playground turned into a battlefield. The winners got to choose their playmates and decide who could join their games and who couldn't—a right they exercised without mercy. Meanwhile, the losers got left out. Unable to choose their play-mates, they often weren't chosen either.

No matter how old we are, the reign of the ego is brutal. "Being told you can't play is a serious matter," Paley writes. "It hurts more than anything else that happens in school."

Just how badly it hurt became clear to Paley when her older students began sharing their memories of kindergarten: "The children, it would seem, have not forgotten a single rejection to which they may have been subjected during the previous kindergarten year. Each incident is recalled with clarity, as if it just happened."

Was it possible to teach children a new way, a way of open-heartedness, gentleness, and compassion? Paley wanted to find out. She decided to try out a new rule: *You can't say you can't play.* What this meant was that outside of the classroom, no child would be allowed to exclude any other child from their games.

At first, Paley's idea was met with utter disbelief. She re-ported: "Only four out of twenty-five in my kindergarten class find the idea appealing, and they are the children most often rejected."

With disarming sincerity, the children articulated their objections. As one little girl explained: "Some people—even me—want to own things. They say you can't come here and you can't come there. They say they are the boss and other people agree. Even me. If that stopped, then your plan could work."

Young as she was, this child had already resigned herself to living in a world of ruthless competition and power struggle. Paley began to wonder: Was it really possible to topple the tyranny of the control-addicted ego? Was she being overly idealistic in her belief that adults could, if they so chose, teach children the art of heart-thinking?

Patiently, Paley spent hours, days, and weeks talking with children of all ages, listening to their stories, addressing their concerns, and learning from their objections. Finally, the day came when the new rule was to officially take effect. Paley was both excited and nervous.

But within short order, she realized, to her amazement, that a small but significant revolution was underway. Previously, each child had been only dimly aware

Heart-thinking, along with all the values it nurtures, such as kindness, tolerance, and respect, can be taught. And if we want to create healthy, peaceful communities, it must be taught.

of how the others felt. Sure, they had sensed the loneliness and sadness of the unwanted outsiders. But this awareness had stayed on the periphery of their vision.

Now, Paley found, every child was fully conscious of how much exclusion hurt, and fiercely determined to protect other children from the searing pain of rejection. Former outcasts were welcomed into the circle of their peers, and over the following weeks and months, they began to thrive and blossom.

Even those who'd initially opposed the new rule for fear that it might diminish their status gradually changed their mind as they discovered the benefits of enjoying new playmates. Within short order, they discovered what at some point everyone on the path of heart-thinking discovers: we feel happiest when everyone around us is happy, too.

Two weeks after the new rule had been installed, Paley knew that her experiment had been a success. In her journal, she recorded with elation: "It is happening. Because the children are learning that it is far easier to open the doors than to keep people out."

For years, Paley had dreamed of the day when the sad and rejected would be welcomed and included. Yet she had always dismissed her dream as a utopia. Today, she knows it's no utopia. Heart-thinking, along with all the values it nurtures, such as kindness, tolerance, and respect, can be taught. And if we want to create healthy, peaceful communities, it must be taught.

Deep Listening

Among all the skills that relational education imparts, the undisputed queen is listening. Nobody can maintain good relationships if they're not good listeners.

On one level, listening simply means that we pay attention

to what someone is saying. But there's another kind of listening—some call it deep listening— that engages not just our ears and mind but our heart and soul. In deep listening, we listen not so much to the words as much as through them. Conscious of the goodness and wisdom that lie within ourselves, we listen for it in others, and in doing so, we draw it forth. Perhaps this is why in Kabala, the mystic branch of Judaism, the soul is described as the Nehemiah—"She Who Listens."

Wherever relational education is taking place, deep listening is a key practice. In many types of circle gatherings, people use a "talking stick," a tool derived from Native American tradition, to encourage deep listening. Only the person holding the talking stick may speak. Everyone else listens. There's no cross-talking, no arguing, no interrupting.

This in itself can be an eye-opening experience. We realize how much of what we say is superfluous, and that what seems of such burning importance to us in one moment actually turns out to be quite unimportant.

Gradually, the very act of listening quiets our mind until we find that we are truly listening—without judgment, resistance, or reactivity. Then, we begin to hear what lies behind the spoken words. Just as a dog follows an enticing scent, nose to the ground, we follow the scent of a person's authentic truth.

Jack Zimmerman, the creator of a group process called Council, is a relational educator who leads circle gatherings for both adults and children. He too uses the talking stick as a tool for teaching the children to listen. As the following glimpse into one of his circles shows, this is no easy task for children used to blurting out whatever goes through their minds:

"I've got to speak again or I'll blow my stack!"

"Shush! Lynda has the stick. You've had your turn."

"But I can't let Sam spout all that stuff without—"

"We're in council, please!"

"I can't—"

"If you can just hold on until we've completed the round, we'll put the talking piece in the center. Then anyone who needs to speak again can pick it up."

"If I last that long!"

How Listening Can Heal Communities

As in our personal relationships, so also in relationships between communities, races, nations, and religions, listening is also an essential key to harmony. As the Vietnamese Buddhist teacher and peace activist Thich Nhat Hanh points out, our failure to really listen to one another is a great obstacle to global peace:

"America has the potential to listen to the suffering of her own people and to remedy discrimination and injustice within. If you cannot listen to your own people, your fellow citizens, how can you listen to and understand the suffering of others? How can you understand the suffering in Afghanistan, Iraq, Israel, or Palestine?"

What Thich Nhat Hanh says here is extremely important,

because it points to the fact that listening can heal not just individuals but entire communities. In fact, we know it can heal communities, because it's been tried and proven.

> *Compassionate listening has one purpose: to help the other person suffer less. You have to nourish the awareness that no matter what the other person says, you will keep calm and continue to listen. You do not judge while listening. You keep your compassion alive. The other person may be unjust, may say inaccurate things, blame, attack, or judge. Yet you maintain your energy of compassion so that your seed of suffering is not touched.*
>
> — Thich Nhat Hanh

One example is the South African Truth and Reconciliation Commission, founded by Bishop Desmond Tutu after the end of Apartheid. Based on the concept of restorative justice, the Commission's goal was not to punish evildoers, but to create a space where both victims and perpetrators of atrocities could tell their stories and be witnessed in ways most of them had never experienced before.

Between 1995 and 1999, a total of 22,000 victims and 7,000 perpetrators testified. Obviously, not everyone experienced healing, but many did, and for South Africa as a nation, the process laid a foundation of hope for the future. Thanks to the South African Truth and Reconciliation Commission, scores of ordinary men and women unearthed within themselves a nobility and strength they did not know they possessed. Forgiveness, they discovered, is an act of supreme generosity—not so much to others as to oneself.

> *I believe that when people sit in a circle and listen deeply to each other, miracles happen. That is the belief that I bring to my work with people in conflict, and it's been confirmed over and over. Miracles happen when we tell our stories and listen.*
>
> — Circle Leader

We who are so easily awed by what is complicated can hardly believe that something as simple as listening can have such a powerful impact. Yet it's true: by listening deeply and with compassion, we initiate a magical, life-giving process of healing. When people feel heard, things that were twisted straighten out, and feelings surface that never before had a safe place to show up. As they offer their story into the hands and hearts of a compassionate, caring community, their soul breathes a sigh of relief.

From the beginning, the members of the Commission approached their work as a form of spiritual service. Before they took on their monumental task, they all went on a retreat together. Alex Boraine, the deputy chairperson, recalls how during the retreat an Anglican priest quoted the saying of a rabbi: An angel walks before every human being saying "Make way, make way for the image of God."

"For me," Boraine wrote, "this summed up the goal of the Commission. I listened in awe as many of the tortured, the mourning, the insulted, the damaged, and the poor shared with us not only their experiences as victims but their triumph as survivors. More than that, many expressed their willingness to forsake revenge and committed themselves to forgiveness and reconciliation. It is this truth which gives me hope for the future."

Relational Education as a Collective Imperative

It's often been said that for democracy to work, citizens must be educated. Democracy doesn't work well in countries where a major portion of the citizenry is illiterate. But, I would add, neither does it work when citizens are relationally illiterate. Relationally illiterate people tend to support leaders who mirror their own bias and reinforce their own prejudices. Thus, people governed by tribal conditioning will typically support politicians who habitually engage in us-versus-them thinking and advocate for war. People governed by heart-shame will gravitate towards leaders who put on a show of being rational and tough. Relational illiteracy makes us perceive reality through the distorting filter of unconscious beliefs and assumptions. As a result, our political choices miss the mark.

Every time I go to Israel or Palestine, I wonder why so little is being done to address the issue of relational illiteracy. The conflict between Jews and Arabs is one among many that

the international community has repeatedly attempted to resolve by political and legal means. Yet despite the enormous
energy and resources expended, their efforts have by and large
failed. Perhaps it's time to face the fact that something is fundamentally amiss with an approach that focuses exclusively on
changing outer circumstances yet ignores the inner dynamics
that perpetuate the violence.

Of course, political negotiation is necessary and important.
But to avoid facing the immense underswell of relational illiteracy that fuels our conflicts is like fixing potholes in a road
while ignoring the smoldering volcano beneath it.

Every year, we chalk up thousands of deaths to such factors as political struggle, poverty, and religious strife. Yet these
deaths could with equal justification be viewed as the tragic
price we pay for our abysmal relational skills. Were we better able to communicate, cooperate, and co-exist, these deaths
need never have occurred.

In our society, many people still view all forms of inner
work, including relational education, as narcissistic hobbies for
people determined to ignore life's more pressing problems. Yet
when you look at the major problems on our planet, you'll see
how many of them can be traced back to relational illiteracy.
Therefore I believe it's high time that we stop viewing relational education as a mere personal hobby and recognize it for
the urgent collective imperative it is.

We typically categorize relationships, not as an issue of
imminent public concern but as a personal, private matter. Indigenous peoples, on the other hand, believe the exact

opposite is true: Nothing is more important to the community than the quality of people's relationships. For example, the Dagara teacher Sobonfu Some explains that in her culture, everyone feels a sense of responsibility for maintaining harmony within the community. Therefore, any conflict between two people is considered a matter of grave concern.

She writes: "One of the principles of the Dagara concept of a relationship is that it's not private. When we talk about "our relationships" in the village, the word "our" is not limited to two. And this is why we find it pretty hard to live a relationship in a modern culture that is lacking true community. In the absence of community, two people are forced to say, "This relationship is ours," when in fact, a community should be claiming ownership."

To avoid facing the immense underswell of relational illiteracy that fuels our conflicts is like fixing potholes in a road while ignoring the smoldering volcano beneath it. It's high time that we stop viewing relational education as a mere personal hobby and recognize it for the urgent collective imperative it is. Our current state of relational illiteracy is a time bomb that needs to be diffused before it pulverizes us all.

I think it's high time that we, as a society, claimed ownership over the relational problems that are decimating our communities. Our current state of relational illiteracy is more than just an inconvenience—it's a time bomb that needs to be diffused before it pulverizes us all. If we want to create a more peaceful world, we should demand that more of our tax dollars be devoted to relational education. It would be money well spent, for the stakes are higher than ever. As Martin Luther King once said, "A nation that continues year after year to spend more money on military defense than on programs of social uplift is approaching spiritual death."

Suggested Exercises (See Appendix II)

Exercise 11. Giving Honor

Exercise 24. What's in Your Closet?

CHAPTER 15

THE RETURN OF CIRCLE GATHERINGS

A circle is not just a meeting with the chairs rearranged. A circle is a way of doing things differently than we have become accustomed to. The circle is a return to our original form of community as well as a leap forward to create a new form of community.

— Christina Baldwin

In a large room, twenty women are sitting in a circle. The warm evening breeze ripples lazily through the gauze curtains, and the sound of children's laughter mingles with the distant warble of birdsong. It's a peaceful, idyllic scene.

Yet looks are deceptive. What has drawn us here is not the beauty of the environment but the bitter knowledge of trauma, warfare, and injustice. For this is Israel, a country that's been plagued by relentless violence since its founding in 1948.

Christians, Muslims, and Druze, Israelis, Bedouins, and Palestinian Arabs, these women all know the damage that unhealed trauma can do. They've watched it fester and explode. They've seen how it reproduces itself and creates new wounds like the demon whose every drop of blood engenders a hundred more of his kind.

Many of these women are mothers who want a better future for their children. Most are engaged in some form of political or social activism. But that alone, they know, is not enough. Since the roots of violence lie within the human psyche, that is where the change must begin.

They also know there is only one alternative to violence: communication. And so they *are* communicating, even against enormous odds. My task, as facilitator, is to help them co-create a strong circle where they can receive the support they need. The issues are complex, the wounds run deep, and conflict is inevitable.

Yet through it all, we've been riding a powerful wave of healing. Here, the women have been able to relax, drop their defenses, and reveal their true feelings, no matter how raw or edgy. Truths that couldn't be shared anywhere else have been spoken honestly. Now, after two days of intense work, the deepening gentleness between them is beautiful to see. Slowly but surely, they're falling in love—with one another, and with life itself.

They all understand how vital it is that they tell their stories—not in order to cast blame, but because sharing pain is an essential step towards healing it. And so, they listen intently as Danya speaks. A short, plump woman in her forties, Danya is a strong, outspoken activist with fiery red ringlets, clear blue eyes, and a joyful laugh that reminds me of a bubbling brook. But now, her voice breaks as she speaks of devastation, heartbreak, and loved ones lost forever.

"So many were killed," Danya says through her tears. "Among them my father, my dear father."

The other women can relate. They too have lost friends and family members, and many eyes well up in sympathy as Danya's body begins to shake like a tree in a fierce storm. But then, suddenly self-conscious, she stops and looks at the Arab women sitting across from her. They too have lost loved ones. They too live under the constant threat of further violence and were raised in an atmosphere of mutual blame and judgment.

Cautiously, Danya asks, "When you sit there, I wonder— how is it for you to hear my grief? What's going through your mind when I speak of these things?"

There's a moment of silence. Then, a young Arab woman called Nada says quietly, "When you mourn your father, I mourn with you. I too have a father, and I too know the pain of loss. Jewish or Arab, we are one."

Heart-thinking always unites people, and in this moment, Nada is thinking and speaking from her heart. And so, her words connect us as women who share the same grief, the same sense of tragedy and loss, and the same longing for peace.

These women are not alone. Remember Medina, the Bosnian woman whose story we heard in Chapter 7? To heal trauma, we must hold it in love, and no tool is better suited to this than a caring, compassionate circle. This is why around the world, people are gathering in circles to heal the wounds of war and to encourage reconciliation. In the wake of inconceivable trauma, circles are helping people forge a path from hatred to forgiveness, and from despair to inner peace.

Invoking Tribal Conditioning in Service of Healing

"Circles have the potential for letting ordinary people experience the truth-telling and reconciliation that can heal wounded hearts and spirits. Globally, people are experimenting with truth and reconciliation processes for people who have done or experienced horrendous things, for example among the Hutus and the Tutsis in Rwanda. Similar processes are happening in Eastern Europe. Still, very few people get to go through that experience. The more that kind of healing is done for ordinary folk, it will change the direction of history and of evolution."

— Circlework Leader

We've spoken of the enormous toll that tribal conditioning is taking on our world. We've seen how it conditions us to divide humanity into us and them and to demonize those who don't share our own belief system.

Nowhere are its toxic effects more obvious than in Israel and Palestine, where two ancient tribes are locked in a seemingly insoluble conflict. And yet, in order to break their impasse, Israeli and Palestinian peacemakers are reaching for an ancient tribal tool: *The circle*. What a strange paradox! The very group format that, more than any other, triggers tribal conditioning, has in recent times emerged as our most powerful tool for transforming it.

When I started leading circles, I knew nothing about

tribal conditioning. Of course, I was aware that circles had been around for a very long time. Yet I couldn't have foreseen how working with them would send me on a journey into the depths of our collective consciousness.

One of the first symptoms of tribal conditioning I noticed in my circles was that people kept commenting on how safe they felt. "I feel a safety here that goes beyond the individuals who are present," one woman remarked. I felt the same thing myself. But why? Objectively, our circle was no safer than any other place. So how come we experienced it that way?

Today, I understand that these feelings are rooted in our collective history. The sight of people sitting in a circle—especially when they're sitting on the ground—triggers ancestral instincts that reach back through the millennia to a time when circle and tribe were synonymous. In the midst of a harsh and often terrifying world, the tribal circle provided refuge, comfort, and support. For our early ancestors, the tribal circle really *was* the safest place on Earth.

The sight of people sitting in a circle triggers ancestral instincts that reach back through the millennia to a time when circle and tribe were synonymous.

Sara, a therapist in her sixties, says that for her, being in circle has awakened ancient memories: "This circle seems to carry within it the memory of things I've learned for thousands of years. It feels very sacred, ancient, and mysterious, as if it were echoing other circles and helping me tap into ancestral memories. I know that I have been in circles for a long, long time."

She's absolutely right. At Benot Ya'aqov in northern Israel, archeologists have uncovered proof that as early as 790,000 B.C.E., humans were already controlling fire and using it to cook food. And presumably, they gathered around their fires, much as we do today.

Clearly, gathering in circles is something we've been doing for an inconceivably long time. We know circles in our blood and bones. Our familiarity with them is not just ancient, it's instinctual—for when a species does something for millennia, that activity becomes part of its nature. Whether we realize it or not, every circle we form today links us back through the millennia to the first peoples who ever gathered around the warming flames of a fire. And though our world has changed radically, the circle still retains its power to unite, heal, and empower us.

No wonder, then, that when people first stumble upon circle gatherings, they often experience them as strangely familiar, as if they had finally found their way home.

"What have I been doing for all these years?" one woman lamented. "Where have I been? I've missed this so much."

Tribal conditioning may be responsible for many of our toughest problems, including fundamentalism and terrorism, yet paradoxically, it's also what allows us to sit down in a circle of caring people, heave a deep sigh of relief, and feel that, finally, finally, we are safe. This sense of safety is crucial if we want to practice heart-thinking in community. Have you ever tried to open your heart when you felt anxious, tense, or scared? It simply doesn't work. To open our hearts, we need to feel safe.

Just as baby birds need a nest, we need protected spaces where our most vulnerable and raw feelings can surface. By delivering an ancient, primal message of reassurance in a language we intuitively understand, the circle calms our restless mind and softens our fearful ego. Not only does this facilitate healing and transformation, but it also makes circle gatherings a potent antidote to the stress and anxiety so many of us struggle with.

For anyone involved in peacemaking, conflict resolution, and reconciliation work, the tribal echoes of the circle have an additional benefit: They can trigger a palpable lessening of hostility between enemies. Without knowing why, people begin to perceive each other differently when they're in a circle. They become more open to hearing the other's point of view and more willing to empathize and forgive.

To understand this phenomenon, we need to consider that during the tribal era, people never shared their circle with enemies. Everyone in the circle was kin. Today, our unconscious mind still perceives the circle as a place reserved for friends and allies. The only times our ancestors *did* share their circle with enemies was when they wanted to resolve a conflict and invite reconciliation.

Tribal Fear

If the first symptom of tribal conditioning I noticed in my circles was a striking sense of safety, the second were surges of intense terror. What just a minute ago seemed like the safest place on Earth could suddenly feel like the most dangerous.

At first, I found this puzzling. Why would a person abruptly plummet into a state of fear, even though nothing particularly scary seemed to be happening? What was going on? Had some childhood trauma been activated?

Sometimes it had, but more often, it hadn't. Like so many phenomena I witnessed in the circle, this one too eluded the explanations of traditional psychology. Western psychology does a great job of helping us understand emotions that are sourced in our personal history, but it offers little help with emotions that are sourced in our collective consciousness.

Gradually, I came to understand that the human psyche holds memories, not only of the circle as a safe refuge, but also of traumatic incidents in which tribes viciously turned on their own members. We need only consider how in the late Middle Ages, an estimated 800,000 women were burned at the stake, or how more recently, millions of Jews were betrayed by their German neighbors. Granted, these events didn't occur during the tribal era, but no doubt similar ones did. Completely dependent on their tribe as our ancestors were, when it attacked them, they had no recourse.

You might object that we have no way of remembering events that occurred long before we were born. Yet based on what I've witnessed in my circles, I believe we *do*. How such memories get lodged in our psyche, I can't tell you. Are we remembering past lives? Are we tapping into what Rupert Sheldrake calls "morphic fields"? Are we merely fantasizing?

We really don't know, but our purposes, it doesn't matter. Our intention is after all not to construct an accurate record of the past. Rather, we want to heal our collective psyche in the present. And as anyone who works with circles is likely to discover, our psyche bears the unmistakable scars of traumatic incidents in which people were rejected, banished, tortured, and killed by their own communities.

No matter how many times we've encountered what I call *tribal fear*, when it surfaces, it's invariably painful. Nonetheless, I always welcome its emergence as an opportunity to heal ancient wounds that continue to alienate us from our own species, even to this day. Within the container of a strong circle, we can consciously face, heal, and release the terror that rises up from the deep crevices of our collective consciousness.

Western psychology does a great job at helping us understand emotions sourced in our personal history. However, it offers little or no help with emotions that are sourced in our collective consciousness.

If you're someone who tends to fear and distrust groups, you might want to ask yourself whether tribal fear might be at play. Perhaps you've tried to deal with it by avoiding groups. But this isn't always possible, nor is it desirable. For in our times, we can't accomplish anything significant in isolation. To initiate meaningful change, we need to connect. As spiritual teacher Jacquelyn Small says, "Everything today is done in groups; it's not done by individuals anymore. The world has gotten too complicated for people to do much of anything alone."

The Circle Archetype

Circlework, the practice I teach, stands in two lineages. So far, we've spoken only of one: the tradition of using circle gatherings to build and sustain community.

The second, equally ancient lineage I draw on is equally ancient. It approaches the circle as a *mandala*—a geometric form imbued with sacred power. Throughout the ages, around the world, human beings have recognized that in the universal language of form, the circle spells unity, wholeness, and oneness. Today, we can still see the circles and spirals that our ancestors painted on rocks and cave walls and walk among the huge stone circles they erected.

To this day, most indigenous peoples honor the circle as a sacred medicine that can treat physical ailments, cure emotional imbalance, and restore mental health. The Navaho use sacred circles in their healing rituals. Australian Aboriginals draw circles to invoke the womb of creation. Tibetan monks paint elaborate mandalas, circular maps of the cosmos, while Hindus meditate on round diagrams called *yantras*. And when the Sioux chief Black Elk was asked to explain his culture to the white race, the circle was the first thing he mentioned:

> You have noticed that everything an Indian does is in a circle. And that is because the Power of the World always works in circles, and everything tries to be round.... This knowledge came to us from the outer worlds with our religion. Everything the Power of the World does is done in a circle. The sky

is round, and I have heard that the earth is round like a ball, and so are all the stars. The wind, in its greatest power, whirls. Birds make their nests in circles, for theirs is the same religion as ours.

As Black Elk emphasizes, the circle, far more than a mere geometric form, is a key to understanding the cosmos. By aligning ourselves with its teachings, we, who have fallen out of harmony with nature, can find our path back to wholeness.

"You know the way," the circle tells us, "because wholeness is what you are." And in our circles, we realize it's true: we do indeed know the way.

Until the advent of industrial society, Europeans too revered the circle. Many early Christian churches were round. Similarly, the stained glass rosettes that adorn cathedrals like Chartres were by no means intended to serve as mere ornaments. Rather, they were tributes to a God whom medieval theologians defined as "the circle whose center is everywhere and circumference nowhere."

Far more than just a geometric form, the circle is a key to understanding the cosmos. By aligning ourselves with its teachings, we, who have fallen out of harmony with nature, can find our path back to wholeness.

Yet with the industrial revolution, we lost touch with the circle as a source of wisdom, guidance, and healing—this despite the fact that industrial society was itself founded on the power of spinning wheels.

Ours may well be the first society ever in which people don't regularly gather in circles. This, however, may be changing. Circles are appearing everywhere, each one part of the great birthing that is underway—the birthing of a new consciousness, a new global community, and new forms of spirituality.

Now, however, we are beginning to remember. One of the pioneers in this process was C.G. Jung, who described the circle as an *archetype*—that is, an image so ancient and so universal that it's imprinted upon the psyche of every human being. The circle, Jung claimed, always elicits a healing response, even in people who know nothing about its symbology. His work with mentally ill patients proved that the circle, used with a healing intention, could help restore psychic integrity and wholeness.

Tribal conditioning was not a term Jung used. Yet our instinctual recognition of the circle as a healing force evolved during the tribal era, when we first began to view the circle as an expression of Divine truth—holy, sacred, and imbued with Spirit. For untold generations, our ancestors used the circle as a medicine, a centering tool, a religious symbol, and as the foundation of community. Today, their experience lives on within us: intuitively, we too understand the circle's message of oneness and wholeness.

Millions of Circles

We're not going to wake up individually anymore; it's about a collective effort. It's about coming together, and of course it has to start within…. When enough people wake up to oneness in themselves, it will run through the whole of the planet.

— Paul Lowe

In ancient times, each tribe had its own set of spiritual beliefs and customs. There was no spiritual language that all humans shared in common, nor did they need one. We, on the other hand, *do*. For in our situation, the realization of our oneness as children of a single planetary community is no mere luxury. Rather, it's the basis for peace between people of diverse races, nations, and religions. The knowledge of our oneness has, in other words, become a prerequisite for our continued presence on this planet.

In theory, we might recognize that we are interconnected. Yet abstract knowledge rarely inspires the kind of radical change we need today. Real, lasting change usually occurs in the wake of experiences that touch us deeply and evoke a direct, immediate, and personal sense of oneness.

Circles very naturally facilitate this kind of experience. Remember Nada, the Arab woman whose words bonded us across light years of difference? These are the kinds of encounters that change us, and no tool is better suited to inviting them than the circle. Circles can open our eyes to the beauty and sacredness of people who we would otherwise tend to avoid. And as this awareness becomes part of our flesh and blood, it strengthens our commitment to peace and justice.

No wonder, then, that at a time when our need for unity is greater than ever, the circle is increasingly emerging within our collective awareness. After a brief period of forgetfulness, we're once again remembering its power to help us become what it is: centered, balanced, unified, and whole.

Ours may well be the society ever in which people don't regularly gather in circles. This, however, may be changing. Since the '60s, circles have been popping up everywhere, like mushrooms after a summer rain, each one part of the great birthing that is underway—the birthing of a new consciousness, a new global community, and new forms of spirituality. Circles have always played an important role in community life. But today, I believe they have the potential to tip the balance of our collective fate.

In this view, I'm by no means alone; rather, I belong to a growing community of relational educators who have fallen passionately in love with circle gatherings and are using them in service of planetary healing

Jean Bolen, author of *The Millionth Circle*, has inspired thousands of women to use circles as a tool for self-remembrance, healing, and empowerment. Jack Zimmerman uses circle gatherings as a tool for building and healing community. Sedona and Joshua Cahill lead ceremonial circles. Parker Palmer's circles offer sanctuaries for the soul to speak and be heard, while Christina Baldwin's circles serve as vessels where people can open to communion with Spirit. Kay Pranis, author of *The Little Book of Circle Processes*, uses circle gatherings as a tool for restoring justice and peace in diverse communities. The list could go on. Though each teacher has his or her own approach to the circle, they all agree that circles can open our hearts, nourish our souls, and heal our communities.

Just fifty years ago, circle gatherings were rare. Now, social activists have them. So do churches. There are circles for cancer patients, caretakers, the bereaved, children, and teenagers. Circles are forming in schools, colleges, and hospitals. Circles like the ones I facilitate in Israel are becoming increasingly common as well.

There are therapy circles, discussion circles, men's and women's circles, drumming and singing circles. Even corporations like Hewlett Packard and Bank of America are hiring circle leaders to teach them the secrets of effective teamwork. Almost unnoticed, the circle has gone mainstream.

- As a geometric form, the circle signifies oneness.
- As a healing tool, it centers, balances and unifies us.
- As an archetype, it awakens our sense of wholeness.
- As a social structure, it supports a communal experience of oneness.

Pick up the catalog of any major retreat center in the United States and you'll see a range of workshops on healing, spirituality, and relationships. The circle is rarely mentioned. And yet, if you were to attend any of these workshops, you'd most likely find yourself sitting in one.

If you asked the facilitators why, they might say that circles support community and connection, and that in a circle, everyone can see everyone else. They might point out that in a circle, there's no "special" place—everyone is at equal distance from the center, a fact that fosters a sense of equality.

All this is true. And yet, it's just the tip of a huge iceberg.

That iceberg is the new Gaia-centered consciousness that has been emerging since the '60s. As the circle echoes the shape of our planet, it's also one of the main channels through which this new consciousness is streaming into our world.

The circle echoes the shape of our planet, and is one of the main channels through which a new Gaia-centered consciousness is streaming into our world.

For many people, the circle has taken the place of the traditional village square. It's where they go to meet up, hang out, get inspired, learn new things, and have fun. Initially, they might be drawn by a desire to connect more deeply with themselves or to improve their relationships with loved ones and co-workers. But the circle has more to offer than personal healing. Used skillfully, it can awaken us to the larger context within which our personal journey is unfolding.

In a circle, nobody has to tell us that we belong to a greater whole: we can see it with our own eyes. In its gentle way, the circle dissolves our ego attachment to being special. Sure, we are special, we matter, we have our place in the circle—but so does everybody else.

As old structures crumble, circles are helping us create non-hierarchical communities that are strong enough to survive, yet flexible enough to adapt to changing circumstances. Best of all, the circle levels the playing field between rich and poor. It requires no technology—it's a tool available to anyone, whether they're sitting in a dusty village square or in a Beverly Hills mansion. And so, circles are emerging everywhere—not just in wealthy countries, but also throughout the third world.

Developing Skill

Circlework is life-altering. It's completely outside of any experience I've ever had. It quenches a longing for connection that so many people feel but that's really hard to find in our world. Until I experienced coming together in this very loving, compassionate, and deeply honest way I didn't know that it was really possible. The circle has given me that experience, the experience of a true alternative. Out of that, hope has come.

— Circlework Graduate

Half a century ago, when circle gatherings first began to reemerge in the West, we didn't really understand their true potential. Most people dismissed them as a pastime for hippies and "alternative" types. In the eyes of the mainstream, circles were suspect—understandably so, given the highly experimental methods some used.

But then, how could our initial attempts at reclaiming the circle have been anything but clumsy? We sensed their importance, but when it came to actually working with them, we were groping around in the dark. Our elders never taught us how to use circle medicine—we had to figure it out for ourselves. Not surprisingly, we messed up a few times before we got it right.

Part of the problem was—and to some extent still is—that our only role models were tribal. Inevitably, some tried to imitate tribal traditions. While we can and should learn from the wisdom of tribal peoples, we can't turn back the clock. As our species is evolving, so must our circles. We are contemporary men and women, planetary citizens, children of the global era, and pioneers exploring new frontiers. Our goal is not to resurrect an old form but rather to create something brand new that has never existed before. Today, our circles are no longer limited to members of our own tribe. Rather, they reflect the diversity that is the hallmark of our times. Instead of being born into a circle, we create and recreate our circles according to our changing needs. Instead of having just one, we

As our species is evolving, so must our circles. Our goal is not to resurrect an old form but rather to create something brand new that has never existed before.

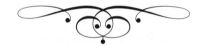

might have many overlapping circles, each one a point of light in a luminous healing web we are weaving around our planet.

No one knows how many circles meet every day on our planet, but they surely number in the tens of thousands, and their number is sure to increase in coming years. Given their diversity, you might assume that beyond their format, they'd have little in common. But look more closely and you'll find that they're overwhelmingly concerned with healing, transformation, empowerment, and awakening. Whether or not it's explicitly acknowledged, they overwhelmingly support the evolution of a new collective consciousness and the birthing of a new world.

Now, two things are needed. First, the thousands of circles

that are already facilitating our shift from head-thinking to heart-thinking need to realize that they are working towards a single goal, albeit from different angles. Currently, this sense of connection is largely lacking. If you already belong to a circle, whether it's a book club, discussion group, women's circle, AA meeting, or meditation group, I invite you to honor it as a droplet in a swelling river that's bringing the healing waters of a new consciousness to our parched world.

Second, we need to become more skillful in working with circles. I wish I could tell you that when people gather in a circle, heart-thinking will automatically prevail. Unfortunately, this isn't the case. The circle has tremendous healing power, but to what extent we realize its potential will depend on our own consciousness. Remember how Medina's circle almost fell apart? Her story can remind us of how complex the dynamics of circle gatherings can be, and how much skill their facilitation can call for.

At present, counselors, psychologists, and ministers are often expected to lead circles without sufficient training. Few are adequately prepared to deal with the challenges that can and often do arise in circles.

This is why for the past two decades I've been on a mission to educate the public about the value, importance, and skillful use of circles. The better we understand their dynamics, the more effectively we'll be able to use what is, without doubt, a potent medicine for healing ourselves and our planet.

Individually, a thousand rays of sunlight can't start a fire. But take a lens and focus them all on one point, and they can.

Individually, we cannot heal the planet. Together, we can. Circles are the lenses that can help us collectively focus our intention. Anything we want to do as a community, they can help us do more effectively.

Suggested Exercises (See Appendix II)

Exercise 25. Circle of Stones

Exercise 26. Making Ripples

CHAPTER 16

CELEBRATING LIFE

Do not cease to drink beer, to eat, to intoxicate thyself, to make love, and to celebrate the good days.

— Egyptian proverb

What can we do, in the face of our collective insanity, other than sink into abject depression? What can we do, other than howl at the moon or bury our heads in the sand?

Strange though it may sound, I believe one thing we can do is *celebrate*.

In our society, we think of celebrations as optional. They're the icing on the cake. They can be fun, but do we really need them? Surely we can do just fine without them. Yet most other cultures would disagree. Across the board, indigenous peoples treasure their celebrations and believe that to neglect them would be to endanger the well-being of the entire community. Over time, the spirit of a people that fails to celebrate will surely shrivel up like a parched plant.

The Minianka healer Yaya Diallo explains that in his tribe,

celebrating is viewed as an important pillar of communal life. He says, "In celebrating together, we find no place for questions such as 'What am I doing in this world?' or 'Does life have a meaning?' It is community preventive therapy. Life feels good.... It is a great harmonizing measure."

I think he's right: we need to celebrate—not just now and then, but often. By laughing, feasting, playing, and dancing together, we shake off our stress and remember why life is worth living and why our planet is worth saving.

Obviously, I'm not talking about people lounging around making small talk or getting drunk. In a true celebration, we amplify positive energy by sharing it. We offer the light of our single candle and in return receive the warmth of a blazing fire. Together, we create a force field that carries us way higher than we could possibly fly on our own.

In our society, we don't celebrate anywhere near enough. That, at least, is my opinion. Perhaps you disagree. "I don't like being in groups," you might say. "I don't like loud music and

---

The Benefits of Celebrating

A celebration is a communal experience co-created by people who want to amplify positive energy by sharing it. Its benefits include:

- Pleasure, joy, and a sense of physical, emotional, and spiritual well-being
- Affirmation of positive values
- Access to healing energy
- Connection to community
- Connection to Spirit
- Renewed energy, courage, and hope

I hate to dance. I'd much rather be alone or enjoy a quiet meal with a friend."

Fine. But even a hermit is part of the human community. On your own, you can't survive. A celebration is, among other things, a way of bowing to your community and saying, "Thank you. Thank you for giving me life and sustaining me." Such gratitude is a great medicine that heals our sense of lack, warms our hearts, and re-bonds us with life.

Coming together to share our happiness with friends, or even with an entire community, is something that comes naturally to us; people do it the world over. But that doesn't mean we do it well. Just like heart-thinking, listening, skillful communication, and all the other relational skills we've discussed, the art of celebration is one that many of us never learned.

To celebrate well, we need to relegate head-thinking to the back seat—at least temporarily. Otherwise, why bother? Head-thinking takes all the fun out of it. Head-thinking is governed by the ego, and to the ego, social gatherings are all about judging and being judged. So when the ego is in charge, celebrations turn into competitions.

The control-addicted ego typically heads off to social events with all the grim determination of a warrior marching onto the battlefield. Afterwards, it anxiously revisits the experience. Did I look okay? Did people like me? Did I make a fool of myself? So torturous is the whole ordeal that many people can only endure it by numbing themselves with alcohol, loud music, or drugs.

Heart-thinking completely changes this picture. It allows

us to truly enjoy ourselves and have fun. Centered in our hearts, we can feel the current of warmth and affection flowing between us. Our laughter is authentic, our joy palpable.

We who love life should take every opportunity to celebrate our love, not just in solitude but in community. For it is as a global community that we need to affirm life's goodness and sacredness.

Our ego hates to let go of its gripes and grievances, its complaints and resentments. But that is exactly what a true celebration requires of us. It asks us to loosen our grip on everything that's going wrong or has gone wrong or might go wrong, and instead embrace the moment and affirm what's *right* in the world. Instead of postponing our joy to some imaginary future when everything will finally be just right, we accept that this is it: it's now or never. As James Baraz writes in his book *Awakening Joy*, "The secret to awakening joy is being present with whatever part of life we're tasting right now."

Heart-thinking enables us to be true friends to one another, and to sincerely support, appreciate, and encourage each other without jealousy or competition. Every celebration is an affirmation of the fact that we really can live together harmoniously. No one said it would be easy, but we are capable of it, and that knowledge in itself is a tremendous source of happiness.

Steeped in the steady heartbeat of our community, we find the strength to face our challenges. Who knows what the future will bring? Life may never be perfect, but it will always be worth celebrating. And by celebrating today, we renew the sense of hope and courage we'll need tomorrow.

> *The more you praise and celebrate your life, the more there is in life to celebrate.*
>
> — Oprah Winfrey

Good celebrations are powerful antidepressants. This stands to reason, given their ingredients: community, abundant food and drink, music, rhythm, dance, laughter, and play. They're like a nutrient without which we can survive but not thrive. They give our collective immune system a big boost and remind us that life is not just a struggle for survival but a song of praise, a dance of joy, and a gift of grace.

A good celebration can renew our will to live and our hope for the future. We have survived another day, another year, another decade. We are alive, something we should never take for granted. For that, we give thanks to our community, to Earth, and to Spirit. For a little while, we stop trying to keep everything under control and instead offer a whole-hearted, unconditional yes to this wild, terrifying, exhilarating journey we're on.

Coming together to express this yes is important, for if something is never expressed, it shrivels and dies. Therefore, we who love life should take every opportunity to celebrate our love, not just in solitude but in community. For it is as a global community that we need to affirm life's goodness and sacredness.

The Bonfire Dance

Some years ago I was at a huge outdoor dance festival. Well past midnight, I wandered into a distant corner of the grounds that I hadn't yet explored. There, I chanced upon a celebration I will never forget.

From a distance, all I could see was a blazing bonfire. But as I approached, I realized about sixty young people were gathered around it. Two girls, perhaps fifteen years old, were dancing around the fire, their smooth young faces serious and concentrated. Lit by the flames, they moved dreamily with undulating arms and half-shut eyes, as if entranced by the mystery of their sleek bodies. Seated in a wide circle around them, a dozen or so drummers, mostly young men, were playing with total concentration, perfectly in sync with the movements of the dancers.

After a few minutes, the girls dissolved back into the crowd. Meanwhile, the drumming continued unabated, growing even more intense, as if to match the leaping flames. Within short order, a lanky boy with tattoos on his bare arms entered the circle and began to dance, awkward yet beautiful in his long-limbed body.

Gradually, all sense of time dissolved. At some point, some didgeridoo players had joined the drummers. Now, they began sending shivers up my spine with the deep, otherworldly drone of their instruments.

With a wild shriek, a girl leapt into the circle, her long black hair flying as she whirled and swooped around the flames.

Soon after, a boy threw himself face down on the ground and before our eyes transformed into a fish swimming through invisible waves. Nobody was being pressured to perform, nor was anyone holding back. Nobody hogged the center space. Nobody had to tell one dancer to make room for another, or remind the musicians to stay focused and attentive.

Every now and then, the musicians would pause for a few minutes. Soft laughter rippled through the warm night. Friends sat arm in arm, their faces open and peaceful. Patiently, with no sense of hurry, everyone waited for the ceremony to resume.

Spellbound, I watched, transported into a world both old and new. I heard the echoes of ancient laughter, felt the pulse of ancient drums, and sensed the presence of men and women long gone. And I thought to myself, "If humans still roam the earth a thousand years from now, they too will gather around their fires to celebrate."

When life gets me down and I am tempted to despair, I often think of those young people. No doubt they are inheriting a wounded world. Yet they come, not with empty hands but with knowledge, wisdom, and powers honed over millions of years. For their sake, and for the sake of their children's children, I offer the Pueblo prayer:

> I add my breath to your breath that our days may
> be long on the earth,
> that the days of our people may be long,
> that we shall be as one person,
> that we may finish our road together.

Suggested Exercises (See Appendix II)

Exercise 27. Visioning a Celebration

Exercise 10. Gratitude Practice

EPILOGUE

In the face of all the challenges we face today, is my optimism about the future of humanity idealistic? Perhaps it is. Is it unrealistic? Certainly not. To remain indifferent to the challenges we face is indefensible. If the goal is noble, whether or not it is realized within our lifetime is largely irrelevant. What we must do therefore is to strive and persevere and never give up.

— The Dalai Lama

We live in times of immense turmoil and collective upheaval. Old ways of life are shattering, old values are disintegrating. Environmental pollution, crime, warfare, nuclear missiles, global warming—danger looms on all sides. What, other than extinction, might lie on the other side of war, terrorism and tsunamis, overpopulation and famine?

No one can say. But in the midst of it all, it can be helpful to remember that the Chinese symbol for crisis also means opportunity. The global crisis is presenting us with an unprecedented opportunity for evolution, and upon our response will depend the quality of life on Earth for centuries to come. Collectively, we've reached a dead end—quite literally so, for unless our collective consciousness changes, life as we know it will cease to exist. As Eckhart Tolle, author of *A New World*, puts it, we're facing a stark choice: "Evolve or die."

When I first heard these words, I was puzzled. Surely he couldn't be talking about evolution in the literal sense? Evolution, I'd learned in school, was an excruciatingly slow process that spanned millions of years. This being the case, it seemed unlikely that our species would evolve in any significant way anytime soon. That kind of thing simply didn't happen overnight.

Today, I know I was wrong. New research reveals that we had completely misjudged the speed of evolution. As ecologists Peter and Rosemary Grant explain in their Pulitzer Prize winning book, *The Beak of the Finch*, evolution can actually be measured from one generation to the next. "Darwin did not know the strength of his own theory," they conclude.

"He vastly underestimated the power of natural selection. Its action is neither rare nor slow. It leads to evolution daily and hourly, all around us, and we can watch."

This is good news because it means that we too are potentially capable of rapid change. Even though toxic habits like us-versus-them thinking and thought addiction have ruled us for thousands of years, we may be capable of transforming them.

There's a hook, though. In the past, evolution was always an involuntary process. We had no awareness of what was happening to us or why: nature was in charge. Today, our situation is different: *The evolutionary leap we need to make cannot occur without our conscious participation.*

We aren't used to thinking of evolution as a goal we can

consciously pursue. After all, in the past, it never was. Today, it *is*. For the first time ever, a species has the option to either resist or embrace its own evolution. Instead of being blindly pushed around by forces beyond our comprehension, we're looking at an extraordinary and totally unprecedented opportunity to serve as nature's willing partners.

> *We have been on a very long journey already....*
> *Where our journey takes us next will depend upon*
> *what kind of beings we humans choose to be. To*
> *put it another way, our decision about the way we*
> *choose to live will determine whether the journey*
> *takes us, or whether we take the journey.*
>
> — Al Gore in The Future: Six Drivers of
> Global *Change*

Of course, to take advantage of this opportunity, we have to believe that we're capable of evolving. Just as no athlete will win the Olympic gold medal if she's convinced she can't, we will never become a heart-centered species if we declare it impossible.

Unfortunately, that is exactly what many people do. "Just look at our ancestors the chimpanzees!" they say. "See how aggressive they are? Violence is just in our nature."

I believe this is nonsense. For one, we're genetically just as closely related to the bonobos, a gentle race of primates who, like the flower children of the '60s, prefer to make love not war.

Moreover, it makes no sense to talk about human nature as if it were written in stone, given that we already know it isn't. Human nature has been changing since the beginning of time. This being the case, there's no reason to assume that our future is destined to equal our past.

Of course, doomsday fantasies have a strong appeal to our ego, which is conditioned to focus on potential danger. Most people can imagine Armageddon at the drop of a hat. And since they can envision a clear path leading from here to there, they perceive their fantasies as potential realities. But ask them to describe a peaceful, happy future for our world and they're likely to draw a blank—or, if they do come up with a vision, to dismiss it as a mere utopia.

Yet our assessment of what's realistic and what isn't is often skewed. This is a lesson I myself had to learn repeatedly before I really got it. One experience that helped me recognize the fallibility of my own mind was fire-walking. Fire-walking is nowhere near as dangerous as it looks. One appears to be standing on red hot coals when, actually, one is standing on a thin layer of ash—just enough to protect one's feet, as long as one keeps moving along at a brisk pace. At the time, however, I didn't know this, and my mind insisted there was no way I could walk on fire without suffering serious injury.

I spent the night before the fire walk tossing and turning as my mind conjured up dire visions.

"You're crazy," it whined. "Do you realize that the nearest hospital is fifty miles away?"

Nonetheless, when the time came, I walked proudly and

confidently across the glowing coals—not just once but twice.

Afterwards, I sat down on a log to examine my feet.

No blisters, nothing! My mind had been wrong. What else, I wondered, was I missing out on because my mind had declared it unrealistic?

Clearly, our mind is not a trustworthy judge of what is and isn't possible. We need to remember this whenever it says that there's no hope for us, and that we're incapable of evolving into a gentle, wise, and peaceful species.

Truthfully, we have no idea of what's possible. Just as a caterpillar might laugh if told it was destined to become a butterfly, we too often have a hard time believing in our evolutionary potential. Let us keep this in sight, lest we undercut our own chances of completing our collective metamorphosis.

We have a long history of violence and warfare. But we also have a history of tremendous adaptability and creativity that has enabled us to survive everything from ice ages to radical displacement.

Some say that long ago, our ancestors lived in trees. At some point, however, they took to the ground. If they were capable of transforming in such fundamental ways, why should we declare ourselves incapable of overcoming our addiction to violence? We have changed deep-seated habits before and can do so again.

Many of us have spent years or even decades healing our emotional and spiritual wounds. All the while, whether or not we realized it, we were midwifing a new consciousness. Every step we took towards our own wholeness sent out ripples of healing energy that touched and encouraged others. Now, the same tools we used to heal ourselves can also help transform our collective consciousness. The skills we acquired, the experience we gathered, and the techniques we developed have all prepared us for this journey of collective evolution.

No question, what's happening is scary. The danger is real, our survival is at stake, and the odds are against us. How could we not feel afraid? And yet, fear is not the main force driving our evolution.

"Fear," says the Sufi mystic Hafiz, "is the cheapest room in the house." And with wry humor he adds, "I'd like to see you in better living conditions."

Indeed, an instinct deeper and more potent than fear is at work. Of course we want to survive and see our children and grandchildren survive. But above all, we want to live a life aligned with our true nature and congruent with our deepest desires.

Having worked with thousands of people, I know, without a doubt, that the human psyche *wants* to evolve, to become wiser, more loving and peaceful. Evolution is not just what the planet is demanding of us. It's also what we ourselves most want, difficult and painful though the process may be.

In the face of our insane world, we can easily get overwhelmed with feelings of powerlessness and futility. We are so small, and the issues so huge! But let's not lose sight of the fact that collective transformation depends on individual transformation.

So what if you're no larger than an ant? If you've ever seen the inside of an anthill, you know that ants build amazing cities. If each individual ant sat down and pondered the size of its contribution, it would surely lose heart, and those cities would never come into being. Fortunately, ants don't do that—and neither should you. Whether your contribution is large or small doesn't matter. The only thing that matters is that you make it fully, wholeheartedly, and courageously.

Immersed as we are in a difficult and sometimes frightening process of global transformation, it can be helpful to remind ourselves that everything we think, say and do ripples out into the world in widening rings that extend far beyond the limited range of our sight. Therefore our choices really *do* matter and do make a difference. Every time we break through old barriers, heal an old emotional wound, or shed a layer of shame or contraction, we help others do the same. Our quest for personal wholeness is not mere self-indulgence, but serves others, as well. This awareness can give us the courage we need to overcome seemingly insurmountable obstacles.

In the face of a world gone insane, it's natural to feel afraid. But we also sense the mounting pressure of an inner force that yearns to live, blossom, and dance, to feel passion, ecstasy, and love. This urgent need to express ourselves and give our gifts to the world might look like a very private, personal impulse. Yet what we are actually feeling is the collective human heart that, through us, is begging to live life to the fullest, to come out of hiding and reveal itself.

Those of us who have said yes to our own transformation—and our numbers are growing with every passing day—are doing so, not just because our survival is at stake, but above all because it's what our hearts and souls want, more than anything.

We have nothing to lose and everything to gain. Though none of us knows what the future will hold, one thing is sure: our souls rejoice when we set ourselves free to fly on the wings of love. That is, after all, what we came here for.

QUESTIONS FOR CONTEMPLATION AND DISCUSSION

The questions listed here are designed to stimulate ideas and discussion. Pick the ones you find most interesting, and remember that the journey of exploration is more important than the answers you come up with.

Many people find that they benefit from having a study circle. A study circle can help you deepen your understanding of the ideas and concepts presented in this book and explore how they apply to your own life.

To receive a free guide to starting and running a study group, please visit www.evolvingtowardpeace.com. If you would like us to list your study group on our website, let us know where you're located, whether you're open to new members, and how you can be contacted. We also love hearing your thoughts, experiences, and stories!

Chapter 1: They Say They Think with Their Heads

- Do you know anyone whom you might describe as a great heart-thinker? What do you notice about them? What's it like to be in their company?

- In what ways might you change were you to think less with your head and more with your heart? How might it affect your relationships?

- This book describes heart-thinking as an essential key to harmonious relationships, both on the personal and the global level. Do you agree?

- Does head-thinking have any advantages over heart-thinking? If so, what are they?

- What are the factors that cause you to get stuck in head-thinking?

- If open-heartedness were your first priority in life, how would you live? What would you do? What would you stop doing?

- Can you imagine a society in which people's relationships were governed by heart-thinking? What would it look like? How would it differ from ours?

- Have you ever experienced a conflict that could only be resolved by a shift from head – to heart-thinking?

- Has your heart ever inspired significant change in your life? If so, what was it?

- Do you believe that we're the most intelligent species on the planet? If so, why? Why not?

- What kind of intelligence do you personally have? Is it the kind that can figure out how machines work? The kind that knows how to comfort a child? The kind that allows you to find your way around a foreign city? Try to identify at least three types of intelligence you recognize in yourself.

- Do you believe that love is all we need? Why, or why not?

- Ask your heart whether it feels happy about the way you're living your life at this time. Take your time, breathe, try to feel your heart and listen to what it has to say.

- Do you believe it matters whether we feel a sense of love for people we don't know and will never meet? Does it make a real difference?

Chapter 2: Re-educating the Ego

- Do you view the ego as a spiritual hindrance? Why? Why not?

- Are there aspects of your own ego that you consider problematic and would like to change? If so, what are they?

- Try to identify some of the survival strategies that were passed down to you from your parents, grandparents, or more distant ancestors.

- To what extent do the survival strategies you inherited

serve you? Are there any that you have let go of or would like to let go of?

- Do you agree that we can create a peaceful global civilization without giving up our ego?

- Do you believe that your own ego has undergone a process of education or transformation? If so, what were the experiences or influences that contributed most to this process?

Chapter 3: The Racist's Transformation

- Have you ever experienced the kind of unconditional acceptance that Justin offered his racist client? Tell the story.

- When someone provokes you, are you able to keep your heart open, or do you become defensive?

- What advice would you give someone who is easily carried away by defensiveness?

- Are there people you know or experiences you've had that you are unable or unwilling to accept? What would it take for you to accept them?

- Justin's client was in a program designed to offer an alternative to incarceration. Do you see incarceration as helpful or harmful? If it were up to you, how would criminals be treated?

Chapter 4: The Toxic Legacy of Belief Addiction

- Do you have any beliefs you feel strongly attached to? What are they?
- What groups of people do your beliefs bond you to?
- Have you ever experienced fanaticism, either in yourself or in others? What was it like?
- Have you ever interacted with a cult, or a cult-like organization? What happened, and what did you learn?
- Can you think of a time when someone you were with expressed views that you found offensive? How did you respond? Looking back, would you do anything differently?
- Do you believe people need a sense of tribal identity?
- How would you define the difference between a tribe and a community?
- Do you presently belong to a group that feels like a tribe? Have you ever? Do you long for the experience, or do you fear it? Why?
- What beliefs and stories were you raised with? To what extent do you still identify with them?

Chapter 5: Religion and Spirituality

- What does spirituality mean to you?
- Do you consider yourself spiritual? If so, why? If not,

why not?

- Do you believe there are universal spiritual values that all humans share in common? If so, what are they?

- Are there people you know or have known who embody these values? Describe them.

- Are there environments where you avoid speaking about spiritual matters? If so, why?

- In *The End of Faith*, Sam Harris argues that since the scriptures of all major religions discredit members of other faiths, religion and world peace are inherently incompatible. Do you agree or disagree, and why?

- Do you follow a religious path? If so, which aspects of your religion are universal, and which are unique to your path? What do you value most about it? What does it offer its members that is special?

- If you belong to a spiritual or religious community, in what ways does it either foster or undermine people's sense of solidarity with members of other religions?

- What would your ideal spiritual community look like? What would it do for you? Set yourself free to fantasize and play.

- How do you see the role of the intellect on the spiritual path? In what ways have you personally experienced it as an asset or an obstacle?

6: Why Judgment is Obsolete

- Do you agree that judgment is obsolete, or do you believe it still serves a purpose?
- Marshall Rosenberg, author of *Non-Violent Communication*, claims that every judgment is a tragic expression of unmet needs. Do you agree?
- Describe a time when you were wounded by judgment, or when your judgments wounded someone else.
- Have you ever held a judgment about someone and then witnessed its dissolution? What happened?
- Have you ever experienced successful conflict resolution? What happened? What were the key factors that led to reconciliation?

Chapter 7: Medina's Story

- Has your life been directly or indirectly affected by war? If so, how?
- Has your life been directly or indirectly affected by other acts of violence?
- Do you belief that warfare is inevitable?
- What does non-violence mean to you? Do you think it's practical? Explain why, or why not.
- Had you been a participant in Medina's circle, how would you have felt about the Serb men?

- What do you see as the foremost needs of those who've been traumatized by violence?
- Do you think our society does enough to address the needs of people traumatized by war, including veterans? If not, what would you like to see happen?

Chapter 8: The Toxic Legacy of Control Addiction

- In his autobiography, Jung describes the face of Western culture as "The face of a bird of prey seeking with cruel intentness for distant quarry—a face worthy of pirates and highwaymen." Do you agree with this view? Why? Why not?
- Do you agree that Western civilization has been driven by a strong need for control? What benefits has this had? What disadvantages?
- Do you see signs of control addiction in yourself? What are they?
- What forms of control do you consider positive and life-affirming? What forms are negative? Why?
- Do you believe that men and women tend to pursue different forms of control? If so, how would you describe the differences?

Chapter 9: Thought Addiction

- Do you consider yourself a thought addict? If so, how does it affect you?
- How would you describe your relationship to your own mind? Are you happy with it?
- If the mind were an employee and you its boss, what feedback would you give it? How might it improve its performance?
- What feedback might your mind give you, its boss? What type of support might it need from you? Does it need you to sleep more, drink more water, or avoid certain activities?
- Have you ever experienced true inner stillness? Under what circumstances?
- Do you agree that thought addiction fuels our economy?
- What are the most effective tools or methods you have experienced for calming the mind?

Chapter 10: Samantha's Story

- Have you ever intentionally switched from head – to heart-thinking? Tell the story.
- Have you ever been guided by something other than your conscious mind? Tell the story.
- Do you agree that our own state of consciousness affects

others? Where have you experienced that happening?

- Have you ever met someone whose presence felt calming and healing? Who were they? Why do you think they had that effect on you?

- Have you ever realized you were going down a wrong path, and changed course? Tell the story.

- Can you think of a time in your life when you, or someone you know, chose to follow the guidance of the heart despite the mind's objections? What happened?

Chapter 11: The Feminine: Our Key to Global Healing

- What messages did your upbringing give you about being a man or a woman?

- To what extent were your parents affected by patriarchal values?

- What aspects of the feminine do you embody? What aspects would you like to embody more fully?

- Do you know men who have embraced their feminine power? What does this look like? How does it manifest?

- What forms of gender inequality, if any, do you see in your society?

- How would the world be different if men and women were equal partners in all aspects of life?

- What purpose, if any, do you believe patriarchy has served in human evolution?

- What messages did you receive concerning emotions such as grief, fear, anger, joy, and love?
- Are you familiar with heart-shame? What triggers it? What might you do, if you were free of it?
- Look at the list of common ways in which our fear of the feminine manifests. Do you see anything that touches a nerve for you personally? If so, why?
- Can you think of people who model emotional shame-lessness? How do you feel about them?

Chapter 12: Understanding the Roots of Greed

- How do you feed your heart?
- Is happiness a priority in your life? If not, why not?
- Do you shop for reasons other than need? If so, what are they? In what other ways might you satisfy those needs?
- Is there any area of your life where you model the path of simplicity? Are there areas you'd like to simplify?
- Do you feel that you have too much stuff? If so, why?
- Do you agree that greed is making us stupid?
- Is there any one change, no matter how small, you could make right now that would bring greater simplicity and spaciousness into your life?
- Is anything about that possibility of having more time or space in your life that scares you? If so, why?

Chapter 13: Working with the Magic of Connection

- Have you ever reached out to a total stranger? What happened?

- Has a total stranger ever reached out to you? What happened?

- What types of religious, racial, ethnic, cultural, social, sexual, and political diversity are currently present in your circle of friends and acquaintances? What types are absent?

- Do you feel a sense of kinship with people around the world?

- Are there certain groups that you have a harder time opening your heart to than others? Are there certain groups of people whom you fear and avoid? If so, why?

- What activities, environments, or experiences have deepened your sense of belonging to a planetary community?

- Are there groups of people you would like to learn more about, yet never meet in the course of your daily life? What steps might you take to do so?

- What experiences have helped strengthen your sense of connection with people around the world?

- Have you ever had an experience similar to the one Naomi Shihab Nye describes in her story-poem?

Chapter 14: Why We Need Relational Education

- How would being a highly skilled communicator affect your life?

- Where has your emotional education come from? Who have your primary teachers been?

- Is there any type of educational or emotional support you wish you had received in your youth, but didn't?

- If you were in charge of redesigning children's schooling, what would it look like? What subjects would you have them study?

- Imagine you've been given the task of creating an educational program for kids designed to strengthen tolerance, understanding, and mutual respect. What would it look like?

- Can you remember someone who made a difference in your life by really listening to you? Can you remember a time when you listened deeply to another?

- Do you agree that listening can heal communities? Under what circumstances can you envision it being most useful?

- Do you believe a sense of kindness and compassion can be taught or nurtured, and if so, how?

Chapter 15: The Return of Circle Gatherings

- For millennia, circle gatherings were an integral part of communal life. Why do you think this changed?

- Do you believe that we share a collective consciousness?

- Have you ever seen signs of collective consciousness in humans or other species?

- How would you expect global-era circles to differ from tribal-era circles?

- If you were to join a circle, what kind might it be? Would it be a meditation circle? A women's circle? A drumming circle? A book group? List all the kinds of circles that you can imagine might interest you.

- Is there anything about circles that scares you? If so, try to articulate what it is.

- What would help you feel safe in a circle?

- Imagine a world in which circle gatherings were common. Take five minutes to make a list of ten ways in which they might be used.

- Have you ever experienced a circle that felt like a sacred space? How was that achieved? What advice might you give a friend who wanted to create such a circle?

- What are the qualities you think a good circle leader should have?

- Everyone is a leader in some way. Take a look at your own life and try to identify some situations in which you demonstrated the qualities you associate with positive leadership.

- Can you imagine wanting to lead circles? If so, what kind? What attracts you about it, and what deters you?

Chapter 16: Celebrating Life

- Have you ever experienced a gathering that was memorable because of how joyful and special it felt? If so, describe it.
- Can you remember times of feeling a sense of strong connection with your community? What caused it?
- How do you feel about movement and dance?
- If you're inhibited, what would it take for you to overcome your inhibitions? Are you willing to try?
- Have you ever experienced a non-religious celebration that felt profoundly sacred? If so, what were the elements that invoked a sense of sacredness?
- Do you know people who are role models for you in terms of their ability to celebrate life?

Epilogue

- Do you believe human consciousness is evolving? If so, in what direction? What signs of evolution do you notice?
- Do you think it's possible for humans to evolve into a

species capable of living peacefully on our planet, or is this a utopia?

- How do you feel about the future of our species? Are you optimistic? Pessimistic?
- What gives you hope for the future of our species?
- Have you ever had an experience where something you considered impossible actually turned out to be possible after all? What happened?
- Try to imagine a world where people live in peace. What do you see? Pick a detail, whether it's transportation, health care, the arts, celebrations, or whatever draws your interest, and try to envision what this aspect of life might look like.

EXERCISES FOR INDIVIDUALS AND GROUPS

1. Five Easy Ways to Connect with Your Heart

To commune with your heart you need to feel it. If you've spent a life time thinking with your head, you may find this difficult. Don't be discouraged! With a little practice, you can regain that exquisite sense of connection to your body that every animal is born with. Here are five simple exercises that may help.

1. As you breathe, imagine that each in-breath gently touches your heart. Each time you inhale, it's as if your breath were ever so gently caressing your heart. Notice any sensations that arise in your chest—warmth or coolness, a sense of openness, softness, or tension. Do this for five minutes.

2. Gently place your palm on the center of your chest and turn your attention to your breathing. Notice how your hand moves as you inhale and exhale. After a minute

or so, drop and relax your hand. Notice how your chest feels. Again, place your hand on your heart and repeat this process. Do it at least three times. Notice whether you feel any aftereffects.

3. When we think of our loved ones, our heart naturally opens. So think of something or someone you love dearly—a baby, a pet, a landscape—and see whether you can sense that opening. Just notice and welcome whatever happens.

4. Throughout the day, check into your heart/chest/belly area as often as possible. Check in while you're driving, when you look up from your computer screen and as you walk into the supermarket. No big deal—it takes just a second, and the more you do it, the stronger your sense of connection with your heart will grow.

5. Play some slow, gentle music that you enjoy and that seems to touch your heart. Stand quietly, with your eyes closed.

Now, invite your heart to initiate some form of movement. Move however you want, allowing your heart to lead you. Perhaps you'll find yourself swaying side to side, arms extended like branches in the wind, or perhaps you'll want to lie down so your heart can feel closer to the earth. Whatever happens, allow it.

2. *Where did It Come From?*

Pick any man-made object in the room you're in right now. Take a close look at it. Notice how it's put together.

Now, think about its genesis. What materials were used to create it? Where did they come from? Who were the people who manufactured it, packaged it, transported it, and sold it?

If the answer is, "I have no clue," just take note of that, too. No matter how much or how little you know about the people who created this object, acknowledge them inwardly, honor their labor, and offer them your gratitude.

3. *What Do I Really Want?*

Spend at least ten minutes writing in response to the question: "What is it that I really want?"

4. *Dear Ego*

Sit down with paper and pen. And say to your ego, "Dear ego, please tell me who you are. Tell me what you want. Tell me what scares you and what makes you feel good. I promise I will try to listen without judging you."

Then, pick up your pen and write:

Dear (your name), I am your ego.

Now, try to get out of the way and just let your ego say

whatever it has to say. Write for at least ten minutes, or more, if you like.

If you run out of steam, just repeat the invitation: "Dear ego, please tell me who you are. Tell me what you want. Tell me what scares you and what makes you feel good. I promise I will try to hear you without judging you."

When you feel complete, close your eyes. Did you learn anything that surprised you? Is there anything about your ego that you feel grateful for? If so, express your gratitude. Inwardly, bless your ego, and ask that it honor and support the needs of your heart and soul. And as you do so, feel that you are also blessing the collective ego. Pray that we might learn to use its powers in ways that bring healing and peace to our world.

5. Making Space

When we judge something or someone, we are in essence saying: "There's no space in my world for this." But given that it exists, God obviously doesn't agree with us. In God's world, there *is* space for it. So by making space within ourselves to accept this situation, we align ourselves with reality—and, insofar as God is truth—with God. We stop waging war, and instead give ourselves permission to be at peace with what is.

To make space for something, you don't have to like it, approve of it or condone it. You'd like to change it? Fine. But remember that the most effective way to change things is *not* to wage war on them. The less energy you waste fighting reality, the more power you'll gain to transform it.

Start practicing with something small. Let's say you're stuck in traffic. Your kneejerk response might be to say, "This is bad. This shouldn't be happening." In other words, "There's no space in my life for this."

To shift from a feeling of "no space" to a sense of inner spaciousness, try using these five steps:

1. Name what's happening: "I'm stuck in traffic. I may be late for a meeting."

2. Remind yourself that your anger, irritation, annoyance, and resistance won't change the outer situation. They'll only pollute your inner world. In light of this awareness, affirm your willingness to release them.

3. Breathe deeply. Feel that with each exhalation, you are letting go of your negativity. With each inhalation, you are becoming more open and spacious. Do this for at least five breath cycles.

4. Imagine that you are watching yourself, as if in a movie. The person you're looking at is totally relaxed and peaceful.

5. *Become* that person as you affirm: "In the midst of this situation, I give myself permission to be at peace."

6. Our Children's Children

Imagine: A thousand years have passed. Humankind has made it through the major crisis with which the previous millennium began. Of course, the external world has changed in many ways. Technology looks different, social structures are different.

But most importantly, the people themselves are different. They are, quite simply, more evolved than we are. To survive, they had to learn to relate in new ways. They had to learn alternatives to judgment, violence, and warfare—and they *have*. They educate their children differently than we do, and possess social and relational skills that are still rare in our day and age.

Imagine that a young man or woman who lives in this future era is writing a letter to you. In it, he explains the differences between the people of the future and those of the present era. He describes what changes took place, what habits they had to let go of, and what skills they have cultivated.

Set your imagination free, and write whatever comes to mind, without censoring or editing. Just have fun, and explore. The more clearly we can see where our evolutionary journey is headed, the more likely we are to complete it successfully.

7. Detachment Practice

Try using this practice when you find yourself getting defensive or feeling angry or hostile towards someone whose beliefs or opinions class with yours. You might be talking to them, or perhaps you're listening to them on the radio or watching them on television. Either way, the following three steps can be helpful:

Take a deep breath and remind yourself: It's just a belief.

It's okay if we see things differently.

Let your attention drop from your mind to your heart. Breathing in, imagine the oxygen nourishing your heart; and on the out-breath, relax.

Imagine that a warm stream of golden light is flowing between your heart and that of the person you're engaged with.

8. Five Breaths

This is a simple practice that you can do anywhere, anytime, within less than sixty seconds. It consists of five breaths—five inhalations and five exhalations. With each breath cycle, say, think, and feel a single word or a phrase. Here are five I like to use, but feel free to replace them with your own:

- Presence
- Silence
- Peace
- Beauty
- Happiness

Whether you say the words out loud or just think them doesn't matter, as long as you allow yourself to feel their meaning fully. Let each word ring like a bell and resonate through your body.

You can also use this practice to let go of judgment or negativity. In that case, simply affirm your willingness to do so, and speak or think the words "let go" on each exhalation.

9. Twelve Ways to Align Your Religious Practice with Heart-Thinking

1. Honor yourself as the highest spiritual authority in your life.
2. Relate to the spirit of your religion, not the letter.
3. Make sure any religious rituals you perform feel meaningful. If they don't, change or discard them.
4. Have the courage to examine your beliefs and to let go of any that your heart does not sanction.
5. If your religion favors certain groups over others, such as heterosexuals over gays, or men over women, demand that they be given equal rights.
6. Study other religious traditions besides your own.
7. Ask that your religious community organize interfaith meetings, so that members of your community can connect with members of other faiths.
8. Incorporate music, dance, and art into your religious practice.
9. Connect with people within your tradition who walk the path of the heart.
10. Ask your religious community to organize ongoing circle gatherings where people can speak honestly and from the heart about their spiritual lives.
11. Initiate a discussion about heart-thinking in your religious community.
12. If you notice elements of belief addiction in your religious community, try to initiate a respectful conversation about it.

10. Gratitude

Every day, we're given a bounty of gifts. But unless we allow them to awaken a delicious sense of fullness and abundance within our being, we haven't really received them at all.

We speak of gratitude as something we give to others. But really, it's first and foremost a gift we give to ourselves. As Brother David Steindl-Rast says, we mistakenly believe that happiness makes us grateful. In reality, gratitude makes us happy.

The practice of gratitude is simple: You notice the gifts you've been given. Then, you allow the natural swelling that is your heart's response to this awareness.

The problem is that we tend to forget. Caught up in head-thinking as we are, our focus tends to lie on everything that is lacking in our life. So even though gratitude makes us happy, we often fail to practice it. This is why it can be useful to formulate a practice that helps us stay aligned with our intention. Below, I've listed a few examples of what such a practice might look like. Use them to help you come up with a daily practice that appeals to you. Then, commit to working with it for just one week.

Make a note to yourself to check in after a week and take stock of what happened. Did you enjoy the practice? Would you like to continue, and if so, is there anything you'd like to change? If you find that you had resistance to doing your practice, or forgot about it entirely, don't beat yourself up. Try to approach your psyche with an attitude of friendly curiosity.

Remember, you're not trying to improve yourself. Your only goal is to fully enjoy the sense of richness and contentment that gratitude awakens.

- When you wake up in the morning, lie quietly for a few minutes, giving gratitude for this new day and everything it will bring you.
- When you go to bed at night, spend a few minutes giving gratitude for everything this day has brought you.
- Every day, write a list of twenty things you feel grateful for.
- Every day, give gratitude for yourself. Make it specific. Appreciate yourself for something you did or let go of or learned, for a risk you took or an act of kindness you performed.
- Commit to inwardly thanking everyone you encounter for their presence in your life. Do this regardless of whether you like or dislike them and of whether they bring you joy or suffering.
- Give gratitude before eating or drinking anything.
- Every day, think of one person who has made a positive difference in your life. Then, spend a few minutes sending them gratitude.
- Commit to consciously appreciating all the gifts that nature brings you, whether it's the grass growing by the sidewalk, the sweet birdsong outside your window, or the sight of the full moon.

11. Giving Honor

Begin this practice first thing in the morning. As soon as you get up, find a place where you can be quiet and undisturbed (and no, God will not feel insulted if you do your spiritual practice in the bathroom).

Place your palms together, and close your eyes. This posture is used in many traditions around the world both to express honor and respect, and to center oneself. I call such postures body-mantras. They are sacred syllables, spoken through the language of the body, that connect us with the realm of the sacred.

Try to let go of any religious associations you might have with this posture, and simply experience it for yourself. Experiment until you find the way of standing and holding your arms that feels best to you.

Now, close your eyes and inwardly greet the world. Bow to it, honor it. Offer it your respect, your devotion, your caring. Affirm your willingness to share your gifts today, without holding back.

Next, set a strong intention of mentally bowing to everyone you meet today, throughout the day. Determine that inwardly, you will bow to cashiers, colleagues, children, friends—everyone. Begin right now by bowing to yourself—to the amazing, flawed, and sacred human being that you are.

At the end of the day, notice what happened. Did you remember to honor people? Did you forget? What happened? No matter what your experience was, don't judge yourself. Simply pay attention, and take note.

12. *Listening to the Heart of Humanity*

Sit in a quiet place with pen and paper. Open to the possibility that the human heart has an intelligence of its own, and might want to speak to you. Affirm the intention that for the next few minutes, you'll listen and write down whatever it might have to say to you.

If there is a specific issue you would like to focus on, or a question you would like your heart to address, write it down. Now, affirm your intention to listen and to serve as a scribe to whatever you hear. I'm not suggesting that you'll literally hear a voice. That can happen, but more often words rise up in our consciousness that have a different tone or quality than our ordinary thoughts.

Now, please write down the words: "I am the heart of humankind." By doing this, you are opening the door and communicating your receptivity.

Now simply listen quietly, and if something emerges, write it down. Don't edit, don't censor—just write it down. Set aside the question of whether what you're "hearing" is really the voice of the human heart, or just a figment of your imagination.

If nothing happens, let that be okay, too. Don't try to "think up" anything. Just stay open and alert. If your mind begins to wander, gently bring it back to your breath, to the present moment, and to your intention of listening.

Sometimes, the main response you get might be silence. Other times, words may rush in faster than you can write them down. Either way, just accept whatever comes. If images or colors appear, write them down, too.

Finish by inwardly thanking the heart of humanity.

If you are doing this practice in a group, you may want to share your writings. There should be no pressure to do so, but neither should you hold back out of shyness. The message that seems meaningless to you may be exactly what someone else needs to hear.

13. Where Did You Come From?

Think of an acquaintance or a friend whom you feel comfortable talking to. Do you know where their parents came from or who their ancestors were?

If the answer is no, look for an opportunity to ask them. If it feels appropriate, create the opportunity by asking them to share a cup of coffee or a meal with you. You could even invite a group of friends over with the specific intention of spending an evening listening to each other's stories.

Don't be pushy or invasive, but communicate your sincere interest. Most people love to talk about their ancestry, given the opportunity. Listen, ask questions, and try to understand better where they're coming from, both literally and figuratively.

If some of your friends are refugees or immigrants, spend a few minutes on the Internet or at the library educating yourself about where they came from and the situation they left behind.

Are you yourself a refugee or an immigrant? Have you had the opportunity to tell your story? Know that whether it's happy or sad, your story is a gift that's been entrusted to you and can help others on their journey. If it's too painful to share with strangers, start looking for someone you trust and feel comfortable with. Whatever you do, don't just hold it inside. When we keep painful stories inside for too long, they begin to fester.

14. I Want You to Feel Safe

What are the things people do that help you feel safe around them? And what are the things that make you feel unsafe? Write down ten of each.

Now take a look at your list. Assuming that other people feel the way you do, do you see any way in which you could help them feel safer around you? If so, try to put it into practice over the next few days whenever you encounter someone.

15. Moving at the Speed of Your Body

I'd like to invite you to spend one whole day moving at the speed of your body. If you feel that a whole day is too much, try it for half a day— even for an hour. But bear in mind that it takes a while to really get into the experience. Even one day is barely enough to taste the sweetness of moving in harmony with the natural rhythms of your body.

Think of a cat, how she can lie for hours sleeping. Every now and then she rouses herself for a brief, voluptuous stretch, only to curl up once again, close her eyes, and return to her feline dream world. Other times, she seems to transform into a miniature tiger. She stalks, leaps, races around and performs crazy dances.

Yet whether she's lying motionless or whirling like a banshee, she's always moving at the same speed: the speed of her body. The speed of your body is the one that feels most pleasurable to you at any given moment. Of course, this fluctuates from moment to moment. Like that cat, you too may sometimes feel like dancing and other times like resting.

All animals move at the speed of their bodies. But for us, it can take a bit of practice because we're so alienated from our natural rhythms. Our body is always telling us what it wants, but often, we don't listen.

Chose a time that will be dedicated to moving at the speed of your body. Obviously, this can't be a busy work day. Pick a time when you are free to determine your own pace. During this time, you can do anything you like, as long as you allow your body to set the speed. You can play with your kids, go for a walk, wash the dishes—it's all fine. But whatever you do, don't move out of rote habit. When you get up from the couch or wash your hands, be present with what you're doing. Feel that each movement is special. Each movement is a celebration of life in the body.

Watch out for transitions! You're taking a walk, you're present and mindful. But then you walk in your front door and something new begins. Maybe it's a conversation with your partner or a chore you want to take care of. It's during those moments that you're most likely to plunge into forgetfulness.

To prevent this, it can be helpful to label transitions whenever they happen: Now I'm transitioning from being outside my house to inside. Now I'm transitioning from taking a shower to having breakfast. Now I'm transitioning from answering emails to ordering something online.

To the extent that you're governed by control-addiction, you may find it difficult to move at the speed of your body for an extended amount of time. The control-addicted ego wants to get things done as quickly as possible. It doesn't understand that, as Martin Luther King, Jr., used to point out, peace is not just our destination but our path. But if you're free from control-addiction, moving at the speed of your body will feel delicious and deeply healing.

16. Being Peace

One mark of our evolution is the capacity to *choose* our state of consciousness, instead of letting circumstances dictate how we feel. Instead of hoping for the peace that comes from being carefree, can we consciously *choose* to be at peace, regardless of circumstances? The purpose of this exercise is to help you strengthen your capacity to do just that. Peace then ceases to be a gift that the world may or may not you. Instead, it becomes a gift that *you* can give the world.

During the next week, pay close attention to everything that disturbs your peace, focusing especially on the small things—the niggling worries and the minor irritations. Perhaps you realize your parking meter has run out and you might get a ticket. Perhaps it suddenly occurs to you that you forgot a friend's birthday. Perhaps someone makes a snide comment that raises your hackles. Think of these minor disturbances as the weights you can use to strengthen your peace muscles. Don't start with the 100 pound dumbbells. Start off light.

To choose peace, you need to know what it feels like. Peace isn't an idea. It isn't something abstract. It's a state of being that involves every part of you. So your first step is to become familiar with the experience. Whenever you notice you're feeling peaceful, pay close attention: How am I breathing? What does my heart feel like? What's going on in my body?

Once you have a clear sense of what the state of peace feels like, try evoking it at will when you're in a neutral state, neither agitated nor ecstatic. Just as you might learn the way to a certain address, you can learn the way to peace. Initially, this may seem challenging, but the more you do it, the easier it will get.

Many people find it helpful to use certain words or affirmations. Here are a few examples:

- Peace, peace, peace
- Om shanti, shanti, shanti (shanti means peace in Sanskrit)
- Spirit of peace, be with me.
- Breathing in, I am peace. Breathing out, I am peace.

Find an affirmation that works for you, and start using it throughout your day.

Your next step is to practice peace in the face of those small challenges that we encounter every day by the dozen. When you do, you may find that your ego is quite attached to its suffering. It may not want to let go of irritation, annoyance and worry. It's used to these states, and if you aren't conscious, it will drag you into automatic patterns of reactivity before you even realize what's going on. But whenever you do, shift your focus from the outer to the inner world. Affirm your attention to be at peace, and call on your affirmation for support.

Every time you successfully shift from reactivity to peace, acknowledge yourself. Perhaps the shift you made was tiny—so tiny that no one else even noticed. Nonetheless, it's cause for celebration. For in that moment, you proved that we are indeed capable of evolving towards peace.

17. Five Minutes of Presence

Sit down in a comfortable position and hold a firm intention to stay present for five minutes. By being present, I mean that you stay aware of your surroundings and don't get caught up in your thoughts. Keep it simple. Don't think of what you're doing as meditation. Just think of it as downtime, a short vacation for body and mind.

To help yourself stay present, pay attention to your breath and your physical body. Your body lives in the present, and is always happy to meet you there.

The thought-addicted mind gets bored at the drop of a hat, and may complain bitterly at being forced to sit still for five minutes. But five minutes of boredom have never killed anybody, and just beyond boredom lies another state where doing nothing is not boring but blissful.

18. Breaking the Computer Trance

Get a timer. When you start working on the computer, set it to go off after ten minutes. When it does, stop. If you need to save a file or complete an important process, do that, but no more.

Turn your attention towards your body. Adjust your posture, so you're as comfortable as possible. If you're in a private place, you may want to close your eyes and give them a rest.

Now, take three full breaths. As you do, try to stay fully present. With each in-breath, hold the intention of receiving love. With each out-breath, let go into the present moment.

Then, open your eyes, and go back to work after resetting your timer to go off after another ten minutes. When it does, repeat the process. Continue doing this for at least one hour.

19. Heart-centering in Daily Life

It's one thing to connect with your heart while you're meditating or on retreat, and another to do it in the midst of daily life with all the constant stimulation it brings. Yet daily life is the real test of your progress; it's where the rubber meets the road. Use the following seven steps to help strengthen your ability to remain centered in your heart.

1. Sit and listen to your heart for five minutes. When you notice that you've become lost in thought, gently return to heart-awareness.

2. Once you get comfortable with this exercise, try staying centered in your heart while you perform a simple, straightforward physical activity, like doing the dishes or brushing your teeth.

3. Next, try to stay centered in your heart while doing something that requires a little thought, like writing a check.

4. Try to stay centered in your heart while working on a challenging mental problem.

5. Practice staying centered in your heart while talking to someone you feel comfortable and relaxed around.

6. Practice staying centered in your heart while talking with someone who's feeling agitated or emotional.

7. Finally, try to centered in your heart in the midst of a difficult conversation, an argument or a conflict.

20. Creating Beauty

Today, I invite you to create something of beauty. It could be a poem, a painting, a meal. It could be an altar or a flowerbed. You might decide to transform a messy, cluttered space into a spacious, orderly one. You could devote a few extra minutes tomorrow morning to dressing in a way that feels beautiful to you.

As Rumi says, "There are a million ways to kneel and kiss the ground." To create beauty, you don't need to be an artist, only a lover of life.

21. *Invoking the Feminine*

The following eight qualities manifest in both sexes but, consciously or not, we are taught to associate them with the feminine:

- Beauty
- Grace
- Softness
- Tenderness
- Vulnerability
- Receptivity
- Compassion
- Gentleness

Which of these qualities attracts you most at this time? Whichever one you pick, I invite you to spend a few minutes thinking of three practical ways in which you could nurture its presence in your life at this time. Write them down, specifying clearly what the step involves and what your timeframe is to incorporate those actions into your life. Keep your steps small, manageable, and fun. For example, if I decide I'd like to invite more gentleness into my life, I might consider the following steps:

- Tomorrow, I won't rush my daughter as I'm helping her get dressed. I'll be totally present with her.
- For the next week, whenever something doesn't work out the way I want it to, instead of getting angry, I'll take a deep breath and relax.
- Today, when I do the dishes, I'll try to handle each dish gently, as if it were infinitely precious.

After you've come up with your three steps, ask yourself: Am I willing to commit to one of them, and if so, which one?

Later, take stock. Did you follow through with your commitment? If not, why not? Don't beat yourself up, just be curious. If you did take your step, did you like the effect it had on your life? What worked for you and what didn't?

If you feel like repeating the exercise, go ahead; each time you do it, you'll have a different experience.

22. Plastic bags

Facing the facts about our impact on our planet can be depressing. Nonetheless, I'd like to encourage you to take a deep breath and choose just among the many products you use. It might be your computer, your television or air conditioner, a toy, a type of food or cosmetic.

Whatever you chose, spend a few minutes on the Internet educating yourself about how its production, use and disposal are affecting the environment. This needn't take long—an enormous amount of information is readily available.

If you learn something disturbing about the product you selected, ask yourself: What is one step I can take towards making a change? You goal isn't to heal the planet, just to claim and use the healing power you do possess.

When I did this exercise, I decided to educate myself about plastic bags. I already knew they weren't good for the environment, but I had no idea that a plastic bag takes 400 to 1,000 years to break down and that even then, its toxicity doesn't diminish. Nor was I aware of the fact that every year, over 100,000 sea turtles and other marine animals die after ingesting plastic bags.

Now, I never go shopping without my tote bags. Cutting back on my consumption of plastic bags is a small step, but it's an easy one to make.

23. Cash Flow

Money is like a river. It flows from person to person, around the world. If we use it mindfully, it can help us stay in touch with the interconnected web of which we are part. Like any other form of power, it can be used in more or less enlightened ways.

Whenever you spend or receive cash, take a brief moment to inwardly acknowledge that these coins or bills are part of a vast network of energy that is flowing around our planet, and notice how you are choosing to direct its flow.

24. What's in Your Closet?

For this exercise, set aside twenty minutes.

Go to your closet. Select an item and look for the label that says where it was made.

Now, take a close look at *how* it was made. Look at the zippers, buttonholes, pockets, and collars. Check out the seams. Be aware of the people who sewed them.

Do this with at least one dozen items of clothing.

Then, sit down and spread them in front of you. Sit down, and feel your appreciation for all the people who worked on these pieces of clothing. Feel how much time they spent on them. Try to imagine their lives. Acknowledge them inwardly and offer them your gratitude.

25. Circle of Stones

This practice can help you access the supportive power of the circle, regardless of whether you belong to an "official" circle or not. It's a great practice for children, too. I'm going to describe three variations. They all start out the same:

Take a piece of paper and write down the names of the people who are closest to you—your loved ones, your true friends, the people who really care about you, the people who nourish your heart and soul. You can also include pets, ancestors, and spirit guides.

Now, look for a small object to represent each one of these beings. Your objects can all be the same, or they can be as unique as the individuals they represent. For now, I'll call them stones, but they could also be shells, crystals, beads, buttons, acorns—anything that strikes your fancy. Just be sure you have as many objects as you have individuals on your list—plus one to represent yourself.

Now, find a place in your house where you can set up your circle, and where it won't be disturbed—a table, a dresser, or, if you have one, an altar. Your circle can be large or small, as you prefer. A friend of mine filled a small bowl with fine white sand into which she placed a circle of tiny deep-blue glass marbles. Another created a huge stone circle in her front yard. It's entirely up to you. Take the time to arrange your circle in a way that pleases you, and have fun doing it. Some people like to add flowers, candles, or other objects to their arrangement.

Variation 1: Once your circle is set up, just remember, now and then, when you walk by it, to stop, look at it, and remember the people it represents. Let the thought of them warm your heart and give you a shot of courage when you need it. Feel how the sense of connection between you and your loved ones is not diminished by distance.

Variation 2: At times when you want to feel their support, try the following. Find some open floor space in a room where you have some privacy (outdoors is great, too). In the center, place a chair or cushion where you can sit comfortably.

Gather up your stones and arrange them in a circle around your seat. Then, sit down in the center, holding "your" stone in your hand. Close your eyes and take a few deep breaths. Remind yourself of the people or beings whom these stones represent. Ask them to be present with you now.

If your environment permits it, speak to them out loud. Tell them what's going on, and what you're feeling. Talk to them as if they were actually present—which on some level, they *are*. Feel their compassion and concern for you, and let it comfort and strengthen you.

Variation 3: If you want guidance on a specific issue or challenge, begin with Variation 2, but keep a journal and pen at hand.

What is the question you would like your circle to address? Once you know what it is, write it down, and speak it out loud. Then, face one of the stones and ask yourself, "Who is this?" A name will pop up.

Ask: "Do you have a message for me?" Now, just listen. If you don't "hear" anything, that's fine. Turn to the next stone and repeat the process.

You may find yourself getting clear impressions of who wants to speak and what they want to say. If you want, write down any messages you get. Don't analyze or question what happens. Just stay open and receptive. Move all the way around the circle, asking each being for their wise counsel. Sometimes they'll all have something to say. Sometimes just one will respond. Sometimes, their presence might be the only message.

When you feel complete, close your eyes and sit quietly for a few minutes, feeling their love and compassion surrounding you and sending them your gratitude.

26. Making Ripples

Next time you're by a pond or lake, throw a pebble into the water and watch the ripples move out in concentric circles. Try to be totally present with this, just watching and witnessing. Do it a few more times if you like.

Now, make a prayer or a wish for someone you care about, for a community, or for the world. Holding your prayer in your awareness, throw another pebble into the water. As you watch the ripples moving out, feel that you are sending ripples of positive energy into the world.

27. Visioning a Celebration

There are a million ways to celebrate, and as children of the global era we are no longer tied to any one way. Some celebrations call forth the wild laughter that shakes us loose and reconnects us with the untamable, ecstatic freedom of our true Self. Others are quiet and mystical. The purpose of this exercise is to help you explore what celebration means to you.

Set aside a minimum of fifteen minutes. If you are doing this exercise in a group, schedule in additional time for sharing. Have paper and pen at hand.

Now, I invite you to imagine that you've been asked to create a special celebration. What kind? The kind that you yourself would enjoy most. Within the next fifteen minutes, try to map out your celebration in enough detail that you can describe it to others.

Here are some questions to help you get started:

- What will the main ingredients of your celebration be?
- Will there be music, dance, ritual, silence, food?
- Will there be hundreds of people, or just a handful?
- Is this a one-time event, or is it part of a cycle that gets repeated at different times throughout the year?
- Do you want your celebration to be indoors or outdoors? What kind of environment do you envision?

Since this is not a celebration that you are actually planning to produce, feel free to let your imagination go wild. You want jugglers? Live musicians? Great! Build them in. Set yourself free to fantasize. Make your celebration as crazy, extravagant, or eccentric as you please. The only criterion is that it must please you. It must be an event you personally would love to attend. Get as specific as you can, and take copious notes.

Here's the vision that came to me when I did this exercise:

A huge gathering in a beautiful old palace. There's an enormous ballroom, with dozens of softly lit side rooms. The guests have come from all corners of the earth. Their skin colors range from ivory to ebony. They speak many languages, wear many kinds of colorful clothes, and belong to many different religious and cultural traditions.

They've come together to celebrate that they're alive, that the human species is alive, that the planet is alive. They're celebrating the global community, the awesome mystery of the cosmos, and the infinite possibilities that lie folded within the womb of each moment.

The evening begins with everyone sitting in a large circle. For fifteen minutes, we sit together in complete silence as we send our blessings and prayers around the planet and into the cosmos.

Then, a bell rings. Someone steps forward, lights a candle in the center, and holds it in their hands. This light symbolizes the light of the world, and to hold it is both an honor and an expression of one's commitment to the welfare of the entire global community.

One by one, each person steps into the center of the circle, holds the candle in silence for a few seconds, and then walks back to the circumference and offers it to their neighbor. In this way, the candle passes from person to person, until everyone has held it.

Again, a bell rings. Everyone rises and, slowly, with gratitude, bows to the center and to the circle.

And now, the party begins. There are many kinds of mouthwatering food and drinks. People talk, laugh, enjoy each other's company, as well as the beauty of their surroundings. Groups of musicians from many cultures are playing in various locations. There's fabulous dance music, as well as quiet music that transports you to other worlds. There's a sense of joy and laughter in the air, a lightness like bubbly champagne. This is a night everyone will remember as a blessed, magical moment of happiness and grace.

GLOSSARY OF IMPORTANT TERMS

Belief Addiction: A form of mental illness in which we become so attached to a belief or a belief system that we allow it to stifle the voice of the heart.

Circlework: A method of working with circle gatherings developed by Jalaja Bonheim that strengthens our capacity for heart-thinking and helps liberate us from the harmful aspects of tribal and control-era conditioning.

Collective Consciousness: A dimension of consciousness shared by a group or a species.

Control-Era Conditioning: A form of conditioning that originated in patriarchal Europe and that evolved over the past five millennia in response to a collective desire to gain more control, primarily over nature, but also over women and other peoples.

The Ego: The part of our being that evolved to help us survive and cannot help but perceive us as separate entities.

The Feminine: The totality of qualities and attributes that our culture defines as "feminine," though they actually belong to both genders.

Greed: The habit of trying to find happiness and fulfillment in ways that harm others while failing to provide the satisfaction we seek.

Head-Thinking: A state of consciousness in which the mind disconnects from the heart and becomes enslaved to the ego.

Heart-Courage: The courage to bare one's heart, reveal one's vulnerability, open to intimacy, communicate authentically, and take relational risks.

Heart-Shame: Shame in regards to qualities associated with open-heartedness, such as softness, gentleness, sensitivity, and others. Heart-shame is sourced in the patriarchal association of the heart with the feminine, and its rejection thereof.

Heart-Thinking: A state in which heart and mind function harmoniously as a single organ of compassionate wisdom. Any practice that strengthens our capacity to use our mind in service of the heart.

Judgment: The way we rationalize closing our heart to someone.

Relational Education: Education that empowers us to create and maintain healthy, harmonious relationships.

Spirituality: The realization of oneness and the path that leads to this realization.

Thought Addiction: The unwillingness and inability to stop thinking, even for brief periods of time.

Tribal Conditioning: Conditioning that evolved in response to the experience, maintained consistently over hundreds of thousands of years, of living in homogenous and often isolated tribes, upon which we were extremely dependant.

True Intelligence: The ability to think, act, and relate in ways conducive to our survival.

Us-Versus-Them Thinking: The habit of dividing people into those we identify with and consider our friends and allies, and those we dissociate from and view as strangers or enemies.

GRATITUDES

Thank you to all my spiritual teachers, especially His Holiness the Dalai Lama and Eckhart Tolle, for your presence on Earth in these times of turmoil and transformation.

You who came to my circles and turned them into magical, healing sanctuaries have been the greatest blessing in my life. Thank you for having the courage to show up, bare your souls and share your stories. Thank you for your laughter and tears, your honesty, wisdom and heart-stopping beauty.

My deepest gratitude to the many skillful midwives who helped me birth this book. My dear friends Sherry Anderson and Liz Walker both offered invaluable support and feedback. At a crucial moment, Megan Shull's clear-sighted guidance steered me in the right direction. With his vote of confidence and his unconditional support, Randy Cash gave me the courage to persevere. Thanks also to Kevin Quirk, another strong, skillful ally.

When I desperately needed a quiet retreat space to complete this book, Rick and Ronda Sigel appeared out of the blue to offer me, a total stranger, their home, a haven of beauty and peace. Thank you for the gift of sanctuary and, above all, for the gift of your trust.

Gratitude doesn't even begin to describe what I feel for my

friend and soul sister Helena Cooper. Thank you for being by my side throughout this wild journey, and for bringing so much joy, laughter and play to my life. Wherever I go, wherever I am, you will always be in my heart.

ABOUT THE AUTHOR

Jalaja (pronounced DJA-la-dja) Bonheim, Ph.D. is an internationally acclaimed author, teacher and speaker whose previous books include *Aphrodite's Daughters: Women's Sexual Stories and the Journey of the Soul* and *The Hunger for Ecstasy: Fulfilling the Soul's Need for Passion and Intimacy*.

As a German Jew growing up in post-war Austria and Germany, Jalaja witnessed the devastating effects of war up close. Driven by a need to understand why we would chose to create hell on earth, she embarked on a life-long quest for insight into the causes of violence and the means of healing it. Since 2005, she has been travelling to Israel and Palestine, where she empowers Jewish and Palestinian women to serve as agents of peace.

Founder and director of the Institute for Circlework, Jalaja Bonheim is known for her groundbreaking use of circle gatherings to foster inner and outer peace. Herself an exceptionally gifted group facilitator, she has trained hundreds of people in the art of skillful circle leadership. Blessed with a keen, penetrating mind, she is able to communicate complex ideas in clear, easily accessible language. She works with people from all walks of life and reveals how by honoring our desire for peace and happiness, we can support the great birthing that is underway—the birthing of a new consciousness and a new planetary civilization.

To contact Jalaja Bonheim, read her blog, learn about

upcoming workshops and events or book her for speaking engagements, please visit www.jalajabonheim.com.

To download a free guide on creating your own *Evolving Toward Peace Study Group*, please visit www.evolvingtoward-peace.com.

INDEX

Page numbers in **bold** indicate glossary entries.

D